Additional Praise for

Performance Dashboards and Analysis for Value Creation

"Jack Alexander has clearly and concisely shown business leaders how to *proactively* manage and direct their businesses. If you are a business leader and want to achieve a higher level of success, you need to get hold of the concepts and principles in this book."

—Paul J. DiCicco, Vice President, Operations
Summer Infant, Inc.

"Mr. Alexander provides you with the tools to custom-build a dashboard for your specific business and continually reminds us of the need to link business dynamics to the creation of shareholder value."

—Sally J. Curley, Vice President, Investor Relations
Genzyme Corporation

"Having had Jack Alexander as a professor, I can testify that his methodology works both in and out of the classroom."

—Pamela A. Pantos, Financial Analyst
W. R. Grace
and Babson College, MBA 2006

Performance Dashboards and Analysis for Value Creation

Performance Dashboards and Analysis for Value Creation

JACK ALEXANDER

John Wiley & Sons, Inc.

Published by John Wiley & Sons, Inc., Hoboken, New Jersey.
Published simultaneously in Canada.

For general information on our other products and services or for technical support,
please contact our Customer Care Department within the United States at (800) 762-
2974, outside the United States at (317) 572-3993 or fax (317) 572-4002.

Wiley also publishes its books in a variety of electronic formats. Some content that
appears in print may not be available in electronic books. For more information
about Wiley products, visit our web site at www.wiley.com.

EVA is a registered trademark of Stern Stewart & Company.

Designations used by companies to distinguish their products are often claimed as
trademarks. In all instances where John Wiley & Sons, Inc., is aware of a claim, the
product names appear in initial capital or all capital letters. Readers, however,
should contact the appropriate companies for more complete information regarding
trademarks and registration.

Library of Congress Cataloging-in-Publication Data:

Alexander, Jack, 1956–
    Performance dashboards and analysis for value creation / Jack Alexander.
        p.   cm.—(Wiley finance series)
    Includes bibliographical references and index.
    ISBN-13 978-0-470-04797-2 (cloth/cd-rom)
    ISBN-10 0-470-04797-6 (cloth/cd-rom)
    1. Corporations—Valuation.   2. Corporate profits.   3. Performance
standards.   4. Organizational effectiveness—Evaluation.   I. Title.   II. Series.
    HG4028.V3A42 2007
    658.15'54—dc22

                                                                2006011782

Printed in the United States of America.
10 9 8 7 6 5 4 3 2 1

To my family:

My parents, Marian and Jack Alexander
My wife Suzanne, and our sons Rob and Tom
My sisters, Karen and Carol, and their families
My mother-in law, Kay

Contents

List of Dashboards

Preface

WHY THIS BOOK?

There has been substantial progress in a number of business disciplines over the past 15 years, including measuring business and financial performance and managing shareholder value. However, in my experience as a CFO, educator, and consultant, it became clear to me that these subjects were not fully integrated in many organizations or in the minds of many students and managers. Most managers and employees want to do the right things but often do not understand how their role relates to the success of the company, including building long-term value. Over a long period of time, I found that students, managers, and employees responded very positively to progressive attempts at linking performance and value through improved analytical models, performance measures, and "dashboards." In addition to these tools, positive results were achieved by creating various wiring diagrams to provide context and visual integration of value drivers, financial performance, and operating processes and activities. Success with these tools and models led to the development of the Value Performance Framework (VPF). The objectives of the VPF and this book are to strengthen the links among operating performance, financial measures, and shareholder value and to provide tools to enable managers to improve the effectiveness of performance management in their organizations to build long-term sustainable value for shareholders.

USING THIS BOOK

This book presents three major topics:

1. Creating Context and Covering the Basics
2. Linking Performance and Value
3. Driving Performance and Value

Chapter 1, The Management Challenge: Integrating Performance, Finance, and Value, frames the challenges facing managers in building effective performance management systems and provides an introduction to the Value Performance Framework.

Part One, Creating Context and Covering the Basics, provides a foundation for the concepts utilized in the VPF, including basic finance concepts and valuation principles. It contains the following chapters:

Chapter 2. Fundamentals of Finance

Chapter 3. Key Valuation Concepts

Chapter 4. The Business Model and Financial Projections

Part Two, Linking Performance and Value, presents key elements of the VPF. Each of the value drivers is linked to critical business activities and processes. Key performance measures, analytical models, dashboards, and tools for improving each value driver are explored. Chapters include:

Chapter 5. Drivers of Shareholder Value and the Value Performance Framework

Chapter 6. Revenue Growth and Pricing Strength

Chapter 7. Operating Effectiveness

Chapter 8. Capital Effectiveness: Working Capital

Chapter 9. Capital Effectiveness: Long-Term Assets

Chapter 10. Cost of Capital and the Intangibles

Part Three, Driving Performance and Value, describes how managers can use these tools to build shareholder value. Topics include effective implementation of a performance management framework, including integrating with other management practices; using these tools to improve the effectiveness of mergers and acquisitions; and finally a review of best practices and performance results based on the author's research into the performance of more than 125 companies. Part Three includes the following chapters:

Chapter 11. Building a Performance Management Framework

Chapter 12. The Economics of Mergers and Acquisitions

Chapter 13. Benchmark Takeaways and Summary

A glossary of commonly used financial, value, and performance measurement terms is included in the back of the book.

ABOUT THE CD-ROM

A number of illustrative performance dashboards and Excel models used in the book are included in the accompanying CD-ROM. These items are identified in the book with a CD-ROM logo, shown in the margin here. The dashboards and spreadsheets are intended as working examples and starting points for the reader's use. An important theme of this book is to underscore the importance of selecting the appropriate measures and dashboards. It is very important to carefully select the measures that are most appropriate for each circumstance. Accordingly, most of the dashboards and models will have to be tailored to fit the specific needs of the user.

The spreadsheets contain the data used in the examples provided in the book. In all cases, the input fields are highlighted in blue. Readers can save these files under a different name and use them to begin developing dashboards and analysis for their specific needs. Using the models on the CD-ROM requires Microsoft Excel software and an intermediate skill level in the use of that software. Additional information on the use of the CD-ROM can be found in the About the CD-ROM section on page 281.

QUESTIONS FOR CONSIDERATION

Each chapter ends with a set of questions for consideration. These are intended to encourage readers to apply some of the concepts and tools to the company they work for or to a business with which they are familiar. Accordingly, there are no "solutions" to these questions. In many cases, the reader is encouraged to utilize the analytical models and sample dashboards included on the CD-ROM.

JACK ALEXANDER

Southborough, Massachusetts
June 2006

About the Author

Jack Alexander is the founder and president of Value Advisory Group, LLC, a consulting and executive development firm with a focus on business performance management and shareholder value. Prior to establishing the consulting practice, he held a number of senior operating and financial positions in industry. Mr. Alexander served in several financial and operational management positions including corporate controller and chief financial officer at EG&G Inc., a global $2.5 billion technology and services company. He also served as senior vice president and chief financial officer for Mercury Computer Systems.

Mr. Alexander's prior experience includes positions at General Refractories Company and in the Philadelphia office of Coopers & Lybrand, now part of PricewaterhouseCoopers. He is a certified public accountant and a member of the Financial Executives Institute and the American Institute of Certified Public Accountants. He has an MBA from Rider University and a BS in Business Management from Indiana University of Pennsylvania.

Mr. Alexander is also an adjunct professor at Babson College, where he has taught corporate finance and advanced finance electives covering valuation, strategic investments, and mergers and acquisitions in both the MBA and undergraduate programs.

Acknowledgments

As a user and participant in the evolution of performance measures and other tools to build shareholder value, I am appreciative of the good work of others, including Aswath Damodaran and Tom Copeland on the subjects of valuation and shareholder value management.

I have been blessed to have exposure to a number of businesses, work with and for great people, and observe and participate in business from several different perspectives. The experience gained as a division finance and general manager, CFO, educator, and consultant has all contributed to the development of the tools incorporated in the Value Performance Framework and this book. I was first introduced to performance measures in the mid-1980s, primarily related to manufacturing and inventory management. Over time, the scope, depth, and use of performance measures has greatly expanded, as has the need to integrate these with financial results and value.

Prior to embarking on my teaching and consulting track, most of my professional career was with a terrific company, EG&G, Inc. The company had a large and diverse portfolio of businesses that provided ample opportunity for learning, as did the period of radical transformation during the 1990s. I had the pleasure of working with and learning from a number of terrific people at the division, group, and corporate level.

The time spent teaching at Babson College has been both rewarding and enlightening. I have learned a lot by teaching, especially how people learn and process information. I also received encouragement and feedback from students and colleagues on the tools incorporated in this book. The team at Mercury Computer Systems was very receptive to and supportive of many of the tools in the Framework. I also learned a great deal from my time at Coopers & Lybrand in Philadelphia. The exposure to a wide range of client companies, process orientation, accounting and reporting, and great people provided a solid foundation for future growth.

I also benefited greatly by knowing and working with a number of external business partners over the years, including bankers, consultants, and public accountants. Working with many directors, analysts, and investors over the years also contributed to my understanding of business, finance, and value.

A number of friends and colleagues were helpful in providing encouragement and feedback on this project, including Warren Davis, Phil Franchois, Dan Heaney, John Howard, Paul Crivello, Earl Kivett, Mike Vance, and especially Gary Olin. Special thanks to Bob Becker, Will Weddleton, Diane Basile, and Gary Olin for reviewing and commenting on the manuscript. Thanks to the team at John Wiley & Sons for their patience, guidance, and assistance with this first-time author, especially Emilie Herman, Bill Falloon, Laura Walsh, and Mary Daniello.

J. A.

The Management Challenge: Integrating Performance, Finance, and Value

One of the primary objectives of corporate managers and directors is to create value for the company's shareholders. Much has been said and written on this subject over the past 15 years. Yet many managers and most employees still have difficulty in fully understanding the drivers of shareholder value and how their activities relate to these drivers. The objective of this book, and the Value Performance Framework (VPF), is to assist managers and employees in developing a comprehensive understanding of valuation and creating a direct link between shareholder value and critical business processes.

Managers face many challenges in building shareholder value in today's business environment. They face pressure from all fronts, balancing demands from customers, suppliers, employees, regulators, and investors. In addition, they must integrate a number of available tools to build shareholder value. Many managers focus primarily on sales and earnings growth. However, many other factors will also affect shareholder value; it is a significant challenge to evaluate and incorporate them into a single management framework. Figure 1.1 presents many of these tools and illustrates the objectives of the Value Performance Framework:

- Demystify valuation.
- Identify key value drivers.
- Link value and performance.
- Identify high-leverage improvement opportunities.
- Build a comprehensive performance management system.
- Build long-term shareholder value.

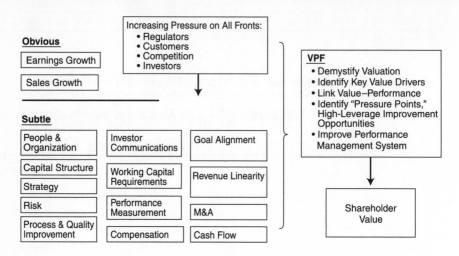

FIGURE 1.1 Managers Face Many Challenges in Managing Factors That Build Long-Term, Sustainable Shareholder Value. The VPF integrates obvious and subtle tools to build value into a single framework.

Note that we are using the verb *building* shareholder value, rather than *creating* value. It is important to recognize that building sustainable shareholder value is more akin to constructing a complex building than to a divine or mystical creation. It takes substantial effort, time, process, and a great team to lay the foundation for building long-term sustainable value. "Creating" also conjures up the images of the dot-com bubble and the unsustainable value created by accounting gimmickry. We will focus on those factors that lead to *building* and *sustaining* shareholder value.

WHAT IS SHAREHOLDER VALUE?

Shareholder value is defined as the market value of the firm's stock held by shareholders. It is commonly referred to as the market cap (capitalization) of the firm. It is calculated by multiplying the number of shares outstanding times the price of the stock. For example:

	Stock price	$25.00
×	Number of shares outstanding	10 million
=	Market value	$250 million

We will discuss the valuation techniques commonly used by investors to establish the stock price and market value of a firm in Chapter 3. For now, we need to simply understand that the market value of both private and publicly held firms will be determined by the expectations of future performance of the firm, primarily future revenues, earnings, and cash flows.

THE MEASUREMENT CHALLENGE

The single greatest challenge in creating an effective measurement system is to ensure that it supports the organization's objective for creating value by executing a strategic plan. Many attempts at building a performance management framework fail to achieve intended results because the context has not been created and the measures are not integrated with other key management practices and systems. Creating context builds excitement and purpose and takes performance management to a whole new level. In addition, operational, financial, and value measures must be understood, linked, and integrated. (See Figure 1.2.)

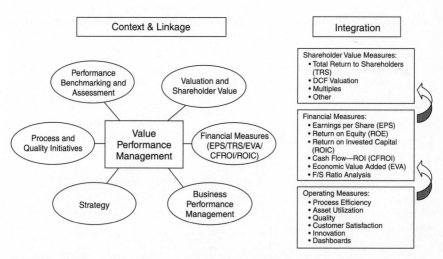

FIGURE 1.2 The Measurement Challenge: Creating Context and Effectively Integrating Value, Financial, and Operational Measures

ABOUT THE VALUE PERFORMANCE FRAMEWORK

The basic architecture for the Value Performance Framework is illustrated in Figure 1.3. The framework recognizes that there are a number of external factors that will affect shareholder value. These factors, such as the general economy, interest rates, and market valuation factors, will impact the value of all firms. Managers need to recognize these factors and understand the impact each has on their business performance and valuation. In this book, we focus on the value drivers that are largely under management's control:

- Sales growth.
- Relative pricing strength (competitive advantage).
- Operating effectiveness.
- Capital management.
- Cost of capital.
- The intangibles.

The critical element of the VPF is to link these value drivers to specific processes, activities, and improvement programs that resonate with managers and employees. Many managers and most employees do not under-

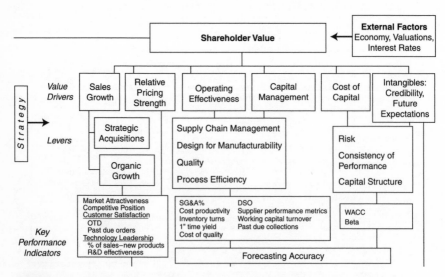

FIGURE 1.3   Building Shareholder Value Requires Performance across All Key Value Drivers
Source: Reprinted by permission of Value Advisory Group, LLC.

stand how their activities relate to shareholder value. For example, engineering groups may understand that their activities affect sales growth, but they may not fully understand the impact the activities have on working capital requirements of the firm. In most companies, a significant driver of inventory levels is the extent to which the products are designed for manufacturability (i.e., the design process has a focus on developing products that can be efficiently manufactured) and use common components. If the engineering group is sensitized to the impact of their practices on downstream business processes such as manufacturing, they have a context for more effective design decisions. If the firm establishes an effective set of performance measures—for example, to track the use of common components and product assembly steps—the future impact of design decisions on the supply chain process and inventory requirements can be measured. We cover more on this subject in Chapter 5.

Linking critical business processes to value drivers and financial performance in this manner can have a profound impact on the firm. Employees are more engaged if they feel connected to the company's overall performance and shareholder value. It becomes easier to choose between compet-

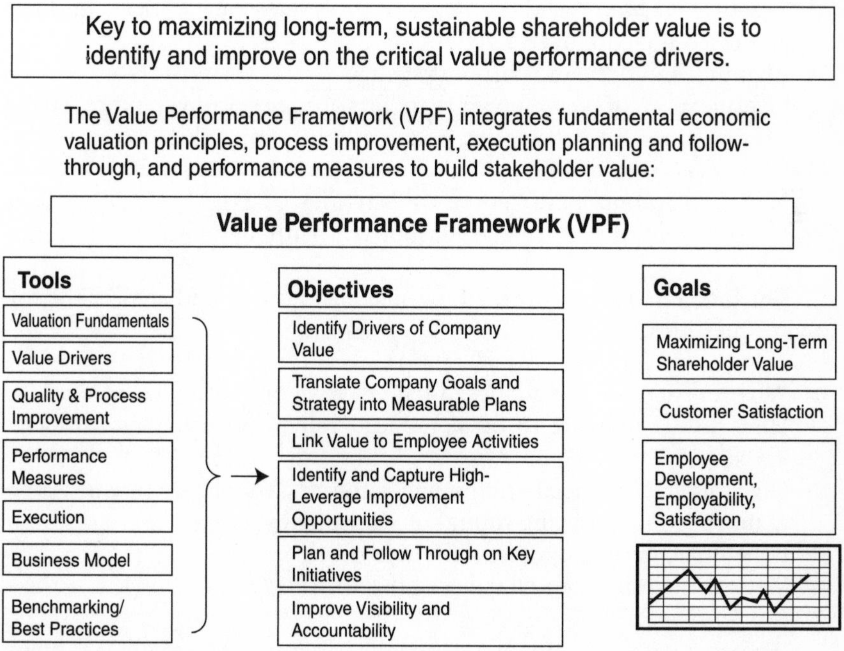

Key to maximizing long-term, sustainable shareholder value is to identify and improve on the critical value performance drivers.

The Value Performance Framework (VPF) integrates fundamental economic valuation principles, process improvement, execution planning and follow-through, and performance measures to build stakeholder value:

Value Performance Framework (VPF)

Tools	Objectives	Goals
Valuation Fundamentals	Identify Drivers of Company Value	Maximizing Long-Term Shareholder Value
Value Drivers		
Quality & Process Improvement	Translate Company Goals and Strategy into Measurable Plans	Customer Satisfaction
Performance Measures	Link Value to Employee Activities	
	Identify and Capture High-Leverage Improvement Opportunities	Employee Development, Employability, Satisfaction
Execution		
Business Model	Plan and Follow Through on Key Initiatives	
Benchmarking/ Best Practices	Improve Visibility and Accountability	

FIGURE 1.4 Value Performance Framework Overview

ing initiatives or projects when we can evaluate the potential contribution of each to long-term shareholder value. One of the great aspects of this link between shareholder value and process is the realization that shareholder value is not at odds with satisfying customers or employees. To the contrary, the framework underscores the need to attract, retain, develop, and motivate a competent workforce that exceeds customers' expectations. This in turn will lead to building long-term sustainable value for shareholders.

The key to implementing sustainable performance improvements and building long-term shareholder value is to integrate valuable business tools including value drivers, benchmarking, quality and process initiatives, and performance management into a cohesive management framework. This integrated framework is illustrated in Figure 1.4. Supported by research covering over 125 companies, the framework emphasizes the importance of linking shareholder value to critical business processes and employee activities. Key elements of the VPF include:

- Understanding key principles of valuation.
- Identification of key value drivers for a company.
- Assessing performance on critical business processes and measures through evaluation and external benchmarking.
- Creating a link between shareholder value and critical business processes and employee activities.
- Aligning employee and corporate goals.
- Identification of key "pressure points" (high-leverage improvement opportunities) and estimating potential impact on value.
- Implementation of a performance management system to improve visibility and accountability in critical activities.
- Development of performance dashboards with high visual impact.

The integrated framework allows managers to ask and answer the following questions:

- What impact will my quality initiatives have on shareholder value?
- How do we compare to best practice companies on key performance measures?
- Given limited financial and human resources, should we pursue a program to reduce working capital or warranty expense?
- How do acquisitions affect shareholder value?
- What is the full potential value of this firm?

We begin with a review of key financial concepts and build a common vocabulary in Chapter 2.

Creating Context and Covering the Basics

CHAPTER 2

Fundamentals of Finance

A key building block in our foundation for utilizing the Value Performance Framework is the ability to understand and evaluate financial statements and financial performance. This chapter presents a brief introduction (or refresher) to financial statements and financial ratios. Many of these financial ratios will be used as overall measures of a company's performance or as overall measures of performance on a particular driver of value.

BASICS OF ACCOUNTING AND FINANCIAL STATEMENTS

There are three primary financial statements: income statement, balance sheet, and the statement of cash flows. We need all three statements to properly understand and evaluate financial performance. However, the financial statements provide only limited insight into a company's performance and must be combined with key ratios and ultimately an understanding of the company's market, competitive position, and strategy, before evaluating a company's current performance and value.

Financial statements are based on generally accepted accounting principles (GAAP). A key objective of financial statements prepared under GAAP is to match revenues and expenses. Two significant conventions arise from this objective: the accrual method of accounting and depreciation. These two conventions are significant in our intended use of financial statements for economic evaluation and valuation purposes, since they result in differences between accounting income and cash flow.

Accrual Accounting

Financial statements record income when earned and expenses when incurred. For example, the accrual basis of accounting will record sales when the terms of the contract are fulfilled, usually prior to collection of cash.

TABLE 2.1 Comparison of Common P&L Measures

	Abbreviation	P&L	EBIT	EBIAT	EBITDA	EP
Sales		$100,000	$100,000	$100,000	$100,000	$100,000
Cost of Goods Sold	COGS	50,000	50,000	50,000	50,000	50,000
Gross Margin	GM	50,000	50,000	50,000	50,000	50,000
% of Sales		50.0%	50.0%	50.0%	50.0%	50.0%
Research & Development	R&D	5,000	5,000	5,000	5,000	5,000
Selling, General, & Administrative Expenses	SG&A	15,000	15,000	15,000	15,000	15,000
Depreciation and Amortization	D&A	10,000	10,000	10,000	—	10,000
Operating Profit	OP	20,000	20,000	20,000	30,000	20,000
% of Sales		20.0%	20.0%	20.0%	30.0%	20.0%
Interest Expense		3,000				
Profit Before Tax	PBT	17,000				
Income Tax	35.0%	5,950		7,000		7,000
Net Income (Profit After Tax)	PAT	$ 11,050				
%		11.1%				
Earnings Before Interest and Taxes	EBIT		$ 20,000			
Earnings Before Interest *After* Taxes	EBIAT			$ 13,000		13,000
Earnings Before Interest, Taxes, Depreciation, and Amortization	EBITDA				$ 30,000	
Capital Charge						10,000
Economic Profit	EP					$ 3,000

Similarly, expenses are recorded when service is performed rather than when paid for.

Depreciation

Generally accepted accounting principles require that an expenditure for such things as property, plant, and equipment with long lives be recorded as an asset and depreciated over the expected useful life of the asset. As a result, when a firm spends cash to purchase equipment, it records it as an asset on the balance sheet and depreciates the cost of that asset each year on the income statement.

Income Statement (aka Profit and Loss)

The income statement, or what is frequently referred to as the profit and loss (P&L) statement, is a summary of all transactions completed during the period (year, quarter, etc.). Typical captions and math logic for a basic income statement include:

Sales	+	$1,000
Cost of goods sold	–	500
Gross margin	=	500
Operating expenses	–	200
Operating income	=	300
Income tax expense	–	100
Net income	=	200

Many different measures, terms, and acronyms are used in practice to describe various elements of the P&L. Table 2.1 illustrates how some of these common measures are determined as well as how they relate to one another.

Following are definitions of some key terms used in Table 2.1:

- *Net income.* Residual of income over expense. Sometimes referred to as profit after tax (PAT).
- *Earnings before interest and taxes (EBIT).* This measure reflects the income generated by operating activities (generally equals or approximates operating income) before subtracting financing costs (interest) and income tax expense.
- *Earnings before interest after taxes (EBIAT).* Also known as net operating profit after taxes (NOPAT) or operating profit after taxes (OPAT), this measure estimates the after-tax operating earnings. It

excludes financing costs but does reflect income tax expense. It is useful in comparing and evaluating the operational performance of firms, excluding the impact of financing costs.

- **Earnings before interest, taxes, depreciation, and amortization (EBITDA).** EBITDA adjusts EBIT (operating income) by adding back noncash charges, depreciation, and amortization. This measure is used in valuation and financing decisions, since it approximates cash generated by the operation. It does not reflect capital requirements such as working capital and expenditures for property and equipment.

- **Economic profit (EP).** Economic profit measures, including Economic Value Added (EVA™) developed by Stern Stewart & Company,[1] subtract a capital charge from the earnings to arrive at an economic profit. The capital charge is computed based on the level of capital employed in the business.

Balance Sheet

The balance sheet is a critical financial report. It is a summary of the company's assets, liabilities, and owner's equity and represents a snapshot of all open transactions as of the reporting date. For example, the inventory balance represents all materials delivered to the company, work in process, and finished goods not yet shipped to customers. Accounts payable represents open invoices due vendors that have not been paid as of the balance sheet date.

The balance sheet can be a good indicator of the efficiency of an operation. A firm with a very effective manufacturing process will have lower inventory levels than a similar firm with less effective practices.

The balance sheet is constructed as shown in Table 2.2.

Another way to look at the balance sheet is to reorder the traditional format (Table 2.2) to identify the net operating assets and the sources of capital provided to the organization. This presentation is more useful in understanding the dynamics of the balance sheet. The net operating assets are those assets that are required to operate and support the business. The net operating assets must be funded (or provided to the firm) by investors, either bondholders or shareholders, as illustrated in Table 2.3.

---

[1] EVA is a registered trademark of Stern Stewart & Company.

TABLE 2.2   Balance Sheet: Assets = Liabilities + Shareholders' Equity

Assets		Liabilities and Equity	
Cash	$150	Accounts Payable	$100
Receivables	200	Accrued Liabilities	100
Inventories	200	Debt	200
Fixed Assets, Net	50	Total Liabilities	400
		Stockholders' Equity	200
Total Assets	$600	Total Liabilities and Equity	$600

TABLE 2.3   Net Operating Assets/Invested Capital Illustration

Net Assets		Sources of Capital	
Cash	$150		
Receivables	200		
Inventories	200		
Fixed Assets, Net	50		
		Debt	$200
Total Assets	$600		
Less Operating Liabilities		Shareholders' Equity	200
Accounts Payable	−100		
Accrued Liabilities	−100		
Net Assets	$400	Total Invested Capital	$400

Statement of Cash Flows

The statement of cash flows (SCF) summarizes the cash generated and uti-lized by the enterprise during the specific period (year, quarter, etc.). Since cash flow will be a focus of our economic valuation and is an important business measure, we will pay particular interest to cash flows in the VPF framework. The statement of cash flows starts with the net income gener-ated by the company over the period, as reported on the income statement.

Since net income is based on various accounting conventions, such as the matching principle, the SCF identifies various adjustments to net in-come to arrive at cash flow. In addition, we also will have to factor in vari-ous cash flow items that are not reflected in net income, such as working capital requirements, dividends, and purchases of equipment.

A simplified format for a statement of cash flows is shown in Table 2.4.

TABLE 2.4 Cash Flow Statement

Net Income	$200
Depreciation and Amortization	10
(Increase) Decrease in Working Capital	–25
Purchases of Property and Equipment	–25
Operating Cash Flow	$160
Dividends	0
Debt Repayments	–60
Cash Flow	$100

The three primary financial statements just discussed are interrelated. Understanding these relationships is critical to evaluating business performance and valuation and is presented in Figure 2.1. For example, net income (or PAT) flows from the income statement to increase shareholders' equity in the balance sheet. Net income for the period is also the starting point for the statement of cash flows. Other elements on the statement of cash flows are the result of year-to-year changes in various balance sheet accounts, including capital expenditures, changes in working capital, and reductions or increases in borrowings. Finally, fi-

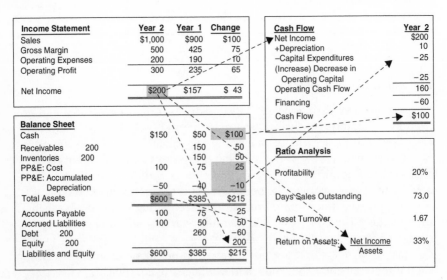

FIGURE 2.1 Financial Statement Interrelationships

nancial ratios look at the relationship of various line items both within each financial statement and across all financial statements (e.g., return on assets).

FINANCIAL RATIOS AND INDICATORS

Financial ratios can be very useful tools in measuring and evaluating business performance. Ratios can be used as tools in understanding profitability, asset utilization, liquidity, and key business trends and in evaluating overall management performance and effectiveness.

Usefulness

Using financial ratios can provide a great deal of insight into a company's performance, particularly when combined with an understanding of the company and its industry. In addition to providing measures of performance, financial ratios can be used to monitor key trends over time and in comparing a company's performance to peers or best-practice companies.

Variations

There are a number of different financial terms and ratios, and variations of each of these are in use. This leads to potential confusion when similar-sounding measures are computed differently or used interchangeably. It is important to clearly define the specific ratio or financial measure used.

Key Financial Ratios

To illustrate key financial ratios we will use the information in Table 2.5 for Simple Co. Unless otherwise indicated, the ratios will be computed using the estimated results for 2006 (2006E).

OPERATING MEASURES

Operating measures include ratios that provide insight into the operating performance of the company. These measures typically utilize the information presented in the income statement.

TABLE 2.5 Simple Co. Historical and Estimated 2006 Financials

	2003	2004	2005	2006E
P&L				
Net Sales	$79,383	$85,734	$92,593	$100,000
Cost of Goods Sold	35,722	38,580	41,667	45,000
Gross Margin	43,661	47,154	50,926	55,000
SG&A	25,403	27,435	29,630	32,000
R&D	6,351	6,859	7,407	8,000
Operating Income	11,907	12,860	13,889	15,000
Interest (Income) Expense	600	600	600	600
Other (Income) Expense	5	7	6	5
Income Before Income Taxes	11,302	12,253	13,283	14,395
Federal Income Taxes	3,843	4,166	4,516	4,894
Net Income	$ 7,460	$ 8,087	$ 8,767	$ 9,501
Balance Sheet				
Cash	$ 25	$ 2,404	$ 4,400	$ 7,944
Receivables	15,877	17,147	18,545	20,000
Inventories	14,289	15,432	16,667	18,000
Other	200	800	975	900
Current Assets	30,391	35,783	40,587	46,844
Net Fixed Assets	15,877	17,147	18,750	20,000
Net Goodwill and Intangibles	14,000	13,000	12,000	11,000
Other Noncurrent Assets	200	210	428	205
Total Assets	$60,467	$66,140	$71,765	$ 78,049
Accounts Payable	$ 3,572	$ 3,858	$ 4,167	$ 4,500
Notes Payable, Bank	—	—	—	—
Accrued Expenses and Taxes	4,000	4,500	4,750	5,000
Current Liabilities	7,572	8,358	8,917	9,500
Long-Term Debt	10,000	10,000	10,000	10,000
Other	3,000	3,100	2,900	3,300
Stockholders' Equity	39,895	44,682	49,949	55,249
Total Liabilities and Equity	$60,467	$66,140	$71,765	$ 78,049

TABLE 2.5 *(Continued)*

		2003	2004	2005	2006E
Other Information					
Stock Price		9.22	9.78	10.00	10.59
Shares Outstanding (in Millions)		16.7	16.8	16.9	17.0
Market Value of Equity		$153,974	$164,304	$169,000	$180,030
Interest Rate	6%				
Income Tax Rate	34%				
Dividends		$3,000	$3,300	$3,500	$4,200
Capital Expenditures		$3,000	$4,200	$4,800	$5,000
D&A		$2,800	$2,930	$3,197	$3,750
Employees		411	450	460	490

Other Information
Comparable companies are trading in the following ranges (trailing 12 months):

	Low	High
Sales	1.3	2.0
Earnings (P/E)	16.0	20.0
EBITDA	8.0	10.0
PEG	1.3	2.0

Cost of Capital (WACC)	12%

Sales Growth

Sales growth is an important determiner of financial performance. Based only on information in the income statement, we are limited to measuring the sales growth rate over periods reported. Two key sales growth measures are year-over-year growth and the compound annual growth rate.

Year-over-Year Growth Simple Co.'s sales are expected to grow from $92,593 in 2005 to $100,000 in 2006. This represents a growth of 8 percent in 2006:

$$\text{Growth Rate} = \frac{\$100,000}{\$92,593} - 1 = 8\%$$

Compound Annual Growth Rate   This measure looks at the growth rate over time (n years). The compound annual growth rate from 2003 to 2006 is computed as follows:

$$
\text{Compound Growth Rate} = \left(\frac{\text{Sales } 2006}{\text{Sales } 2003} \right)^{-1/n} - 1
$$

$$
= \left(\frac{\$100,000}{\$79,383} \right)^{1/3} - 1
$$

$$
= 8\%
$$

Revenue growth contributed by acquisitions has significantly different economic characteristics. As a result, total revenue growth is frequently split between "acquired" and "organic" growth.

Gross Margin % Sales

How Is It Computed?   Gross margin % is simply the gross margin as a percentage of total revenues.

$$
\text{Gross Margin } \% = \frac{\text{Gross Margin}}{\text{Sales}}
$$

$$
= \frac{\$55,000}{\$100,000}
$$

$$
= 55\%
$$

What Does It Measure and Reflect?   Gross margin % is an important financial indicator. Gross margins vary widely across industries, ranging from razor-thin margins of 10 to 15 percent to very high margins approaching 70 or even 80 percent.

The gross margin % will be impacted by a number of factors and therefore will require substantial analysis. The factors affecting gross margin include:

- Industry.
- Competition and pricing.
- Product mix.
- Composition of fixed and variable costs.

- Product costs.
- Production variances.
- Material and labor costs.

Research and Development (R&D) % Sales

How Is It Computed?

$$R\&D\ \%\ Sales = \frac{R\&D}{Sales}$$
$$= \frac{\$8,000}{\$100,000}$$
$$= 8\%$$

What Does It Measure and Reflect?   This ratio determines the level of investment in research and development (R&D) compared to the current period sales. This ratio will vary significantly from industry to industry and from high-growth to low-growth companies. Some industries, for example retail, may have little or no R&D. Other firms, such as pharmaceuticals or technology companies, will likely have large R&D spending. Firms in high-growth markets or investing heavily for future growth will have very large levels of R&D, occasionally exceeding 20 percent of sales.

Selling, General, and Administrative (SG&A) % Sales

How Is It Computed?

$$SG\&A\ \%\ Sales = \frac{SG\&A}{Sales}$$
$$= \frac{\$32,000}{\$100,000}$$
$$= 32\%$$

What Does It Measure and Reflect?   Since this measure compares the level of SG&A spending to sales, it provides a view of spending levels in selling and distributing the firm's products and in supporting the administrative aspects of the business. The measure will reflect the method of distribution, process efficiency, and administrative overhead. In addition, SG&A will often include costs associated with initiating or introducing new products.

Operating Income (EBIT) % Sales

How Is It Computed?

$$\text{EBIT \% Sales} = \frac{\text{Operating Income}}{\text{Sales}}$$
$$= \frac{\$15,000}{\$100,000}$$
$$= 15\%$$

What Does It Measure and Reflect?   This is a broad measure of operating performance. It will reflect operating effectiveness, relative pricing strength, and level of investments for future growth.

Return on Sales (Profitability)

How Is It Computed?

$$\text{Return on Sales} = \frac{\text{Net Income}}{\text{Sales}}$$
$$= \frac{\$9,501}{\$100,000}$$
$$= 9.5\%$$

What Does It Measure and Reflect?   This is an overall measure of performance. In addition to the factors described under Operating Income (EBIT) % Sales, this measure reflects taxes and other income and expense items.

ASSET UTILIZATION MEASURES

Asset utilization is a very important element in total financial performance. It is a significant driver of cash flow and return to investors.

Days Sales Outstanding (DSO)

How Is It Computed?

$$\text{DSO} = \frac{\text{Receivables} \times 365}{\text{Sales}}$$
$$= \frac{\$20,000 \times 365}{\$100,000}$$
$$= 73 \text{ days}$$

What Does It Measure and Reflect?   Days sales outstanding (DSO) is a measure of the length of time it takes to collect receivables from customers. It will be impacted by the industry in which the firm participates, the creditworthiness of customers, nature of distribution channels, and even the countries in which the firm does business. In addition, DSO is affected by the efficiency and effectiveness of the revenue process (billing and collection), product quality, and even by the pattern of shipments within the quarter or the year.

Inventory Turns

How Is It Computed?

$$\text{Inventory Turns} = \frac{\text{Cost of Goods Sold (COGS)}}{\text{Inventory}}$$

$$= \frac{\$45,000}{\$18,000}$$

$$= 2.5 \text{ times (turns per year)}$$

What Does It Measure and Reflect?   Inventory turns measure how much inventory a firm carries compared to sales levels. Factors that will affect this measure include effectiveness of supply chain management and production processes, product quality, degree of vertical integration, and predictability of sales.

Days Sales in Inventory (DSI)

How Is It Computed?

$$\text{DSI} = \frac{365}{\text{Inventory Turns}}$$

$$= \frac{365}{2.5}$$

$$= 146 \text{ days}$$

What Does It Measure and Reflect?   This measure is impacted by the same factors as inventory turns. The advantage to this measure is that it is easier for people to relate to the days sales in inventory (DSI) number; it is easier to conceptualize the appropriateness (or potential improvement opportunity) of carrying 146 days' worth of sales in inventory than it is 2.5 inventory turns.

Operating Cash Cycle

How Is It Computed?

$$\text{Operating Cash Cycle} = \text{DSO} + \text{DSI}$$
$$= 73 + 146$$
$$= 219 \text{ days}$$

What Does It Measure and Reflect?   Operating cash cycle measures the overall efficiency and cycle time in the business by combining the number of days' worth of inventory on hand with the length of time it takes the firm to collect invoices from customers. The factors impacting this measure are the aggregate of those affecting DSO, inventory turns, and DSI.

Operating Capital Turnover and Operating Capital % Sales

How Are They Computed?

$$\text{Operating Capital \% Sales} = \frac{\text{Operating Capital}}{\text{Sales}}$$
$$= \frac{\$29,400}{\$100,000}$$
$$= 29.4\% \text{ or } 3.4 \text{ turns per year}$$

Operating capital is computed as follows:

Receivables	$20,000
Inventory	18,000
Other current assets	900
Accounts payable	– 4,500
Accrued expenses	– 5,000
Operating capital	$29,400

What Do They Measure and Reflect?   These measures reflect the net cash that is tied up in supporting the operating requirements of the business. The factors impacting them are the aggregate of those affecting DSO and inventory turns, as well as the timing of payments to vendors, employees, and suppliers.

Capital Asset Intensity (Fixed Asset Turnover)

How Is It Computed?

$$\text{Capital Asset Intensity} = \frac{\text{Sales}}{\text{Net Fixed Assets}}$$
$$= \frac{\$100,000}{\$20,000}$$
$$= 5 \text{ turns per year}$$

What Does It Measure and Reflect? This measure reflects the level of investment in property, plant, and equipment relative to sales. Some businesses are very capital intensive—that is, they require a substantial investment in capital—whereas others have modest requirements. For example, electric utility and transportation industries typically require high capital investments. On the other end of the spectrum, software development companies would usually require minimal levels of capital.

Asset Turnover

How Is It Computed?

$$\text{Asset Turnover} = \frac{\text{Sales}}{\text{Total Assets}}$$
$$= \frac{\$100,000}{\$78,049}$$
$$= 1.28 \text{ turns per year}$$

What Does It Measure and Reflect? This measure reflects the level of investment in all assets, including working capital, property, plant and equipment, and intangible assets, relative to sales. It reflects each of the individual asset utilization factors discussed earlier.

CAPITAL STRUCTURE/LIQUIDITY MEASURES

Capital structure and liquidity measures are indicators of the firm's source of capital (debt vs. equity), creditworthiness, ability to service existing debt, and ability to raise additional financing if needed.

Our definition of debt includes all interest-bearing obligations. The following measures include notes payable, current maturities of long-term debt (long-term debt due within one year), and other long-term debt.

For Simple Co.:

Notes payable	$ —
Current maturities of long-term debt	—
Long-term debt	10,000
Total debt	$10,000

Debt to Equity

How Is It Computed?

$$D/E = \frac{Debt}{Equity}$$
$$= \frac{\$10,000}{\$55,249}$$
$$= 18.1\%$$

What Does It Measure and Reflect?   The debt to equity (DE) percentage measures the proportion of total book capital supplied by bondholders (debt) versus shareholders (equity).

Debt to Total Capital

How Is It Computed?

$$D/TC = \frac{Debt}{Debt + Equity}$$
$$= \frac{\$10,000}{\$10,000 + \$55,249}$$
$$= 15.3\%$$

What Does It Measure and Reflect?   This measure computes the percentage of total book value (as recorded on the books and financial statements) of capital supplied by bondholders. A low debt to total capital percentage indicates that most of the capital to run the firm has been supplied by stockholders. A high percentage, say 70 percent, would indicate that most of the capital has been supplied by bondholders. The capital structure for the latter example would be considered highly leveraged. This measure is also computed using market value of debt and equity.

Times Interest Earned (Interest Coverage)

How Is It Computed?

$$TIE = \frac{\text{EBIT or Operating Income}}{\text{Interest Expense}}$$

$$= \frac{\$15,000}{\$600}$$

$$= 25 \times$$

What Does It Measure and Reflect?   This measure computes the number of times the firm earns the interest expense on current borrowings. A high number reflects slack, indicating an ability to cover interest expense even if income were to be reduced significantly. Alternatively, it indicates a capacity to borrow more funds if necessary.

OVERALL MEASURES OF PERFORMANCE

The following measures provide a basis for evaluating the overall effectiveness of business performance.

Return on Assets (ROA)

How Is It Computed?

$$ROA = \frac{\text{Net Income}}{\text{Assets}}$$

$$= \frac{\$9,501}{\$78,049}$$

$$= 12.2\%$$

What Does It Measure and Reflect?   This measure computes the level of income generated on the assets employed by the firm. It is an important overall measure of effectiveness since it considers the level of income relative to the level of assets employed in the business.

Return on Equity (ROE)

How Is It Computed?

$$ROE = \frac{\text{Net Income}}{\text{Equity}}$$
$$= \frac{\$9,501}{\$55,249}$$
$$= 17.2\%$$

What Does It Measure and Reflect?   This measure computes the income earned on the book value of the company's equity.

Note that ROE is greater than ROA. This is because part of the capital of the firm is furnished by bondholders and this financial leverage enhances the return to stockholders (ROE).

Understanding ROE   A very useful analytical tool that can be used to understand the drivers of ROE is to break the measure down into components. This methodology, often called the Dupont Model or return tree, is illustrated here:

$$ROE = \text{Profitability} \times \text{Asset Turnover} \times \text{Financial Leverage}$$
$$= \frac{\text{Net Income}}{\text{Sales}} \times \frac{\text{Sales}}{\text{Assets}} \times \frac{\text{Assets}}{\text{Equity}}$$

For Simple Co.:

$$17.2\% = 9.5\% \times 1.28 \times 1.41$$

Using this formula, we can compare the performance of one company to another by examining the components of ROE. It is also useful to examine ROE performance over time and to determine how a change in each of the components would affect ROE. For example, if we improve profitability to 10.5 percent, ROE will improve to 19 percent. The individual components (profitability, asset turnover, and financial leverage) can be further broken down into a tree to highlight the contributions of individual measures, for example, DSO or SG&A % Sales.

Return on Invested Capital (ROIC)

How Is It Computed?

$$\text{ROIC} = \frac{\text{EBIAT (Earnings Before Interest After Tax)}}{\text{Invested Capital}}$$

$$= \frac{\text{EBIT} \times (1 - \text{Tax Rate})}{\text{Debt} + \text{Equity}}$$

$$= \frac{\$15,000 \times (1 - .34)}{\$10,000 + \$55,249}$$

$$= \frac{\$9,900}{\$65,249}$$

$$= 15.2\%$$

What Does It Measure and Reflect? ROIC measures the income available to all suppliers of capital (debt and equity) relative to the total capital provided from all sources (debt and equity). Another way of looking at ROIC is that this measure indicates the amount of income a company earns for each dollar invested in the company, including both debt and equity.

Return on Invested Capital—Market (ROICM)

A variation to the ROIC measure is to use the market value of capital, rather than the historical book value.

How Is It Computed?

$$\text{ROICM} = \frac{\text{EBIAT (Earnings Before Interest After Tax)}}{\text{Invested Capital (Market)}}$$

$$= \frac{\text{EBIT} \times (1 - \text{Tax Rate})}{\text{Debt} + \text{Equity (Market)}}$$

$$= \frac{\$15,000 \times (1 - .34)}{\$10,000 + \$180,030}$$

$$= \frac{\$9,900}{\$191,030}$$

$$= 5.2\%$$

What Does It Measure and Reflect?   ROICM measures the income available to all suppliers of capital (debt and equity) relative to the total capital provided from all sources (debt and equity) at current market values. While ROIC is a good measure of management effectiveness, ROICM relates current income levels to the market value of a company. A very low ROICM may indicate that the company's market value is high compared to current performance. This may be due to extremely high expectations for future growth or a potential overvaluation of the company's stock.

Total Return to Shareholders

One of the best overall measures of financial performance is total return to shareholders (TRS). It reflects the return provided to shareholders considering both stock appreciation and any dividends paid over a period of time. The only limitations to this measure are that it is a *historical* measure looking back several years and is impacted by fluctuations in the stock market that may be independent of the company's performance.

Public companies in the United States are required to report TRS to shareholders annually in their proxy statements filed with the Securities and Exchange Commission. In addition to the TRS for the firm, the company must provide two benchmarks, typically an industry comparison and an overall comparison to the broad market. The analysis assumes that $100 was invested in the company's stock and in the comparative benchmarks at the beginning of the period. A related measure computes the compound annual growth rate (CAGR) embedded in the TRS over that time:

$$\text{TRS CAGR} = \left(\frac{\text{TRS Value Year 5}}{\text{Investment Year 0}} \right)^{1/5} - 1$$

Figure 2.2 presents the TRS information reported by Procter & Gamble (P&G) in its 2005 proxy statement. The first graph is the required presentation of stock performance over the five-year horizon from mid-2000 to mid-2005. The second graph reflects the value of the $100 investment in P&G stock and benchmark comparisons at the end of the five-year period and includes the compound annual growth rate over that time.

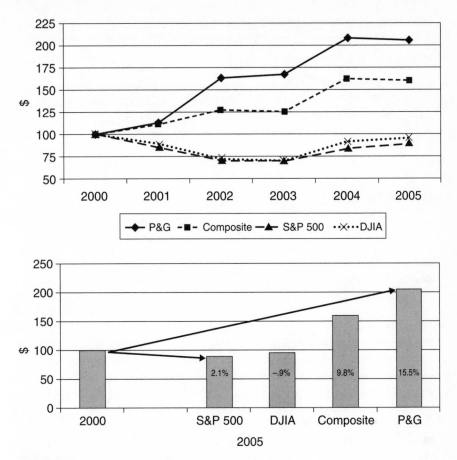

FIGURE 2.2 TRS Disclosure for Procter & Gamble
Source: P&G 2005 proxy statement filed with the Securities and Exchange Commission.

CASH GENERATION AND REQUIREMENTS

In addition to measures such as EBITDA, others have been developed to measure and evaluate cash flow.

Cash Effectiveness (CE%)

Some managers and analysts measure the operating cash flow relative to the income generated as a measure of cash effectiveness.

TABLE 2.6 Cash Effectiveness for Simple Co.

OPAT	$9,900	100%
Depreciation and Amortization	3,750	38
Capital Expenditures	−5,000	−51
(Increase) Decrease in Operating Capital	−2,130	−22
Operating Cash Flow	$6,520	66%

How Is It Computed?

$$\text{Cash Effectiveness \%} = \frac{\text{Operating Cash Flow}}{\text{Operating Profit after Tax}}$$

The cash effectiveness for Simple Co. for 2006 is estimated to be 66 percent (see Table 2.6).

What Does It Measure and Reflect? The cash effectiveness ratio (CE%) can be an insightful measure of the relationship between reported income and cash flow. A significant decrease in the ratio may signal that receivables collections are slowing or inventories are growing faster than income. Conversely, an increase in the percentage may indicate that the company is doing a better job in managing receivables, inventories, and capital investments. However, this measure is highly dependent on the rate of growth and maturity of a business. A fast-growing company may have a very low or even negative cash effectiveness percentage, since asset levels must grow to support future sales growth. A company that is shrinking may find it easy to post CE% greater than 100 percent since capital investment levels will often decline faster than sales.

Self-Financing or Internal Growth Rate (IGR)

Managers must understand whether the company is generating enough cash flow from operations to meet requirements to support future growth. A company that is self-financing will generate enough cash from operations to satisfy working capital and other requirements to support growth. Many companies test this requirement with future cash flow projections. Others use rules of thumb; for example, in order to support future growth levels of 15 percent a company needs an ROIC of 20 percent. Ross et al. have developed a formula to estimate the self-financing growth rate given a firm's ROA and cash retention policy.[2]

How Is It Computed?

$$IGR = \frac{ROA \times r}{1 - (ROA \times r)}$$

where r is the percentage of net income retained in the business (i.e., not paid out as dividends to shareholders). For Simple Co.:

$$r = 1 - \frac{\text{Dividends and Share Repurchases}}{\text{Net Income}}$$
$$= 1 - \frac{\$4,200}{\$9,501}$$
$$= .5579$$

$$IGR = \frac{12.2\% \times .5579}{1 - (12.2\% \times .5579)}$$
$$= 7.3\%$$

What Does It Measure and Reflect?   This measure provides a good estimate of the rate at which the firm can grow without requiring outside financing. If Simple Co. grows at a rate faster than 7 percent, it will need to raise additional funds. If growth is under 7.3 percent, then the firm is generating enough cash to fund the growth. If the firm desires to increase the internal growth rate, it can retain a greater percentage of earnings or increase ROA.

---

[2]S. A. Ross, R. W. Westerfield, and B. D. Jordan, *Fundamentals of Corporate Finance*, 5th ed. (McGraw-Hill, 2000), 102.

LIMITATIONS AND PITFALLS OF FINANCIAL RATIOS

Since the measures are based on financial statements that are prepared after the close of the period, these ratios are referred to as "lagging" measures of performance. We will discuss leading/predictive indicators a bit later, as we consider each of the value drivers in detail, beginning in Chapter 5.

Some managers place too much emphasis on blindly comparing ratios from one company to another. In order to effectively compare ratios across companies, it is important to understand the strategy, markets, and structure of each company. For example, a company that is vertically integrated will likely post significantly different financial results than one that is not. A company with a strong value-adding product in a growing market will likely have very different characteristics than a company participating in a competitive, slower-growth market.

Financial ratios should be used as part of a broader diagnostic evaluation. These ratios will provide a great basis to identify trends, will complement other aspects of an overall assessment, and will be a great source of questions. Think of them in the same way a medical doctor uses key quantitative data about a patient's health. Even in routine examinations, doctors monitor key factors such as weight. But a patient's weight provides limited insight until combined with other insights, observations, and comparisons. How does the weight compare with the weight of others of the same age, height, and frame? Has the patient gained or lost weight since the last exam? Lost weight? Why? This obviously could be good if intended as part of a fitness program or bad if a result of a health problem. Only through observation, discussion with the patient, and perhaps additional testing can the doctor reach a conclusion. So it is with many elements of financial performance.

Another potential limitation is that a great variety of similar ratios are employed in business. An example is return on capital. There are a number of potential definitions for both the income measure and the capital measure in such a ratio. It is important to understand exactly what is being measured by a formula before reaching any conclusions.

Similarly, it is important to understand the period to which the measure relates. Many measures could apply to monthly, quarterly, or annual periods. Further, an annual measure could be based on a balance at the end of the period or an average of each of the quarters.

PUTTING IT ALL TOGETHER

These individual ratios and measures take on greater meaning when combined as part of an analytical summary, as shown in Table 2.7.

Creating a set of graphs capturing selected performance measures will typically be helpful to analyze and communicate this information, as shown in Figure 2.3.

Table 2.8 provides a quick reference guide to key financial terms and measures.

SUMMARY

Understanding and interpreting financial statements is a required competency for effective management and investing. Combining this competency with an understanding of the business, industry, and strategic objectives of a firm can significantly improve management effectiveness and decision making. Historical and projected financial statements will serve as the basis for many decisions and are an important part of the foundation in building an effective performance management framework.

QUESTIONS FOR CONSIDERATION

1. Using the Performance Assessment Summary (Table 2.7) on the CD- ROM, assess the performance of your company. If you are unfamiliar with the financial ratios and measures, compute those ratios manually using the formulas provided in this chapter.
2. How is the company performing on key measures?
3. What trends and changes in performance have occurred? What is the underlying cause of any changes?

TABLE 2.7 Simple Co. Performance Assessment Summary: Historical and Estimated 2006 Financials

	2003	2004	2005	2006E	2003	2004	2005	2006E	CAGR
P&L									
Net Sales	$79,383	$85,734	$92,593	$100,000	100%	100%	100%	100%	8.0%
Cost of Goods Sold	35,722	38,580	41,667	45,000	45	45	45	45	8.0
Gross Margin	43,661	47,154	50,926	55,000	55	55	55	55	8.0
SG&A	25,403	27,435	29,630	32,000	32	32	32	32	8.0
R&D	6,351	6,859	7,407	8,000	8	8	8	8	8.0
Operating Income	11,907	12,860	13,889	15,000	15	15	15	15	8.0
Interest (Income) Expense	600	600	600	600	1	1	1	1	0.0
Other (Income) Expense	5	7	6	5	0	0	0	0	0.0
Income Before Income Taxes	11,302	12,253	13,283	14,395	14	14	14	14	8.4
Federal Income Taxes	3,843	4,166	4,516	4,894	5	5	5	5	8.4
Net Income	7,460	8,087	8,767	9,501	9	9	9	10	8.4
EPS	0.45	0.48	0.52	0.56					
EBIAT	$ 7,859	$ 8,488	$ 9,167	$ 9,900					
Balance Sheet									
Cash	$ 25	$ 2,404	$ 4,400	$ 7,944	0%	3%	5%	8%	
Receivables	15,877	17,147	18,545	20,000	20	20	20	20	
Inventories	14,289	15,432	16,667	18,000	18	18	18	18	
Other	200	800	975	900	0	1	1	1	
Current Assets	30,391	35,783	40,587	46,844	38	42	44	47	

Net Fixed Assets	15,877	17,147	18,750	20,000	20	20	20	20
Net Goodwill and Intangibles	14,000	13,000	12,000	11,000	18	15	13	11
Other Noncurrent Assets	200	210	428	205	0	0	0	0
Total Assets	$60,467	$66,140	$71,765	$78,049	76%	77%	78%	78%
Accounts Payable	$ 3,572	$ 3,858	$ 4,167	$ 4,500	5%	5%	5%	5%
Notes Payable, Bank	—	—	—	—	0	0	0	0
Accrued Expenses and Taxes	4,000	4,500	4,750	5,000	5	5	5	5
Current Liabilities	7,572	8,358	8,917	9,500	10	10	10	10
Long-Term Debt	10,000	10,000	10,000	10,000	13	12	11	10
Other	3,000	3,100	2,900	3,300	4	4	3	3
Stockholders' Equity	39,895	44,682	49,949	55,249	50	52	54	55
Total Liabilities and Equity	$60,467	$66,140	$71,765	$78,049	76%	77%	78%	78%
Operating Capital	$22,793	$25,021	$27,270	$29,400				
Invested Capital	49,895	54,682	59,949	65,249				
Market Value of Equity	153,974	164,304	169,000	180,030				
Cash Flow								
Net Income	7,460	8,087	8,767	9,501	9%	9%	9%	10%
D&A	2,800	2,930	3,197	3,750	4	3	3	4
Capital Expenditures	-3,000	-4,200	-4,800	-5,000	-4	-5	-5	-5
(Increase) Decrease in OC		-2,228	-2,249	-2,130	0	-3	-2	-2
CF	$ 7,260	$ 4,589	$ 4,914	$ 6,121	9%	5%	5%	6%

(Continued)

TABLE 2.7 (Continued)

	2003	2004	2005	2006E	2003	2004	2005	2006E	CAGR
Employees	411	450	460	490					
Returns/Ratios									
DSO	73.0	73.0	73.1	73.0					
Inventory Turns	2.5	2.5	2.5	2.5					
DSI	146.0	146.0	146.0	146.0					
FA Turnover	5.0	5.0	4.9	5.0					
Asset Turnover	1.3	1.3	1.3	1.3					
ROA	12.3%	12.2%	12.2%	12.2%					
ROIC	15.8%	15.5%	15.3%	15.2%					
ROE	18.7%	18.1%	17.6%	17.2%					
Economic Profit	$7,859	$8,488	$9,167	$9,900					
Interest Earned	19.8	21.4	23.1	25.0					
Debt to Total Capital (Book)	20.0%	18.3%	16.7%	15.3%					
Debt to Total Capital (Market)	8.1%	7.8%	7.7%	5.3%					
Leverage (Assets/Equity)	1.52	1.48	1.44	1.41					
Current Ratio	4.0	4.3	4.6	4.9					
ROE Analysis									
Profitability	9.4%	9.4%	9.5%	9.5%					
× Asset Turnover	1.31	1.30	1.29	1.28					
× Leverage	1.52	1.48	1.44	1.41					
= ROE	18.7%	18.1%	17.6%	17.2%					
WACC	12%								

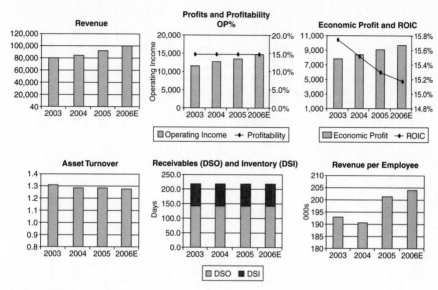

FIGURE 2.3 Key Performance Trends for Simple Co.

TABLE 2.8 Key Financial Terms and Measures: Quick Reference Guide

Measure	Description	Computed as . . .	Application
Value Creation and Overall Effectiveness			
ROE	Return on equity	Net Income/Shareholders' Equity	Measures return to shareholders' capital (equity)
ROIC	Return on invested capital	EBIAT/Invested Capital	Measures return to all providers of capital (equity and debt)
EP or EVA™	Economic profit or Economic Value Added	EBIAT – (Cost of Capital × Invested Capital)	Measures return to all sources of capital (equity and debt)
TRS	Total return to shareholders	Stock Price Appreciation + Reinvested Dividends	Measure of management performance (and comparables)
Operating Measures			
COGS	Cost of goods sold	Total product cost including labor, material, overhead, and variances	Key operating measure
Gross Margin %	Gross margin as a % of sales	Gross Margin/Sales	Key operating measure
SG&A %	SG&A expenses as a % of sales	SG&A/Sales	Key operating measure
Operating Income (Profit)	Income from operations	Sales – COGS – Operating Expenses	Key operating measure
EBIT	Earnings before interest and taxes	Sales – COGS – Operating Expenses	Key operating measure

			Key operating measure
Operating Margin % (Profitability)	Operating income as a % of sales	Operating Income/Sales	Key operating measure
EBITDA	Earnings before interest, taxes, depreciation, and amortization	EBIT + D&A	Adds back noncash expense items (D&A)
EBIAT (OPAT)	Earnings before interest after tax (operating profit after tax)	EBIT$(1 - t)$	Earnings available to all providers of capital
CAGR	Compound annual growth rate	CAGR = [(Last Year/First Year)$^{1/n}$] – 1	Measure growth in a key variable over time (e.g., sales)
Asset Management			
DSO	Days sales outstanding	(Accounts Receivable × 365)/Sales	Measures time to collect from customers
Inventory Turns	Inventory turnover	Cost of Goods Sold /Inventory	Supply chain effectiveness
DSI or DIOH	Days sales of inventory or days inventory on hand	365/Inventory Turns	A more intuitive measure of inventory levels/cycle time
Operating Capital Turnover	Operating capital levels relative to sales	Sales/Operating Capital	Measures operating capital relative to sales
Operating Capital % Sales	Operating capital levels relative to sales	Operating Capital/Sales	Measures operating capital relative to sales
Operating Capital Cycle	Receivables and inventories expressed in days	DSO + DSI	Measures key operating capital elements relative to sales
Asset Turnover	Asset levels relative to sales	Sales/Total Assets	Asset requirements and effectiveness

(Continued)

TABLE 2.8 *(Continued)*

Measure	Description	Computed as . . .	Application
Capital Structure			
TIE/C	Time interest earned/Covered	EBIT/Interest Expense	Measures ability to service debt
Debt to Total Capital	% of capital contributed by lenders	Debt/(Debt + Equity)	Measures financial risk and capital structure
Valuation			
WACC or Cost of Capital	Weighted average cost of capital	$WACC = (ke \times we) + (Kd \times wd)$	Expected returns of equity and debt investors
Invested Capital	Total capital contributed by investors	Book Equity + Interest-Bearing Debt	Historical investment from all investors
Enterprise Value (EV)	Market value of debt and equity	Debt + Equity	Total value of the firm
Market Value or Market Cap	Market value of equity	Shares Outstanding × Share Price	Equity value of the firm

Note: Definitions and uses of ratios often vary.
EVA is a registered trademark of Stern Stewart & Company.
Source: Reprinted by permission of Value Advisory Group, LLC.

CHAPTER 3

Key Valuation Concepts

Nearly all valuation techniques are based on estimating the cash flows that an asset, for example real estate or a firm, can generate in the future. These two critical points are worth emphasizing. First, the value of any asset should be based on the expected *cash flows* the owner can realize by holding that asset or selling it to another party. Second, only the *future* expectations of cash flows are relevant in determining value. Historical performance and track records are important inputs in estimating future cash flows, but "the market prices forward" based on expectations of future performance.

It is important to recognize that valuation is both an art and a science. While we outline a number of quantitative, objective approaches to valuing a business, many other nonquantitative and perhaps even irrational factors do impact the value of the firm, especially in the short term. Commonly used valuation techniques fall into two major categories: (1) estimating the value by discounting future cash flows, and (2) estimating the value by making comparisons to the value of other similar businesses.

This chapter is not intended to be an exhaustive work on business valuation; this has been the objective of some very well written books.[1] The goal in this chapter is to provide a foundation in key valuation concepts that will provide a basis for our focus on driving performance and value.

---

[1] A number of very useful books provide a more comprehensive study on valuation concepts and tools, including Aswath Damodaran's *Investment Valuation* (2nd ed., 2002) and *Damodaran on Valuation* (2nd ed., 2006), and *Valuation: Measuring and Managing the Value of Companies* by Thomas E. Copeland and others (2nd ed., 1994), all from John Wiley & Sons.

ESTIMATING THE VALUE BY DISCOUNTING ESTIMATED FUTURE CASH FLOWS

The discounted cash flow (DCF) valuation method is based on sound fundamental economic theory. Essentially, the value of a firm is equal to the present value of expected future cash flows. These future cash flows are discounted to arrive at the value today. Since DCF is based on projections of future cash flows, it requires that financial statement projections be prepared. In order to prepare financial statement projections, assumptions must be made about the firm's performance in the future. Will sales grow, and if so, at what rate? Will margins improve or erode? Why? What capital will be required to support the future business levels? Financial projections are covered in more depth in Chapter 4. The DCF technique also allows us to determine the magnitude of improvement in key operating variables necessary to increase the value of the firm by say, 20 percent.

Figure 3.1 presents an overview of DCF methodology. Estimates of key financial and operating variables result in projected cash flows. These projected cash flows are then discounted to estimate the value of the firm. The discount rate considers a number of factors, including the time value of money and the level of risk of the projected cash flows. The discount rate, or cost of capital, will be more fully explored in Chapter 10.

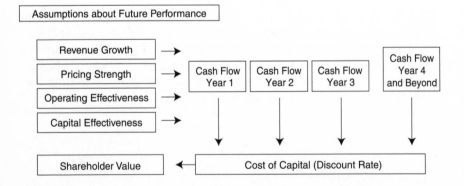

FIGURE 3.1 Discounted Cash Flow (DCF)

A sample worksheet for a DCF valuation is presented in Table 3.1. This example builds on the Simple Co. example introduced in Chapter 2, utilizing the financial performance and other information presented in Table 2.5. This DCF valuation worksheet was developed for the primary purpose of understanding the overall dynamics of a firm's valuation and may require modification to be used as a valuation tool. For example, the model uses a single estimate of future sales growth and other key variables. Generally a valuation would be based on estimates of key financial inputs for each period, supported by detailed projections and assumptions.

At first glance, the model presented in Table 3.1 can be overwhelming. We will review the model by breaking it into five key steps:

1. Review and present the firm's financial history.
2. Project future cash flows by estimating key elements of future operating performance.
3. Estimate the terminal or post-planning horizon value.
4. Discount the cash flows.
5. Estimate the value of the firm and equity.

Step 1: Review and Present the Firm's Financial History

Although the DCF valuation is based on expected future cash flows, it is essential to review and consider recent history and trends in developing the projected financial results. The DCF model should present three to four years of history alongside the projections. In addition to providing a base from which the preparer estimates future cash flows, it provides a basis for others to evaluate the future projections in the context of recent performance. For example, if sales have grown at 3 to 5 percent over the past several years, why are we projecting 8 percent growth over the next several years?

Step 2: Project Future Cash Flows by Estimating Key Elements of Future Operating Performance

After reviewing the historical performance and identifying the key drivers of current and future performance, the analyst or manager can project the expected future financial performance. It is deceptively easy to plug in estimated sales, margins, expenses, and so forth to arrive at financial projections and estimated cash flows. However, significant analysis, understanding, and

TABLE 3.1 DCF Valuation Model ($000s)

Simple Co.	2003	2004	2005	2006	Estimates	2007	2008	2009	2010	2011	2012	2013	2014	Terminal Value
Revenues	$79,383	$85,734	$92,593	$100,000		$108,000	$116,640	$125,971	$136,049	$146,933	$158,687	$171,382	$185,093	
Year-over-Year Growth	8%	8%	8%	8%	8.0%	8%	8%	8%	8%	8%	8%	8%	8%	
Cost of Goods Sold	35,722	38,580	41,667	45,000										
Gross Margin	43,661	47,154	50,926	55,000		59,400	64,152	69,284	74,827	80,813	87,278	94,260	101,801	
% Sales	55%	55%	55%	55%	55.0%	55%	55%	55%	55%	55%	55%	55%	55%	
Operating Expenses	31,753	34,294	37,037	40,000		43,200	46,656	50,388	54,420	58,773	63,475	68,553	74,037	
% Sales	40%	40%	40%	40%	40.0%	40%	40%	40%	40%	40%	40%	40%	40%	
Operating Income (EBIT)	11,907	12,860	13,889	15,000		16,200	17,496	18,896	20,407	22,040	23,803	25,707	27,764	
% Sales	15.0%	15.0%	15.0%	15.0%		15.0%	15.0%	15.0%	15.0%	15.0%	15.0%	15.0%	15.0%	
– Taxes	–3,843	–4,166	–4,516	–4,894	–34.0%	–5,508	–5,949	–6,425	–6,938	–7,494	–8,093	–8,741	–9,440	
OPAT	8,065	8,694	9,373	10,106		10,692	11,548	12,471	13,469	14,546	15,710	16,967	18,324	
+ Depreciation/Amortization	2,800	2,930	3,197	3,750		5,000	5,400	5,832	6,299	6,802	7,347	7,934	8,569	
– Capital Expenditures	–3,000	–4,200	–4,800	–5,000	–5.0%	–5,400	–5,832	–6,299	–6,802	–7,347	–7,934	–8,569	–9,255	
(Increase) Decrease in OC		–2,228	–2,249	–2,130	30%	–2,400	–2,592	–2,799	–3,023	–3,265	–3,526	–3,808	–4,113	

Free Cash Flow	7,865	5,196	5,521	6,726	7,892	8,524	9,205	9,942	10,737	11,596	12,524	13,526
+ Terminal Value					0							$293,190
Present Value Factor					1.000	0.893	0.797	0.712	0.636	0.567	0.507	0.452
Present Value of Cash Flow (PVCF)					7,892	7,610	7,338	7,076	6,824	6,580	6,345	6,118

For terminal value column: 0.452 × 293,190 = 132,624

Sum PVCF	55,784
Present Value of Terminal Value	132,624
Estimated Value of Firm (Enterprise Value)	188,408
Add: Excess Cash and Nonoperating Assets	7,944
Subtract: Value of Debt	10,000
Estimated Value of Equity	186,352
Number of Shares Outstanding	17,000
Estimated Value per Share	$10.96

Cost of Capital	12.00%

Terminal Value (TV) Assumptions	Multiple/Rate	TV
Multiples of Earnings (P/E)	16.0	$293,190
	18.0	329,838
	20.0	366,487
Multiples of Revenue	1.3	240,621
	2.0	370,186
Perpetuity No Growth	0%	112,714
Perpetuity Growth	5%	202,885
Use Multiple of P/E	16.0	$293,190

thought are required to project key variables such as revenue or gross margins. For example, in order to predict revenue for a firm, multiple factors must be considered, including:

- Economic factors (growth, recession, etc.).
- Market size and growth.
- Competitive factors.
- Unit volume.
- Pricing trends.
- Product mix.
- Customer success.
- New product introduction.
- Product obsolescence.

It is extremely important to document the critical assumptions about revenue and all other key elements of financial performance. These assumptions can then be evaluated, changed, monitored, and adjusted to understand the significance of each on the estimated value of the firm. Since no one has a crystal ball, we know that actual results will vary from our projections. Much of the value in business planning results from the *process* of planning, as opposed to the plan or financial projection itself.

Another critical decision in DCF valuations is to determine the forecast horizon, that is, the period for which we project future financial performance in detail. In theory a company has an extended, if not infinite, life. However, it typically is not practical or necessary to attempt to forecast financial results for 20 or 30 years. The forecast horizon should be selected according to the individual circumstances. Most discounted cash flow estimates for ongoing businesses will determine the value of the projected cash flows for the forecast horizon (7 to 10 years) and then add to that an estimate of the value of the business at the end of that period, called the terminal value (TV) or post-horizon value.

Two key factors should be considered in setting the forecast horizon. First, ensure that there is a balance between the value of the cash flows generated during the forecast horizon and the estimated terminal value. If substantially all of the estimated value is attributable to the terminal value, the forecast horizon should be extended. The second and related consideration is to extend the forecast horizon to a point where the financial performance reaches a sustainable or steady state basis. For example, if a firm is in a period of rapid growth, the forecast horizon should extend beyond this rapid growth phase to a point where it has reached a long-term sustainable growth rate. This will ensure that the key variables impacting cash flow reach a steady state, allowing us to use this as a base for estimating the terminal value.

Step 3: Estimate the Terminal or Post-Planning Horizon Value (Terminal Value)

The use of a terminal value or post-horizon value is an effective practical alternative to very long forecast horizons, subject to proper application. First, the factors in setting the forecast horizon as described earlier must be utilized. Second, care must be exercised in selecting the multiple or valuation technique utilized in calculating the terminal value. The TV is usually estimated by using one of two methods:

The first method involves taking the base performance in the last year (or average of the last several years) and estimating the value of the firm by applying a multiple to earnings or sales—for example, taking the final estimated earnings in year 2014 of $18,324 and applying a multiple of 16× to arrive at an expected terminal value of $293,190. Multiples could be applied in this manner to EBIT, EBITDA, and sales, as well as cash flow.

The second method is to determine the economic value of cash flows beyond the forecast horizon by assuming that the cash flows will continue to be generated at the level of the last projected year forever. It is more common to assume that the future cash flows will continue to grow from the last projected year at some level, say 3 to 5 percent, in perpetuity. Assuming no future growth beyond 2014, the estimated value of annual cash flows of $13,526 continuing in perpetuity is:

$$TV = \frac{\text{Cash Flow}}{\text{Discount Rate}}$$

For Simple Co.:

$$TV = \frac{\$13,526}{12\%}$$
$$= \$112.7 \text{ million}$$

Assuming future growth after 2014 at g percent:

$$TV = \frac{\text{Cash Flow}_{\text{Final Year}} \times (1+g)}{\text{Discount Rate} - g}$$

For Simple Co.:

$$TV = \frac{\$13,526 \times 1.05}{12\% - 5\%}$$
$$= \$202.8 \text{ million}$$

Since an argument can be made supporting both methods, I recommend computing a range of estimated terminal values using both multiples and economic value. Understanding the underlying reasons for the different values is informative and should be explored. One of the estimates must ultimately be selected and used for the terminal value. Since the estimate of TV is usually significant to the overall valuation, a sensitivity analysis using multiple estimates of the terminal value should be created. This analysis should provide a more comprehensive understanding of the impact of key assumptions on the valuation of the company.

Common mistakes in estimating the terminal value include using inappropriate price-earnings (P/E) multiples or unrealistic post-horizon growth rates. The P/E multiple used in the TV estimate should be consistent with the performance estimated for the post-horizon growth period. This may be significantly different than current P/E ratios reflecting current performance. Post-horizon growth rates should be modest, since perpetuity means forever! Few companies achieve high levels of growth over extended periods, and most companies' growth rates decline to overall economic growth levels or even experience declines in sales over time.

Step 4: Discount the Cash Flows

The DCF valuation method can be utilized to estimate the total value of the firm or the value of equity. Typically, we estimate the total value of the firm by projecting total cash flows available to all investors, both equity and debt. We then discount the cash flows at the weighted average cost of capital (WACC), which is an estimate of the returns expected by investors. Discount rates and the cost of capital are explored in greater detail in Chapter 10.

Step 5: Estimate the Value of the Firm and Equity

The resultant discounted cash flow is the *total* value of the firm, also referred to as the *enterprise value*. To compute the value of equity, two adjustments must be considered. First, if the firm has a substantial cash reserve, this amount is added to the discounted value of projected cash flows. Second, in order to compute the value of equity, we deduct the value of the debt. The estimated value of an individual share can then be determined by dividing the market value of equity by the number of shares outstanding. Where there are significant stock options or other common stock derivatives outstanding, these should also be considered in the share count.

One of the criticisms of discounted cash flow is that it requires assumptions about the future. In fact, this is actually a major strength of

DCF analysis. We all recognize that it is not possible to predict the future, including specific projections of sales, costs, and numerous additional variables required for completing a thorough DCF analysis. However, by using sensitivity analysis, we can identify and quantify the sensitivity of shareholder value to key assumptions. The analysis allows us to identify the most critical factors impacting the value of a firm, such as revenue growth and profitability.

ESTIMATING VALUE BY USING THE VALUATION OF SIMILAR FIRMS: MULTIPLES OF EARNINGS, CASH FLOW, AND RELATED MEASURES

The other commonly used valuation technique is based on using measures of revenues, earnings, or cash flow and capitalizing these amounts using a multiplier that is typical for similar companies. These methods are essentially shortcuts or rules of thumb based on economic theory. Users of these methods tend to establish ranges for certain industries. For example, retail companies may trade at a multiple of 0.5 to 1.0 times revenues, while technology companies may trade at 2 to 3 times revenues, or higher. The significant difference between the multiple for the two industries is explained by many factors that are independent of the current revenue level. For example, expected growth in revenues, profitability, risk, and capital requirements will impact the revenue multiple. Those familiar with the business characteristics of specific industries, such as market growth, profitability, risk, and capital requirements, can use the method effectively.

In applying multiples, it is important to use consistent measures of income and valuation. Specifically, we must determine whether we are attempting to estimate the value of the firm (enterprise value) or the value of the equity.

To illustrate these techniques, we will use the information provided in Table 2.5 for Simple Co.

Price/Sales Ratio

This ratio computes the value of the firm to the estimated or recent sales levels. For example, Simple Co. has sales of $100 million and an estimated (enterprise) value of $180 million.

$$P/S = \frac{\text{Enterprise Value}}{\text{Sales}} = \frac{\$180 \text{ million}}{\$100 \text{ million}} = 1.8 \times$$

Other companies in this industry have price-to-sales ratios of 1.3 to 2.0. This would indicate a comparable valuation range of $130 million to $200 million for Simple Co. The value-to-sales ratio for Simple Co. is within the range of similar or comparable companies.

Advantages: The price-to-sales ratio is a simple, high-level measure.

Disadvantages and limitations: The measure requires many implicit assumptions about key elements of financial performance including growth rates, margins, capital requirements, and capital structure.

Price-Earnings (P/E) Ratio

This ratio compares the price of the stock to the firm's earnings. Using per share information, the P/E ratio is calculated as follows:

$$P/E = \frac{\text{Stock Price}}{\text{Earnings per Share}}$$

For Simple Co.:

$$P/E = \frac{\$10.59}{\$0.56} = 18.95\times$$

The valuation of companies comparable to Simple Co. indicates a P/E ratio range of 16 to 20 times earnings. Simple Co.'s stock price of $10.59 is within the range indicated by the market research ($8.94 to $11.18) using the comparable P/E range.

This measure can also be computed at the firm level:

$$P/E = \frac{\text{Market Value of Equity}}{\text{Net Income}} = \frac{\$180.0 \text{ million}}{\$9.5 \text{ million}} = 18.95\times$$

Advantages: This method is simple to employ and commonly used in practice.

Disadvantages and limitations: Several problems exist with this technique. First, earnings are accounting measures and not directly related to economic performance or cash flows. This has become an increasing problem in recent years as accounting profit continues to diverge from the underlying economic performance. Second, this measure also requires many implicit assumptions about key elements of financial performance, including growth rates, capital requirements, and capital structure.

Enterprise Value/EBIT

This method compares the total value of the firm to the earnings before interest and taxes. Recall that EBIT generally approximates operating income. Since it is a measure of income before deducting interest expense, it represents income available to all investors, both equity (shareholders) and debt (bondholders). Therefore, we will compare this measure to the total value of the firm (EV).

$$\frac{EV}{EBIT} = \frac{\text{Market Value of Equity} + \text{Market Value of Debt}}{EBIT}$$

For Simple Co.:

$$\frac{EV}{EBIT} = \frac{\$180 \text{ million} + \$10 \text{ million}}{\$15 \text{ million}} = 12.67$$

Advantages: This method is also simple to use. It results in valuations based on earnings available to all investors.

Disadvantages and limitations: This method does not directly take into account other key elements of performance, such as growth or capital requirements.

Enterprise Value/EBITDA

This measure is very close to EV/EBIT, but uses EBITDA as a better approximation of cash flow, since it adds back the noncash charges, depreciation and amortization (D&A).

For Simple Co.:

$$\frac{EV}{EBITDA} = \frac{\$190 \text{ million}}{\$15.0 \text{ million} + \$3.75 \text{ million}} = 10.13$$

Other similar companies are valued at 8 to 10 times EBITDA. Based on comparables, Simple Co. is valued just outside the high end of this range of comparables.

Advantages: This method is simple to apply and is based on an approximation of cash flow.

Disadvantages and limitations: The primary limitation with this method is that it does not explicitly account for growth or future capital requirements.

Price-Earnings/Growth (PEG)

The price-earnings/growth (PEG) ratio is a derivative of the price-earnings ratio that attempts to factor in the impact of growth in price-earnings multiples. The logic here is that there is a strong correlation between growth rates and P/E multiples. Companies with higher projected growth rates of earnings, for example technology companies, should have higher P/E ratios than firms with lower expected growth rates.

The price-earnings/growth ratio is computed as follows:

$$PEG = \frac{P/E}{\text{Estimated EPS Growth Rate}}$$

For Simple Co:

$$PEG = \frac{18.95}{8.0} = 2.37$$

Simple Co. has a very high PEG ratio relative to the peer group. This may reflect a number of factors: perhaps strong cash flows or consistent operating performance relative to the benchmark group.

Advantages: This method reflects a key driver of valuation: expected growth.

Disadvantages and limitations: This measure does not directly reflect other key elements of financial performance.

BUILDING SHAREHOLDER VALUE IN A MULTIPLE FRAMEWORK

Many investors, analysts, and managers use multiples of earnings or sales in investment and valuation decisions. There are two ways to build value using multiples. First, the firm can improve the base performance measure—for example, earnings. The second way is to command a higher multiple. For illustration, let's assume that Simple Co.'s valuation is being driven by capitalizing earnings (P/E ratio). The stock is valued at $10.59 because the firm earned $0.56 per share in earnings and the market has capitalized those earnings at approximately 19 times. The price of Simple Co. stock will rise when the earnings increase and/or if the market applies a higher multiple, for example increasing to 22 times earnings. In this case, the stock would trade at $12.32 (22 × $0.56).

FACTORS THAT AFFECT MULTIPLES

What factors would cause the multiple to expand or contract? A variety of factors can contribute, including some specific to the firm and others that relate to the industry or even the general economy. Examples include expected growth rates, the quality of earnings, cash generation, perceived risk, and interest rates. A firm's P/E multiple should expand if it demonstrates a higher expected growth rate, improved working capital management, and/or more consistent operating performance. It will likely contract if it consistently misses financial targets, utilizes capital less effectively, or increases the perceived risk by entering a new market. In addition, economic factors such as changes in interest rates or expected economic conditions will cause multiples to expand or contract.

USE OF MULTIPLES IN SETTING ACQUISITION VALUES

Most of the multiples used are typically derived from the valuation of other similar companies, industry averages, or broad market indexes. This is commonly referred to as the "trading multiple," that is, the value set by trades in the equity markets. If a company is being considered as a potential acquisition target, the multiples will typically be adjusted to reflect a likely control or acquisition premium. These acquisition values are referred to as transaction values, versus trading values, and the multiples would be derived by looking at transactions involving similar companies.

Control premiums are typical for two reasons. First, boards of directors and management teams are unlikely to surrender control of a company unless there is an immediate reward to the selling shareholders. In addition, the acquirer should be able to pay more than a passive investor, since the acquirer will be able to control the company and should be able to realize growth in earnings and cash flow due to synergies with the acquired company. Valuation for acquisition purposes is covered in Chapter 12, on the economics of mergers and acquisitions (M&A).

Trailing and Forward Multiples

When applying multiples of earnings, sales, and other measures, the analyst must select a base period. The value of the multiple will vary depending on whether the multiple is applied to actual past results (e.g., trailing 12 months earnings) or to a future period's estimated performance (e.g., "forward 12 months earnings"). The multiple applied to trailing earnings

will be higher than the multiple applied to future earnings for two reasons: risk, and the time value of money. There is risk associated with future earnings projections; they may not be achieved. The time value of
money suggests that a dollar to be received next year is not worth a dollar
today. These two factors result in a discount of the multiples used for future periods.

Adjusting or Normalizing the Base

Using multiples requires us to use a measure for a single period, typically a
year. Many of the measures, such as sales or earnings, for the selected period may have been or are anticipated to be significantly impacted by a
number of anomalous, or one-time, factors. For example, the current year
earnings may include income that is not expected to continue into the future. Or perhaps the income includes a nonrecurring adjustment to record
a legal settlement or the closing of a plant. In these situations, companies
and analysts may adjust the base to normalize the earnings, often referred
to as "pro-forma earnings."

This practice became very prevalent in the 1990s and led to a number
of abuses. Certain companies were accused of being selective in choosing
items to exclude, leading to a perceived overstatement of the earnings on a
pro forma basis. The Securities and Exchange Commission subsequently
placed significant constraints on reporting adjusted earnings. These circumstances gave rise to the use of pro forma measures:

- *Deficiencies in generally accepted accounting principles (GAAP) as a
  measure of economic performance.* There has been a continuing diver-
  gence of accounting measures and economic results. Specific issues include accounting for acquisitions, income taxes, stock options, and
  pension plans.
- *Significant restructurings, divestitures, and acquisitions.* One-time or
  nonrecurring charges are reflected in earnings in a specific period based
  on very precise rules established by the accounting rule makers. However, a significant restructuring may be viewed as an investment for
  economic and valuation purposes. Acquisitions and divestitures may
  result in a disconnect between historical performance trends and future projections.

Some advocate using other measures, such as cash flow or economic profits, which adjust the accounting earnings to a measure with greater rele-
vance in evaluating the economic value and performance of the firm.

Problems with Using Multiples

The use of multiples has several inherent limitations, especially for our purposes in linking shareholder value to operating performance.

Circular Reference   The basic logic with multiples is that one company's value is determined by looking at the valuation of other companies. This is very useful in comparing relative valuations and in testing the fairness of a company's valuation. Management teams and boards rely heavily on the use of multiples to review the fairness of acquisition prices. However, if the industry or peer group is overvalued, then this method will result in overvaluing the subject enterprise. This was a contributing factor to the technology/Internet (and other) market bubbles. The logic was that since one dot-com was valued at 50 times sales, so should another dot-com, notwithstanding the fact that neither valuation was supported by basic economic theory.

Basis of Assumptions   Another problem with this methodology is that it is not directly related to key value drivers or elements of financial performance. It is very difficult to understand the assumptions underlying values computed using multiples. If a firm is valued at 18 times earnings, what are the underlying assumptions for revenue growth, working capital requirements, and other similar factors?

The market often attempts to cope with this limitation by increasing or decreasing the multiple over benchmarks to reflect factors such as consistency of performance, quality of earnings, lower or higher risk, and so forth. Such stocks would be described as "trading at a premium to the market based on" certain identified factors.

Selecting Appropriate Comparables   Using multiples requires the analyst to select a set of comparable companies or a peer group. This can be a significant challenge. Few companies are "pure plays" that are serving a single industry or match up closely with other companies. Further, choosing an appropriate benchmark or peer group can lead to great debates, since the process is both subjective and often emotionally charged.

INTEGRATED VALUATION SUMMARY FOR SIMPLE CO.

The individual valuation techniques described earlier should be combined to form a summary analysis of estimated valuation for Simple Co. Each measure provides a view of valuation that contributes to an overall picture.

The numerical summary shown in Table 3.2 can be converted into a more user friendly visual summary in Figure 3.2.

Simple Co.'s current value is at the high end of the 12-month trading range and near or exceeding the top of the range for comparable companies. In this case, it would be important to understand the underlying performance characteristics of the benchmark group compared to Simple Co. Is Simple Co.'s valuation supported by better performance or higher future expectations of growth? The current market value approximates our estimate of the DCF value. This indicates that the market is probably expecting future performance in line with our projections used in the DCF.

 TABLE 3.2 Simple Co. Valuation Analysis: Multiples

				Benchmark Range	
	Value Basis	Value	Simple Co.	Low	High
Sales		2006 Result	$100,000		
		Multiple	1.9	1.3	2.0
	Enterprise	Value/Indicated Range	$190,030	$130,000	$200,000
	Equity	Value/Indicated Range	$180,030	$120,000	$190,000
Earnings		2006 Result	$ 9,501		
		Multiple	18.95	16	20
	Equity	Value/Indicated Range	$180,030	$152,011	$190,014
		Per Share	10.59	8.94	11.18
EBITDA		2006 Result	$ 18,750		
		Multiple	10.13	8.00	10.00
	Enterprise	Value/Indicated Range	$190,030	$150,000	$187,500
	Equity	Value/Indicated Range	$180,030	$140,000	$177,500
Price-Earnings/ Growth		P/E	18.95		
		Estimated Growth (%)	8		
		PEG	2.37	1.3	2.0
DCF	Equity	Value	$186,352	NA	NA

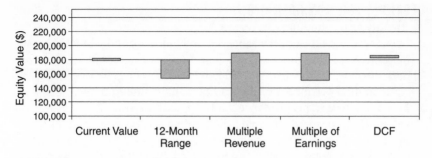

FIGURE 3.2 Simple Co. Valuation Summary Graph

SUMMARY

While each of the valuation techniques has limitations, they do provide insight from a variety of perspectives. It is best to use a combination of measures and techniques in reviewing the valuation of a firm. When an analyst summarizes these measures for a firm and compares them to key benchmarks, significant insight can be gained. Conversely, inconsistencies across the valuation measures for a company are worth exploring and can usually be explained by identifying a specific element of financial performance that the measure doesn't reflect. For example, a company that consistently meets or exceeds operating plans and market expectations will typically be afforded a higher P/E multiple than its peers. This positive factor is reflected in a higher P/E multiple, and the company would trade at a premium to the industry norms.

It is useful to develop a broad set of benchmark references, rather than to rely on the selection of direct comparables. In addition to providing more objectivity, it is useful to compare the company to broad market measures as well as best-practice companies from other industries. Typically, more can be learned by understanding why firms differ on key measures than by selecting a peer group that shares common characteristics. A much richer picture is framed by comparing your firm to market averages and several best-practice companies in addition to a peer group. Further, the use of a broad set of measures, with appropriate benchmarks, would help to avoid the level of valuation errors that were made in the most recent stock market bubble. Given this foundation in valuation, we turn our attention to a focus on business models and financial projections in Chapter 4.

QUESTIONS FOR CONSIDERATION

1. Utilizing the DCF model (Table 3.1) included on the CD-ROM, estimate the value of your company based on your expectations of future
   performance. If the firm is publicly traded, compare the indicated
   value in the DCF model to the trading value of the firm.
2. Based on recent performance and the current trading or estimated
   value of the company, compute the multiples of revenue, earnings, and
   EBITDA. How do these measures for your company compare to other
   companies in your industry? What factors account for differences?
3. Summarize the results of the valuation estimates. Do the estimates
   developed by the different valuation techniques present a consistent
   picture?

CHAPTER 4

The Business Model and Financial Projections

Managers often describe the actual and targeted financial performance of their companies as a "business model." The business model represents the quantification of a company's strategy and business practices. The business model concept provides a useful framework for a number of business decisions ranging from pricing to setting investment and expense levels. However, managers may lock into a single business model concept, limiting their ability to effectively compete or grow into other markets.

The common view of a business model represents a target profit and loss (P&L) model. The manager thinks of the business in terms of the P&L captions and the relationship of each line item as a percentage of sales as illustrated in Table 4.1.

TABLE 4.1 Business Model Illustration: Traditional View

Simple Co.	2006	% of Sales
Sales	$100,000	100.0%
Cost of Sales	45,000	45.0
Gross Margin	$ 55,000	55.0%
SG&A	$ 32,000	32.0%
R&D	8,000	8.0
Total Expenses	$ 40,000	40.0%
Operating Income	$ 15,000	15.0%
Other (Income) Expense	605	0.6
Taxes	4,894	4.9
Net Income	$ 9,501	9.5%

Using this conceptual framework, managers will set prices, establish business plans, evaluate business proposals, set expense levels, and make other critical business decisions. For example, a company that is developing a product with a cost to produce of $450 would likely set a target selling price of $1,000 to maintain the 55 percent margin. In establishing the research and development (R&D) budget, the company may target spending at 8 percent of projected sales.

COMPREHENSIVE BUSINESS MODEL FRAMEWORK

The traditional P&L business model framework, while useful, provides an incomplete view of a company's economic performance since it does not reflect other critical aspects of business performance. Most importantly, it does not consider sales growth rates, capital requirements, cash flow, and returns. The two critical determiners in building long-term, sustainable value are growth and return on invested capital (ROIC). Therefore, any comprehensive business model framework must incorporate these elements to be a useful decision support tool.

A broader, more comprehensive view of the business model is illustrated in Table 4.2. By including the additional measures reflecting growth and invested capital, we present a more complete picture of the company's performance. For example, managers or investors should not reach a conclusion on the reasonableness of R&D spending levels without considering the potential sales growth rates.

In addition, the profitability measures alone are incomplete for evaluating the performance of the organization. Only when we include the capital levels employed in a business can we fully assess the financial performance of that business. The inclusion of a balance sheet and key metrics will allow us to determine the ROIC. Many companies and entire industries generate significant returns despite relatively low profit margins as a result of low capital requirements or high asset turnover. The grocery industry is a prime example. This industry tends to operate with thin margins, but requires lower invested capital by turning assets, primarily inventory, faster than other industries. Many mass merchandisers have a similar low margin, high-turnover model. Wal-Mart's profitability (net income % sales) of 3 to 4 percent is relatively low, but the combination of asset turnover and leverage boosts the company's return on equity (ROE) to over 20 percent.

Conversely, other industries such as equipment manufacturers must post higher profitability to compensate for high capital requirements.

TABLE 4.2 Business Model Illustration: Comprehensive View

Simple Co.		2006	% of Sales
Sales Growth Rate:	8.0%		
Profitability Model			
Sales		$100,000	100.0%
Cost of Sales		45,000	45.0
Gross Margin		$ 55,000	55.0%
SG&A		$ 32,000	32.0%
R&D		8,000	8.0
Total Expenses		$ 40,000	40.0%
Operating Income		$ 15,000	15.0%
Other (Income) Expense		$ 605	0.6%
Taxes		4,894	4.9
Net Income		$ 9,501	9.5%
Asset Utilization			
Days Sales Outstanding			73.0
Days Sales Inventory			146.0
Operating Capital Turnover			3.4
Fixed Asset Turnover			5.0
Intangible Turnover			9.1
Total Asset Turnover			1.3
Leverage			1.4
Debt to Total Capital			15.3%
Returns			
ROE			17.2%
ROIC			15.2%

REVIEW OF BUSINESS MODELS

Table 4.3 provides a summary of various business models. The table presents selected financial information for a number of companies that most of us are familiar with at some level. Take a moment to compare key performance measures across the companies, including growth, profitability, asset turnover, and financial leverage. The companies'

TABLE 4.3 Business Model Benchmark Summary

				Company			
	PG	DELL	DKS	HPQ	WMT	HNZ	EK
Fiscal Year	2005	2005	2006	2005	2005	2005	2004
Revenue ($M)	$56,741	$49,205	$2,606	$86,696	$285,222	$8,912	$13,517
1-year growth	10.4%	18.7%	23.5%	8.5%	11.3%	5.9%	4.7%
3-year growth	12.1%	16.4%	27.0%	6.2%	11.8%	5.4%	1.4%
Profitability/Operating Efficiency							
GM %	51.0%	18.3%	27.8%	23.6%	22.9%	36.0%	29.4%
R&D %		0.9%		4.0%			6.3%
SG&A %	31.7%	8.7%	21.0%	12.9%	17.9%	20.8%	18.5%
Operating Income %	19.3%	8.6%	5.6%	4.0%	6.0%	15.2%	-0.6%
OPAT %	13.4%	5.9%	3.4%	2.7%	3.9%	10.6%	0.6%
Net Income %	12.8%	6.2%	3.6%	2.8%	3.7%	8.3%	0.6%
Asset Utilization							
Operating Cash Cycle	92.6	36.9	105.9	79.6	51.1	125.1	113.0
DSO	26.9	32.7	4.9	41.7	2.2	44.7	68.7
DSI	65.7	4.2	101.0	37.9	48.9	80.4	44.3
Operating Capital Turnover	NMF	NMF	14	NMF	18.3	16.3	NMF
Capital Intensity (Fixed Asset Turnover)	4.0	29.1	7.4	13.4	4.2	4.1	3.0
Intangible Turnover	2.3	NMF	16.6	4.3	26.4	3.0	9.3
Asset Turnover	0.9	2.1	2.2	1.1	2.4	0.8	0.9

	PG	DELL	DKS	HPQ	WMT	HNZ	EK
Leverage	3.52	3.58	2.84	2.08	2.43	4.06	3.87
Debt to Total Capital	58.2%	7.2%	36.5%	12.3%	51.6%	64.3%	37.9%
Returns							
TRS—5-Year (CAGR)	15.5%	1.9%	136.0%	–8.0%	–0.2%	5.4%	–9.7%
ROIC	18.2%	41.7%	13.6%	5.5%	10.9%	12.9%	1.2%
ROE	41.5%	46.6%	22.5%	6.4%	21.6%	27.0%	2.1%
Dividend	Yes	No	No	Yes	Yes	Yes	Yes
Valuation							
Price-Earnings	26.9	24.2	18.3	37.9	18.0	15.7	84.6
Enterprise Value/Sales	3.9	1.5	0.7	1.1	0.8	1.8	0.7

Ticker Symbol
PG   Procter & Gamble
DELL   Dell Inc.
DKS   Dick's Sporting Goods
HPQ   Hewlett-Packard
WMT   WalMart
HNZ   H. J. Heinz Co.
EK   Eastman Kodak

NMF—Not meaningful.
Source: Compiled from company reports and SEC filings.

performance on each of these variables can be related to the key valuation measures, ROE, and total return to shareholders (TRS) over a five-year period.

While this summary is used to illustrate the business model concept, the format is also a terrific way of benchmarking performance across value drivers. Many managers limit benchmarking to a peer group of similar companies or competitors. Their logic is that it is only meaningful to compare performance across companies in the same industry, so-called comparables. Companies in the same industry tend to adopt similar business practices. In addition, their financial performance is shaped by the same market forces, since they typically would share common customers and suppliers. While benchmarking comparable companies is useful, it does not capture many of the potential benefits of a broader benchmarking process.

The potential for learning can be greatly expanded if the universe of companies in the benchmark is expanded. If you want to identify the best and the most innovative practices in supply chain management, do you want to study a competitor that has achieved a mediocre level of performance, or a best-practice or wild card company like Wal-Mart or Dell? While Wal-Mart and Dell may be in a very different business than yours, understanding the business practices that they have employed and the resultant impact on the business model is very enlightening.

It is also helpful to look at the performance of key customers and companies in related or adjacent industries. Comparing your performance to these companies on key metrics such as sales growth, operating costs, and capital requirements can be thought provoking. A primary factor in your company's success will be the performance of your key customers. How fast are they growing? Are they profitable? Cash-strapped or cash-flush? In addition, you may find it meaningful to contrast your business to other models. Understanding the different financial results in light of varying business practices may identify potential improvement opportunities as well as potential vulnerabilities. A comprehensive benchmark approach is illustrated in Figure 4.1.

We will build on this concept of benchmarking business models in Chapters 5 and 11. This one-page summary such as shown in Figure 4.1 will allow managers to easily compare critical elements of their company's financial performance and valuation to competitors and customers as well as most-admired and best-practice companies.

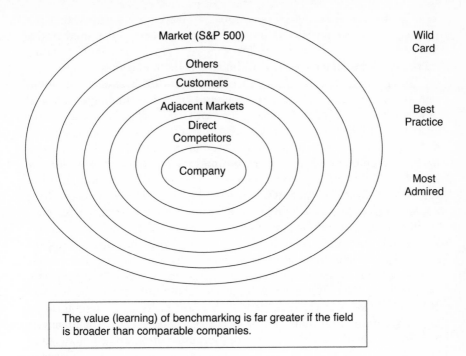

The value (learning) of benchmarking is far greater if the field is broader than comparable companies.

FIGURE 4.1 Expanded Benchmark View

VARYING BUSINESS MODELS WITHIN A COMPANY

Most companies have two or more distinct business units under one corporate roof. When this situation exists, it is important that managers understand the differences in the various businesses and don't attempt to force fit the model from one business to another without due consideration. This is especially important when a company has one dominant business, with smaller but different business units in the portfolio. Managers have a tendency to apply a single business model, expecting similar ratios and performance across the businesses, which can result in dysfunctional decisions and missed opportunities.

This is a frequent problem when managers consider a related but different business opportunity. For example, there may be an opportunity to build a business based on the current product line, but requiring lower pricing and therefore lower costs. Managers may pass on this opportunity because of lower expected gross margins. However, it is possible that this product line may require lower levels of selling, general, and administrative (SG&A) spending and inventory. This may result in returns approximating or even exceeding the levels achieved by the high-end business.

This phenomenon is striking at companies with diversified portfolios such as General Electric (GE), Textron, and United Technologies. Each of these companies contains business units with very different business characteristics. In GE's case, they range from financial services to jet engines to medical systems to plastics. Each of these businesses is shaped by different market and competitive forces. The businesses have different growth rates, gross margins, operating expense levels, and asset requirements. An illustration of a diversified portfolio is presented in Table 4.4. This portfolio has five businesses, each with very different characteristics. These businesses record gross margins that range from 65 percent to as low as 15 percent. Some had very high levels of assets; other businesses required essentially no capital. Some of these businesses are growing and require capital to fund the growth; others are mature and are generating substantial cash flow. This diverse set of businesses could not have a one-size-fits-all business model. If the managers of this firm insist on a single business model, the results are likely to be disastrous. For example, if managers evaluated each of these businesses on operating profitability alone, they could significantly misjudge the economic performance of each. To evaluate overall business performance, managers and investors need to consider

 TABLE 4.4   Varying Business Models under the Same Roof

	Equipment		Components		
	Mature	High-Growth	Mature	High-Growth	Services
Estimated Sales Growth	5%	15–20%	5%	15–20%	3%
Gross Margin	65%	60%	45%	40%	15%
R&D	9%	12%	5%	8%	1%
SG&A	40%	35%	30%	24%	5%
Operating Margin	16%	13%	10%	8%	9%
Net Income	10%	8%	7%	5%	6%
DSO	60	60	50	45	75
DSI	120	90	70	50	0
Other Capital Requirements	Low	Medium	Medium	High	Low
Asset Turnover	3.0	4.0	5.0	4.0	8.0
ROIC	31%	34%	33%	20%	47%

TABLE 4.5   Business Models in a Homogeneous Company

	Base Business						
	End Use 1	End Use 2	End Use 3	Services	Parts	New Market	Combined
Estimated Sales Growth	–2%	10–15%	20%	5%	6%	60%	12%
Gross Margin	60%	40%	54%	35%	30%	50%	53%
R&D	3%	8%	10%	0%	0%	15%	7%
SG&A	28%	20%	35%	7%	7%	20%	25%
Operating Margin	29%	12%	9%	28%	23%	15%	21%
Net Income	19%	8%	6%	18%	15%	10%	14%
DSO	60	60	100	45	45	90	70
DSI	90	115	200	100	160	150	118
Other Capital Requirements	Low	Medium	High	Low	Low	High	Medium
Asset Turnover	5.0	4.0	2.5	5.0	5.0	2.7	3.5
ROIC	94%	31%	15%	91%	75%	26%	48%

expected growth rates and ROIC. Note in this example that the services business has the lowest operating margin, but due to low investment requirements, posts one of the highest ROICs.

Even in companies with a more homogeneous set of businesses, there is likely to be a significant variation in the performance characteristics of business segments. Businesses tend to have different product lines or end-use markets with different business models. Geographic markets and ancillary products and services also contribute differently to financial performance. Managers must understand and evaluate the individual business models and the contribution that each makes to total corporate performance, as well as the interactions and dependencies between the businesses. Table 4.5 presents different business models that may exist in what appears to be a homogeneous business.

OPERATING LEVERAGE: THE BUSINESS MODEL AND VARIABILITY

Another important dimension to the business model is the dynamics of the model in terms of fixed and variable costs. This analysis for Simple Co. is presented in Table 4.6. The analysis starts with the basic P&L model. Then

TABLE 4.6   Cost and Breakeven Analysis

Simple Co.	Fixed	Variable	2006 Variable % Sales	Total	% of Sales
Sales				$100,000	100.0%
Cost of Sales					
Material		$20,000	20.0%	$ 20,000	20.0%
Direct Labor	$12,000	1,000	1.0	13,000	13.0
Overhead	11,000	1,000		12,000	12.0
Total Cost of Sales	$23,000	$22,000	22.0%	$ 45,000	45.0%
Operating Expenses					
Research & Development	$ 8,000			$ 8,000	8.0%
Selling Expense	20,000			20,000	20.0
Commission Expense		$ 3,000	3.0%	3,000	3.0
Marketing Expense	4,000			4,000	4.0
General & Administrative	5,000			5,000	5.0
Other					0.0
Total Operating Expenses	$37,000	$ 3,000	3.0%	$ 40,000	40.0%
Total Costs	$60,000	$25,000	25.0%	$ 85,000	85.0%
Operating Profit				$ 15,000	15.0%
Variable Contribution Margin			75.0%	—	
Breakeven Point Sales per Year			$ 80,000	80.0%	
Breakeven Point Sales per Week			1,538		

costs can be classified into one of two groups: fixed costs and those that vary with changes in sales levels. The schedule also estimates the variable contribution margin representing the additional margin realized on each additional sales dollar.

With these estimates of fixed and variable components of the cost structure, managers can significantly improve their understanding of the business model and the relationship of costs and profitability to sales volume. Given this information, they can estimate the breakeven point in sales and project profit levels at various sales levels.

The breakeven level in sales can be estimated as follows:

$$\frac{\text{Total Fixed Costs}}{\text{Variable Contribution Margin}} = \frac{\$60,000}{75\%} = \$80,000$$

At \$80,000, Simple Co. operating income would be \$0.00, or at breakeven. For every dollar of sales above this level, operating income will increase by 75 cents. Similarly, for every dollar below \$80,000, Simple Co. will lose 75 cents. A summary of this analysis is presented in Table 4.7.

Companies in cyclical industries often attempt to reduce the fixed component of the cost structures in favor of variable costs. If Simple Co. is in a cyclical market with significant variation in sales levels, management may wish to lower the breakeven point or make more of the costs variable. As illustrated in Table 4.8, managers could consider reducing the fixed component of the cost model from \$60,000 to \$40,000, converting these costs to variable costs. Management may accomplish this in a number of ways, for example by outsourcing manufacturing or by using outside distributors rather than internal sales employees. Note that the profits and profitability

TABLE 4.7 Operating Leverage Illustration: Current Sitaution

Current		–60%	–40%	–20%	Base	+20%	+40%	+60%
Sales		\$40,000	\$60,000	\$80,000	\$100,000	\$120,000	\$140,000	\$160,000
Fixed Costs	\$60,000	–60,000	–60,000	–60,000	–60,000	–60,000	–60,000	–60,000
Variable Costs	25.0%	–10,000	–15,000	–20,000	–25,000	–30,000	–35,000	–40,000
Operating Profit		\$–30,000	\$–15,000	\$ 0	\$ 15,000	\$ 30,000	\$ 45,000	\$ 60,000
%		–75.0%	–25.0%	0.0%	15.0%	25.0%	32.1%	37.5%
Breakeven Sales Level	\$80,000							

TABLE 4.8 Operating Leverage Illustration: Revised Cost Structure

Reduce Breakeven		–60%	–40%	–20%	Base	+20%	+40%	+60%
Sales		\$40,000	\$60,000	\$80,000	\$100,000	\$120,000	\$140,000	\$160,000
Fixed Costs	\$40,000	–40,000	–40,000	–40,000	–40,000	–40,000	–40,000	–40,000
Variable Costs	45.0%	–18,000	–27,000	–36,000	–45,000	–54,000	–63,000	–72,000
Operating Profit		\$–18,000	\$ –7,000	\$ 4,000	\$ 15,000	\$ 26,000	\$ 37,000	\$ 48,000
%		–45.0%	–11.7%	5.0%	15.0%	21.7%	26.4%	30.0%
Breakeven Sales Level	\$72,727							

are unchanged at the base sales plan from the levels projected under the current situation in Table 4.7.

The revision to the company's cost structure has several benefits. Simple Co. will achieve profitability at a lower sales level ($72,727) compared to $80,000 in the current situation. Operating losses will be reduced from the current situation under any sales shortfall scenarios. This will also reduce risk, since the firm is more likely to avoid operating losses and resultant liquidity and cash flow problems. It is important to note that converting fixed costs to variable costs is not without downsides. One downside visible from this analysis is that profits will be reduced at the higher end of the sales range under the revised model. Other downsides may include reduced control over key business processes, potentially resulting in reduced information flow or longer cycle times.

LIMITATIONS OF THE BUSINESS MODEL CONCEPT

The use of the business model concept has limitations, and the model can be misused. Blind adherence to the concept may discourage managers from considering sound business opportunities simply because they don't fit the prescribed model for the company. They may indeed be acceptable businesses, but with a variant business model.

Other companies fail to challenge their business models and may be vulnerable to potential competitors that approach the business from a dramatically different direction. Some very successful companies have done just that. For example, Dell Inc. redefined the business model for the personal computer market with a new distribution and supply chain strategy. This reduced costs and increased competitiveness as well as reducing inventory requirements and possible obsolescence risk. Similarly, Southwest Airlines attacked the traditional model for commercial airlines, and Wal-Mart that of the retail industry.

PROJECTING FINANCIAL PERFORMANCE

Forecasting or projecting future financial performance is a key element of many business and financial decisions. The projections used in estimating value, evaluating a capital project, and evaluating financing alternatives will be significant inputs to the decision-making process. In order to provide a complete summary of expected financial performance, financial projections should include the P&L, balance sheet, and statement of cash flows. It is important to recognize that is difficult to predict the future and that all projections incorporate assumptions. Therefore, nearly all projections of long-term performance will be incorrect to some degree. However, there are a number of things that managers can do to improve the financial projections and their understanding of the dynamics affecting future performance. A series of financial projections can be prepared to provide an understanding of how the key decision variables will be impacted under various scenarios and assumptions.

Extrapolation

Most financial projections for established businesses contain some element of extrapolation—that is, basing the projections on recent financial performance trends. We could start with recent financial statements or the target business model and extrapolate financial trends into the future. Recent sales growth rates can be extended into the future. We could assume gross margins, expenses, and asset levels maintain a constant percentage of sales. This method is reasonable in very stable environments, which are increasingly becoming the exception rather than the rule. This is the method we used in developing the DCF valuation for Simple Co. in Chapter 3.

This is generally not the best way to project financial performance. Most businesses are dynamic, and key variables will change over time. However, it may provide a useful view in serving as one potential scenario, assuming that recent trends continue into the future. This can be very useful in cases where other scenarios appear optimistic relative to historical performance.

Considered Approach

For most significant decisions, managers should prepare well-thought-out financial projections. In addition to historical performance and trends, the projections should consider the impact of a number of factors, including:

- Strategic objectives.
- Actions and potential actions of customers and competitors.
- Anticipated changes in prices, costs, and expense levels.
- Investments required in order to achieve the strategic objectives and projects.
- Economic variables.

Managers must carefully address a number of questions in order to estimate future performance on key value drivers. We discuss key financial inputs to each value driver in Chapters 6 through 10. Here are a few examples.

Revenue

- How fast is the market growing?
- Is our market share expected to increase or decrease? Why?
- Will we be able to increase prices or be forced to reduce prices in the future?
- What new products will be introduced (by our company and competitors)?
- What general economic assumptions are contemplated in the plan?

Costs and Expenses

- What is the general rate of inflation?
- What will happen to significant costs such as key raw materials, labor, and related expenses such as employee health care?
- What increases to head count will be required to execute the plan?
- What operating efficiencies and cost reductions can be achieved?

Asset and Investment Levels

- What level of receivables and inventories will be required in the future?
- Will we need to increase capacity to achieve the planned sales levels?

Cost of Capital

- Will we need additional financial resources to execute the plan?
- Do we plan to change the mix of debt and equity in the capital structure?
- Is our business profile becoming more or less risky?
- What is likely to happen to interest rates over the plan horizon?

The answer to each of these questions represents an assumption that must be reflected in the financial projections. All critical assumptions should be documented, evaluated, and tested as part of the planning process. Managers should test the sensitivity of the projections and the decision criteria to each critical assumption. Once identified, these critical assumptions can be closely monitored as leading indicators of the firm's ability to achieve the plan.

Multiple Scenarios and Sensitivity Analysis Provide Context

For significant decisions, it is essential to run several different versions of financial projections, for example:

- *Base case.* The most likely outcome.
- *Extrapolation based on recent performance.* Provides a reference point to evaluate other scenarios.
- *Conservative scenario.* A scenario reflecting lower expectations or downsides.
- *Upside or stretch scenario.* A scenario reflecting the potential of certain upside events.
- *Recession scenario.* What will happen to the projections if a recession occurs?

The impact of each of these cases on key decision criteria can be summarized for the decision makers, providing valuable insight into potential outcomes. While financial projections are an important element of all decisions and plans, it can be argued that there is even more value created by the thinking necessitated in developing the financial projections. For example:

- Identifying critical assumptions that can be tested and monitored.
- Identifying and thinking through different scenarios and developing contingency plans.
- Understanding how critical management decisions impact the financial model and shareholder value.

However, managers need to avoid reaching a state of analysis paralysis that renders them unable to reach a decision or plot a course of action. As Yogi Berra said, "When you come to a fork in the road, take it."[1]

SUMMARY

The business model framework is a powerful management tool. By expanding the traditional P&L model to a more comprehensive model reflecting all

---

[1]Yogi Berra with Dave Kaplan, *When You Come to a Fork in the Road, Take It* (New York: Hyperion, 2001), 1.

value drivers, managers can ensure that key decisions will be evaluated in the context of maximizing long-term value. Managers should also evaluate the mix of fixed and variable costs and the resultant effect on profitability and returns at various sales levels. Financial projections are an essential input to most business decisions. The use of tools such as scenario and sensitivity analysis serves to improve the projections and provide additional insight into the underlying decision.

We build on this concept in Chapter 5, as we consider the key drivers of shareholder value and discuss methods to improve on the performance of each of these drivers.

QUESTIONS FOR CONSIDERATION

1. What is the business model of your company?
2. Does the model reflect key measures of operating and financial performance, including asset requirements?
3. Does your company have a single business model, or is it a composite of multiple business models? If a composite of multiple business models, do you appropriately consider these different characteristics in key business decisions such as assessing performance, pricing, and investment decisions?
4. Do your planning and decision processes identify and recognize the unique aspects of each business model?
5. Does the planning and forecasting process consider alternative scenarios and identify and monitor key assumptions embedded in the financial projections?

PART TWO

Linking Performance and Value

CHAPTER 5

Drivers of Shareholder Value and the Value Performance Framework

With an understanding of financial statements, business models, and basic valuation principles, we can begin to focus on the drivers of shareholder value. In this chapter, we identify and introduce the Value Performance Framework (VPF). In subsequent chapters, we drill down deeper into each of the critical value drivers and discuss key measures and means of improving on each of these drivers.

SIX DRIVERS OF SHAREHOLDER VALUE

The six drivers of shareholder value used in the VPF are:

1. Sales growth.
2. Relative pricing strength.
3. Operating effectiveness.
4. Capital effectiveness.
5. Cost of capital.
6. The intangibles.

Factors such as interest rates, market conditions, and irrational investor behavior will, of course, affect the price of a company's stock. However, the six value drivers identified here are those that management teams and directors can use in order to build long-term sustainable shareholder value.

It is important to recognize that the significance of each driver will vary from firm to firm and will also vary over time for a particular firm.

For example, a firm with increased competition in a low-growth market will likely place significant emphasis on operating and capital effectiveness, whereas a firm with a significant opportunity for sales growth is likely to focus on that driver and place less emphasis on capital management or operating effectiveness. At some time in the future, however, this high-growth firm may have to deal with a slower growth rate and may have to shift emphasis to other drivers, such as operating efficiency and capital management.

In order to attain its full potential value, a firm must understand the potential contribution of each driver to shareholder value. The Value Performance Framework introduced in Chapter 1 is presented again in Figure 5.1. It starts with the six value drivers that ultimately determine shareholder value. Underneath these value drivers are some of the key activities and processes that determine the level of performance in each value driver. In addition, the framework identifies some of the key performance indicators that can be used to measure the effectiveness of these activities and processes. For example, sales growth is a key driver of shareholder value. A subset of sales growth is the level of organic growth, excluding the impact on sales growth of any acquisitions. Organic sales growth will be driven by a number of factors, including customer satisfaction, which can be tracked by key metrics such as on-time deliveries (OTD) and the level of past due orders.

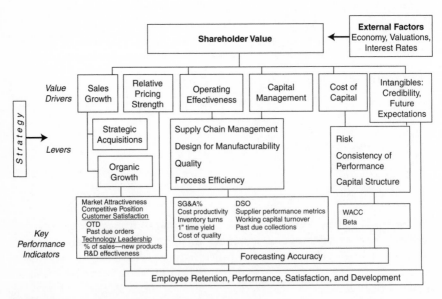

FIGURE 5.1   The Value Performance Framework
Source: Reprinted by permission of Value Advisory Group, LLC.

At the foundation of the Value Performance Framework is the employee. A firm cannot build sustainable value for shareholders without developing and retaining a competent and motivated workforce. This framework is very useful in helping employees and managers throughout the organization link their specific roles and objectives to the value of the company. A brief description of each of the value drivers within the framework follows. In subsequent chapters, each driver will be explored in detail.

Sales Growth

Revenue growth is the most significant driver of shareholder value over the long term. Other drivers are very important, but tend to reach a limit in terms of value creation. For example, a firm can improve management of working capital to a certain level, but will eventually reach a point of diminishing marginal contribution. However, a firm with a strong competitive advantage in an attractive market can enjoy sales growth over an extended period of time. In due course, this driver also tends to slacken for nearly all firms as they approach the mature stage in the life cycle of a company.

Despite its importance, managers must not focus exclusively on sales growth. To reach full potential value, some level of attention must be paid to each value driver. Additionally, it is important to note that not all sales growth leads to value creation. Sales growth must be profitable and capable of generating positive cash flow and economic returns in a reasonable period of time in order to create value.

It is fairly straightforward and relatively easy to measure and track sales growth over time. Two common measures are the growth in sales over the prior year and the growth over an extended period of time, usually measured as compound annual growth rate (CAGR). Predicting future revenue levels, however, is much more difficult and requires considerable thought and analysis. In fact, estimating future sales and sales growth is typically the most difficult element of any planning or forecasting process.

Under the VPF, we understand that value will be driven, to a significant extent, by the expectation of *future* revenue growth. Therefore, considerable emphasis will be placed on understanding the factors impacting future revenue levels. Key factors in evaluating potential revenue growth include the market size and growth rate, the firm's competitive position in the market, pricing pressures, costs, product mix, new product introductions, product obsolescence, customer satisfaction, and impact of foreign currency exchange rates, to name a few. The sales growth driver will be reviewed in greater detail in Chapter 6.

Growing the firm through acquisitions is a very different proposition than organic growth. This subject is reviewed in detail in Chapter 12, on the economics of mergers and acquisitions.

Relative Pricing Strength

The firm's ability to command a strong price for its products and services will have a significant impact on financial performance and building shareholder value. Clearly, if a firm has a strong competitive position, it should have greater pricing flexibility. This will allow the firm to set its pricing at a level that covers its costs and investments, and earns an acceptable return for shareholders. However, if the firm is in a relatively weak position in a highly competitive market, it could be subject to significant pricing pressure that will limit financial returns and drive cost containment and reduction. The subject of relative pricing strength will be explored more fully in Chapter 6.

Operating Effectiveness

Operating effectiveness is a broad term that covers how effectively and efficiently the firm operates. Operating effectiveness is an extremely important value driver and is often measured in terms of costs, expenses, and related ratios. Consider a firm that has operating margins of 15 percent of sales. This firm consumes 85 percent of its revenues in operational costs and expenses. If this firm is able to improve its productivity and reduce costs, a significant improvement in its financial performance, and ultimately its valuation, will occur.

A couple of obvious topside measures of operational effectiveness include gross margin and selling, general, and administrative (SG&A) expenses expressed as a percentage of sales. These measures can be supported by a number of indicators of process efficiency. A less obvious but no less important element of operational efficiency relates to the level of investments a company is making in future growth and the manner in which the firm manages these investments. Many firms have high levels of investment directed toward future growth. The disciplines around evaluating growth programs and eliminating dubious investments are important contributors to future financial performance and value creation. Eliminating investments in dubious investments at the earliest possible time allows managers to redirect the investment dollars to other projects or to improve margins.

An analogous issue for many companies is the frequency and diligence management applies to evaluating business units and/or products that routinely lose money. Thoughtful and disciplined managers can add significant shareholder value by addressing underperforming businesses or product lines. In addition to the ability to make the tough calls on these businesses, managers must have visibility into the true economic performance of the units and/or products.

Chapter 7 explores in further detail these and other business processes and key measures for operating effectiveness.

Capital Effectiveness

An often underutilized lever to improve cash flows and shareholder value is effective capital management. Capital effectiveness has two broad categories: operating capital requirements and investments in property and equipment. Failing to manage investments in operating capital and in property and equipment has a significant impact on cash flows and return on assets, and ultimately on valuations.

Our definition of operating capital in the VPF includes accounts receivable and inventory, offset by accounts payable and accrued expenses. We will focus primarily on the business processes and conditions that drive the levels of receivables and inventories for a firm.

For property, plant, and equipment (PP&E), we will look at the processes for reviewing and approving large expenditures, measuring utilization, and conducting post implementation reviews. In addition, we will address the impact of underutilized assets and the hidden potential value of assets that are quite frequently carried at low accounting values.

Capital effectiveness is explored in detail in Chapters 8 and 9.

Cost of Capital

As we noted in Chapter 3, the firm's cost of capital is a significant value driver because it is the rate used to discount future cash flows. Cost of capital is influenced by a number of factors, including the firm's capital structure, perceived risk of future performance, operating leverage, and stock price volatility. General economic factors, such as interest rates, also play a role in determining the cost of capital for a firm. Cost of capital, capital structure, and related topics are discussed in Chapter 10.

The Intangibles

In addition to the more quantitative, hard factors discussed earlier, there are any number of soft, intangible factors that play a significant role in driving share value. These include expectations of future performance, the reliability and consistency of financial performance, and the credibility of management. The intangibles will be discussed in Chapter 10.

BUILDING THE FRAMEWORK

In order to create a linkage between the day-to-day activities of the employees and the company's share value, we must first create a discounted cash flow (DCF) model for the company. We can start with the model introduced in Chapter 3. We first input several years of historical performance as a baseline, and then project key elements of the expected future performance. The projections should be based on our best estimate of future performance. These estimates should be realistic and should be reviewed against the recent historical performance trends experienced by the firm. This scenario, using your projections for the future performance, can be described as the "base forecast."

If the firm is publicly traded, the preliminary valuation can be tested against the current stock price. If the value indicated by the DCF model is significantly different from the recent trading range of the stock, one or more of your assumptions is likely to be inconsistent with the assumptions held by investors and potential investors. Identifying and testing the critical assumptions that investors are making in valuing the firm's stock can be very enlightening. The DCF model will allow you to easily change key assumptions and observe the potential impact on the value of the stock. It is very informative to iterate key assumptions until you can achieve a valuation consistent with recent market values for your company. For firms that are not publicly traded, this process can be performed for a comparable firm or firms that are in the same industry. Growth rates, other key drivers, and valuation metrics reviewed in Chapter 3 can then be transferred to the private firm to understand value drivers and expectations for the industry.

Since the model requires a number of critical assumptions, for example revenue growth and profitability, you may want to create multiple scenarios to estimate the impact each assumption has on the value of the company. A very useful tool for representing the outcomes of this analysis is a sensitivity chart, illustrated in Table 5.1. This sensitivity chart presents combinations of assumptions for profitability and sales growth and the resultant estimated stock price. Sensitivity analysis provides important context to develop an understanding of value drivers.

After developing a perspective on valuation and value drivers, the second step is to identify the critical activities and processes that impact each value driver. While many of these critical processes and activities are common from business to business, their relative importance will vary significantly among companies. Further, every industry and firm has certain unique characteristics that must be identified and reflected in the framework. In Chapters 6 through 10, we examine each of the value drivers and link them to critical processes and activities.

TABLE 5.1 DCF Value Sensitivity Analysis: Simple Co. Stock Price

Operating Income %	Sales Growth Rate				
	4%	6%	8%	10%	12%
20.0	$12.11	$13.49	$15.04	$16.80	$18.77
17.5	10.52	11.68	13.00	14.49	16.17
15.0	8.92	9.88	10.96	12.18	13.56
12.5	7.33	8.08	8.92	9.87	10.95
10.0	5.74	6.27	6.88	7.57	8.34

The VPF allows managers to evaluate potential improvement projects and identify high-leverage opportunities in the context of value creation. Too often, companies or functional managers embark on initiatives to improve certain aspects of the business without fully considering the impact on value creation—will the initiative be worth the investment of time and valuable resources? The VPF framework allows managers to rank various programs and address the following questions:

- How much value will be created if we accelerate sales growth from 5 to 10 percent?
- How much value will be created if we reduce manufacturing defects by 20 percent?
- How much value will be created if we reduce accounts receivable days sales outstanding (DSO) from 65 to 50 days? If we improve inventory turns from four to six?
- Which of these programs will have the greatest impact on value?

MEASURING PERFORMANCE AND PROGRESS: THE CORPORATE DASHBOARD

Having provided managers with an understanding of the key value drivers for the firm and having identified the key processes and activities that are vital to improving business performance, we must build a reporting mechanism to provide insight into these critical activities. It is essential to provide managers and all employees with critical information about the health of the business and the effectiveness of the activities in which they participate. And if performance improvement is to be achieved, information must be provided consistently and routinely in real time relative to the activity.

Traditional financial reports have several limitations. First, they typically are prepared after the accounting period, on a monthly, quarterly, or annual basis. Once these reports are prepared and distributed, managers attempting to use them for performance monitoring are "looking in the rearview mirror." The report may tell them where they have been, but it will not be helpful in keeping the car on the road! A financial report for March, for example, may indicate that inventories increased above expected levels. While management can review the cause and take corrective actions in April, they were unable to avoid the problem and are left with the unfavorable impact on working capital and cash flows.

A related limitation with traditional accounting reports is that their content is typically focused on the lagging financial measures, such as gross margins, accounts receivable days sales outstanding (DSO), and so forth. Effective managers identify measures of critical business processes and activities that can be monitored on a current basis. This affords them the opportunity to identify exceptions and unfavorable trends and take immediate corrective action. In creating a system of effective performance reports, managers need to identify the leading or predictive indicators of performance. For example, a key but lagging indicator of accounts receivable performance, DSO, requires knowing the ending accounts receivable balance and sales for the period. However, a well-constructed performance report will track key leading indicators such as revenue patterns and collections on a weekly basis throughout the quarter. Management can estimate the ending accounts receivable level based on the interim measures and take corrective action immediately *within* the quarter if exceptions or unfavorable trends emerge. Figure 5.2 identifies critical factors and key performance measures for accounts receivable.

The third limitation with most accounting reports is that they are prepared by accountants in a way that is useful and intuitive to them. They include traditional financial statements, supporting schedules, and spreadsheets that are easily understood by accountants, but are difficult for most nonfinancial managers and employees to understand and digest. Key trends or exceptions may be buried in the statements but are extremely difficult for anyone to identify let alone take action upon.

A far more effective method is to develop a series of reports that present all of the key factors in a high-visual-impact presentation format, including graphs, charts, and tables. These user-friendly reports can be summarized in one or more dashboards that will allow managers and employees to quickly scan the series of charts, as a pilot would scan the instrument panel on an airplane. Figure 5.3 shows the instrument panel in a cockpit of an aircraft, specifically the space shuttle. At a glance, the pilot can get a highly visual report on the plane's altitude and attitude and on every major system in the aircraft. The radar in an airplane allows the pilot

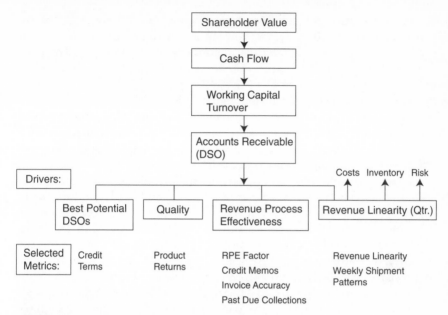

FIGURE 5.2 Drill-Down for Accounts Receivable Drivers

FIGURE 5.3 Space Shuttle Instrument Panel
Photo Courtesy of NASA.

to spot and identify potential threats long before visual contact. At first the panel appears very complex, but you can bet the pilot knows where every needle and dial should be and the importance of any changes! The pilot compares this information with the feel of the plane, visual observation, and intuition and makes adjustments in real time, as indicated, to operate the craft to safely execute the flight plan or mission.

Running a business is similar to flying an airplane. Managers also need timely, visual reports on key aspects of their business. How well is the company performing on major systems? Where is the company now? Where is it headed? Are there any threats on the horizon?

Examples of quarterly and weekly dashboards are presented in Figures 5.4 and 5.5, respectively. Note that at first the dashboards can be visually overwhelming. However, after a few cycles, managers become familiar with where each dial and needle should be on the dashboard. Having a complete and highly visual dashboard covering the business provides great insight across all key value drivers and affords managers the opportunity to assess performance and progress on key strategic objectives.

The quarterly corporate dashboard contains key measures across all value drivers. This summary-level dashboard would be supported by a series of dashboards with additional and more detailed measures that focus on key business processes and activities. This graphic affords managers the opportunity to examine performance and understand the interrelationships of key factors—for example, the relationship between forecast accuracy and operating capital.

Managers should develop dashboards for key performance indicators at various levels in the organization. In addition, the ideal frequency of key measures will vary significantly and may range from annually to weekly. Many key processes or activities are so critical to the performance of the organization that they should be measured daily or on a continuous basis. Examples of such activities may include key measures in continuous manufacturing processes, and accounts receivable collections in a cash-strapped firm. Incorporating key performance indicators into a series of performance dashboards will be discussed in detail in Chapter 11.

People and organizations respond to the use of measures. The mere fact that performance is being tracked often leads to improvements in productivity. This is even more dramatic if compensation plans are tied to the measures. As a result, care must be exercised to select appropriate measures. Establishing measures that are not well vetted may lead to behavior changes that have unintended consequences. In addition, it is critically important to achieve a balance in the measures. For example, measuring inventory turns could lead to the unintended consequence of impacting customer deliveries if not balanced with appropriate measures

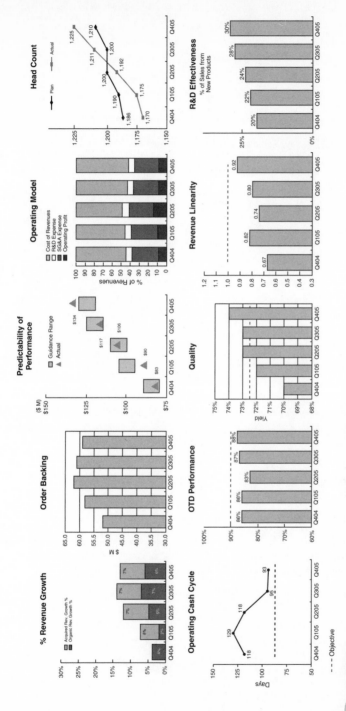

FIGURE 5.4 Example of Corporate Quarterly Dashboard

XYZ Company
Q4' 05 Week #7 of 13/ 54% of Q4
($ in Millions)

Bookings

Week	Unit	QTD	Forecast	% Achieved	$ Required
0.7	BU 1	15.0	30.0	50%	15.0
—	BU 2	0.9	1.0	89	0.1
0.5	BU 3	4.0	6.0	67	2.0
0.4	BU 4	1.7	4.7	37	2.9
0.0	Other	0.1	—		(0.1)
1.6	Totals	21.7	41.7	52%	$20.0

Revenue

Week	Unit	QTD	Forecast	% Achieved	Backlog	Req'd Fill
2.0	BU 1	13.0	28.0	46%	5.0	10.00
0.4	BU 2	3.0	5.0	60	1.0	1.00
0.0	BU 3	3.0	6.0	50	2.0	1.00
2.6	BU 4	3.0	7.0	43	1.0	3.00
—	Other	—	—			
5.0	Totals	22.0	46.0	48%	9.0	15.0

Receivable Collections (Cumulative)

Week	1	2	3	4	5
Actual	1.0	5.0	19.0	28.0	
Target	4.0	9.0	17.0	28.0	35.0

Process Yield

Day	1	2	3	4	5
	77%	80%	81%	68%	82%

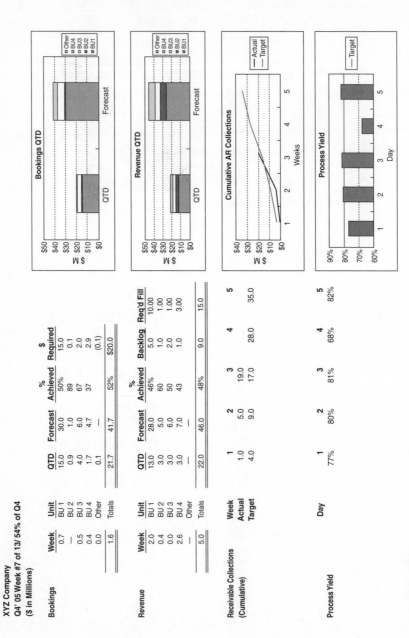

FIGURE 5.5 Example of Corporate Weekly Dashboard

88

of on-time deliveries and customer satisfaction. The selection of performance measures should be done in the context of building a comprehensive performance management framework (PMF), more fully discussed in Chapter 11.

ASSESSING PERFORMANCE AND IDENTIFYING PRESSURE POINTS

Managers have a number of tools to evaluate the performance of their firm. Two objective methods that we emphasize in the VPF are process assessment and benchmarking. We discuss business process assessment as it relates to each specific driver in Chapters 6 to 10. Benchmarking will be discussed here and again in detail in Chapter 11.

Benchmarking can be a great tool in identifying potential improvement opportunities. There are two different types of benchmarking. The first is simply to compare reported financial results and measures across companies. This method is a great way to compare performance on key measures and is illustrated in Figure 5.6. However, it has a number of shortcomings. While it does identify gaps and differences, it stops short of providing insight behind the numbers. Without an understanding of the businesses' practices and other factors, it provides limited benefit. For example, it is noteworthy to identify that Dell Inc. turns inventory over 100 times per year. But just how does Dell do that? Are there best practices here that can be considered in your company?

This more meaningful method of benchmarking requires us to climb under the numbers to understand the practices and drivers of one firm's performance versus another's. This requires detailed knowledge of the market, business model, processes, and practices of the firm. For example, Dell's performance in inventory management is a result of creating a breakthrough business model with significant attention to managing the supply chain, assembly, order fulfillment, and distribution processes. Much has been written and published about best practices at Dell and other innovative companies. Many of these companies have been open about sharing the methods they employed in achieving breakthrough performance in a particular area. In addition, many consulting firms have developed a practice in this area or offer training courses in implementing best practices in various business processes. By comparing your performance to that of competitors as well as best-practice companies, it is possible to identify gaps in your performance that represent significant opportunities to increase shareholder value.

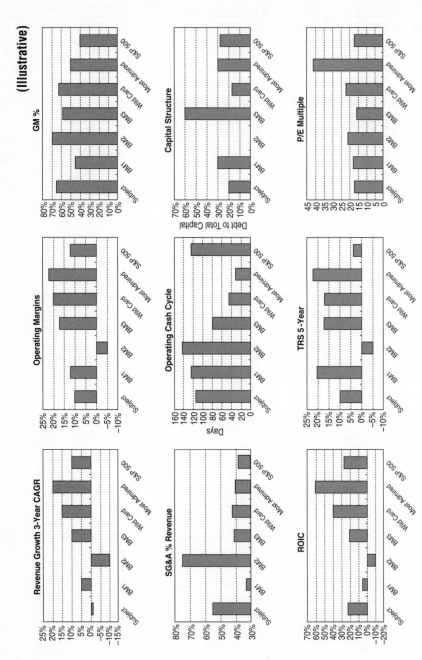

FIGURE 5.6 Benchmarking Dashboard. Benchmarking is a key tool in assessing performance and identifying improvement opportunities.

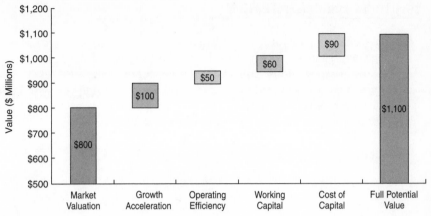

FIGURE 5.7   Estimating Full Potential Valuation

IDENTIFYING HIGH-LEVERAGE IMPROVEMENT OPPORTUNITIES AND ESTIMATING FULL POTENTIAL VALUE

Utilizing the tools including business process assessment, benchmarking, and discounted cash flow analysis, managers can estimate the potential improvements in the value drivers and quantify the effect on the value of the firm if the targeted performance is achieved. The results of this process are illustrated in Figure 5.7. In this example, the firm's current market value of $800 million could be increased to $1,100 million by achieving the performance levels targeted as a result of the performance assessment process.

SUMMARY

We will explore the concepts introduced in this chapter throughout the rest of the book. In Chapters 6 through 10, we will drill down into each of the key value drivers, linking to critical business processes and identifying key performance measures. In Part Three, Chapter 11 covers the implementation of dashboards as part of a comprehensive performance management framework, including the integration of the tools to assess performance and increase shareholder value. Chapter 12 integrates these concepts and tools with the evaluation, valuation, and measurement of mergers and acquisitions. Chapter 13 provides some key findings from our benchmark study covering performance and shareholder value.

QUESTIONS FOR CONSIDERATION

1. Does your company utilize performance measures? Are they part of an integrated framework linked to shareholder value and strategic objectives, or are they a loose collection of independent measures?
2. Do you have a dashboard or instrument panel to provide you with key information to run the business?
3. What are the key value drivers for your company?

CHAPTER 6

Revenue Growth and Pricing Strength

Revenue growth is one of the most important drivers in building and sustaining shareholder value. Understanding the drivers of revenue growth, estimating future revenue levels, and achieving sustainable growth rates are some of the most difficult challenges that managers face. This chapter is not intended to be a work on strategy or marketing. The objective in this chapter is to enable more discipline and analysis in predicting, driving, and evaluating future revenue levels.

REVENUE GROWTH: KEY DRIVERS

Figure 6.1 presents a summary of key drivers of revenue growth. Revenue growth arises from two sources: growth resulting from internal activities and growth resulting from acquisitions. Growth resulting from internal activities is often referred to as organic growth. Growth resulting from acquisitions will have very different drivers and economic characteristics from organic growth. The economics of acquired growth are covered in detail in Chapter 12, on the economics of mergers and acquisitions (M&A). We will focus on organic growth for the remainder of this chapter. Organic growth may result from growth in the overall size of the market, by gaining share from competitors within the market, or by entering new markets.

Market

Whether chosen by luck or as a result of great strategic thinking, the market(s) that a company serves will be a key driver in determining potential sales growth. Some markets are mature and will grow at slow rates. Others are driven by external forces that will result in high growth rates for a number of

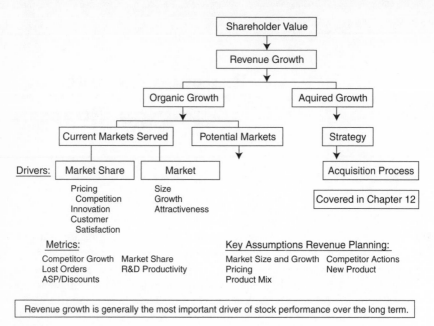

FIGURE 6.1 Drill-Down Illustration: Revenue Growth Drivers

years. In markets with high growth rates, even marginal competitors may thrive as all market participants are raised by the incoming "tide."

Competitive Position

Within a market, the competitive environment and the competitive position of a particular company will determine its ability to grow by increasing market share. A number of factors will determine a company's competitive position, including innovation, customer satisfaction and service, cost and pricing, and the number and size of competitors. Analysis of competitive position should be performed from a customer's perspective. What are the key decision criteria that drive a customer's purchase evaluation and decision? Analysis of competitive position is a relative concept; it is the performance of a company on key factors relative to other firms offering similar products or services.

Innovation Innovation can be a leading source of competitive position. Innovation should be considered in broad terms and not simply limited to product performance. In addition to product innovation, firms such as Dell have differentiated themselves by radically changing the customer fulfillment and supply chain processes to redefine the business model within an industry. Innovations in marketing or packaging can also produce a significant advantage leading to revenue gains.

Customer Satisfaction   Customer satisfaction plays a vital role in revenue growth in three ways. First, customer satisfaction will always be a key factor in retaining existing customers. Second, customers that are satisfied with a supplier's performance are likely to offer additional opportunities to that supplier. Third, a strong reputation for customer satisfaction and underlying performance may also lead to opportunities with new customers. Most markets are small worlds with key customer personnel changing companies. Satisfied customers will often pull a high-performing vendor along with them.

Customer Service   Many companies compete by providing outstanding service beyond the traditional customer satisfaction areas such as delivery and quality performance. Working with customers to solve their problems and participating in joint development programs are both examples of investments that build long-term customer loyalty.

Cost or Pricing Advantages   Price is nearly always a key factor in a customer's procurement decision. The price of a product or service will be driven by the cost of the product, profit targets, and market forces.

The cost of a product or service includes direct and indirect costs. Prices are often set by marking up or adding a profit margin to the cost to achieve a targeted level of profitability or return on invested capital (ROIC). The actual price will have to be set in the context of market forces, including price-performance comparisons to competitor products.

Suppliers can attain a cost advantage in a number of ways, including achieving economies of scale, process efficiencies, or improvements in quality. Most sophisticated customers look at the total life cycle cost of a procurement decision, of which the product selling price is one component. Other elements of life cycle cost may include installation and training, service, maintenance, and operating and disposal costs. Suppliers that can demonstrate a lower life cycle cost can achieve an advantage over competitors, even if the product price component is more expensive.

Competitor Attributes and Actions   The performance of competitors in the areas that are important to customers will have a big impact on a company's ability to grow or even maintain sales. It is not meaningful to project or evaluate revenue projections without a view of competitor intentions, tendencies, and actions. What is the competitor's strategy? How will its financial performance impact its performance in the market? If the competitor has other related businesses, how does that impact its ability to serve this market? What new product or service will the competitor introduce? How will the competitor respond to the introduction of a new product? Do competitors define the market differently? What new competitors may enter the market?

Many revenue projections are prepared without fully considering the answers to these questions. Revenue from new products is assumed to gain market share, without reflecting the competitor response. Again, the value in planning is not found in the precise quantitative values on the spreadsheet, but rather in the evolution in thinking as a result of the planning process.

Entering New Markets: Opportunities to Broaden or Migrate to Other Segments

Many companies have been successful at growing over extended periods of time. In addition to growing with their primary market and gaining share within that market, companies have found ways to expand the size of the market they serve by moving into adjacent markets. Dell, for example, leveraged its competencies in distribution and supply chain management to expand its market from personal computers to other consumer electronics.

PROJECTING AND TESTING FUTURE REVENUE LEVELS

Since revenue growth is an important driver of economic value, it is critical for managers and investors to fully identify, understand, and evaluate the factors impacting future revenues. Despite the relative importance of revenue compared to other drivers, it often suffers from less disciplined analytic approaches than other drivers such as cost management and operating efficiency. This is due in part to the complexity of the driver and due to the significant impact of external forces such as customers, competitors, and economic factors. Managers should develop and improve tools and practices for projecting future revenues and monitor leading indicators of revenue levels. Best practices include:

- Improve the revenue forecasting process.
- Prepare multiple views of revenue detail.
- Measure forecast effectiveness.
- Deal effectively with special issues.

Improve Revenue Forecasting Process

Forecasting   In addition to providing a projection of future performance for planning, budgeting, and investor communication, the revenue forecast typically drives procurement and manufacturing schedules and activities. Forecasting is a very important activity within most companies and is included on our list of pressure points addressed in Chapter 13. Forecasting future business levels is almost always a significant challenge.

Predicting the future is inherently difficult. However, there are a number of things managers can do to improve the forecasting process. First, it is of vital importance that all managers understand the importance of forecasting as a business activity. It impacts customer satisfaction and service levels, costs and expenses, pricing, inventories, and investor confidence, to name a few. Businesses that are predictable and have consistent levels of operating performance will have lower perceived risk, leading to a lower cost of capital. Second, huge gains can be made by measuring forecast accuracy and assigning responsibility and accountability to appropriate managers. Third, there are a number of techniques that can be applied to improve the effectiveness of forecasts, such as using ranges of expected performance, identifying significant risks and upsides, and developing contingency plans. However, because forecasting involves an attempt to predict the future, it will always be an imperfect activity.

Forecast Philosophy and Human Behavior   The starting point in improving forecasting is to recognize tendencies in human behavior. Most managers are optimistic. They are positive thinkers. They are under pressure to achieve higher levels of sales and profits. They are reluctant to throw in the towel by lowering performance targets. They recognize that decreasing the revenue outlook may result in a decrease in value and may necessitate cost and staff reductions, or even the loss of their jobs. Managers who are ultimately responsible for the projections, in most cases the CEO and CFO, must recognize these soft factors and their impact on projections. They must communicate and reinforce the need for realistic and achievable forecasts.

Base Forecast   Many companies have improved their ability to project revenues by using multiple scenarios. A base forecast is developed, which is often defined as the most probable outcome. Managers find it helpful to define an intended confidence level for the base forecast. Is it a 50/50 plan or 80/20? The former would indicate that there is as much chance of exceeding the forecast as falling short. The latter confidence level implies a greater level of confidence in achieving the forecast: There is an 80 percent chance of meeting or exceeding the forecast. A practical way of defining this would be that 8 out of 10 times the forecast would be met or exceeded.

Upside and Downside Events   After planning the base case, upside and downside events can be identified. Examples include economic factors, competitor actions, or acceleration or delays in new product introductions. For each possible event, managers should identify how they will monitor the possible event and the probability of the event occurring during the plan horizon. In most cases, upside and downside events with high probabilities should be built into the base forecast.

Development of Aggressive and Conservative Forecast Scenarios   Using the base case scenario and potential upside and downside events, managers can prepare an aggressive scenario and a conservative scenario. The aggressive scenario can be achieved if some or all of the upside events materialize—for example, if product adoption rates exceed the estimates incorporated in the base case. The conservative scenario contemplates selected downside events.

What actions will we take if it becomes apparent that we are trending toward either the aggressive or the conservative scenario? If trending to the aggressive scenario, do we need to accelerate production, hiring, and other investments? If trending to the downside scenario, do we need to reduce or delay investments or hiring? Pedal harder to close the gap?

Identify, Document, and Monitor Key Assumptions   As with any projection, it is important to identify and document key assumptions that support the revenue forecast. Projecting revenues is typically the most difficult element of business planning and involves many assumptions, including factors external to the organization. Key assumptions for revenue projections typically include:

- Market size and growth rate.
- Pricing.
- Product mix.
- Geographic mix.
- Competitor actions/reactions.
- New product introductions.
- Macroeconomic factors, including interest rates, gross domestic product (GDP) growth, and so forth.

After identifying and documenting these key assumptions supporting revenue projections, these factors must be monitored. Any changes in assumptions must be identified and the potential impact on sales must be quantified and addressed. Critical assumptions should be included on the performance dashboard for revenue growth.

Prepare Multiple Views of Revenue Detail

Key dynamics of revenue projections can be identified by reviewing trend schedules of revenue from various perspectives. Table 6.1 is a sample summary of revenue by product. This level of detail identifies contributions from key products and provides visibility into dynamics including product introduction and life cycles. Other views may be sales by region or geography, customers, and end-use market.

Another insightful analysis is to evaluate the projections in light of recent performance and comparisons to the plan and to prior year results. Table 6.2 compares year to date (YTD) actual and rest of year (ROY) projected performance to last year and the plan. Since it is comparing the same periods, seasonality is accounted for in the analysis.

This forecast needs some explaining! On a year-to-date basis, revenues

TABLE 6.1   Revenue Planning Worksheet: Product Detail

	Actual		Projected		
	2004	2005	2006	2007	2008
Existing Products					
1	$100	$ 90	$ 80	$ 60	$ 50
2	100	100	100	100	100
3	50	40	20	10	0
4	30	60	70	90	110
Subtotal	$280	$290	$270	$260	$260
New Product Pipeline					
5			$ 20	$ 35	$ 60
6			5	20	35
7				20	45
8					
Subtotal	$ 0	$ 0	$ 25	$ 75	$140
Total Sales Projection	$280	$290	$295	$335	$400
Year-over-Year Growth		3.6%	1.7%	13.6%	19.4%
CAGR 2004: 2008P					9.3%

TABLE 6.2 Forecast Evaluation Worksheet

Revenue ($ M)	YTD			ROY			Year		
	Actual	Last Year	Plan	Forecast	Last Year	Plan	Forecast	Last Year	Plan
Product 1	$1,250	$1,208	$1,300	$1,450	$1,325	$1,400	$2,700	$2,533	$2,700
Product 2	1,005	950	1,100	1,200	1,102	1,200	2,205	2,052	2,300
Product 3	1,300	1,310	1,400	1,500	1,433	1,500	2,800	2,743	2,900
Product 4	850	825	900	950	879	950	1,800	1,704	1,850
Product 5	733	715	750	800	775	800	1,533	1,490	1,550
Product 6	1,650	1,612	1,700	1,800	1,725	1,800	3,450	3,337	3,500
Total	$6,788	$6,620	$7,150	$7,700	$7,239	$7,650	$14,488	$13,859	$14,800

Revenue %	YTD		ROY		Year	
	Last Year	Plan	Last Year	Plan	Last Year	Plan
Product 1	103%	96%	109%	104%	107%	100%
Product 2	106	91	109	100	107	96
Product 3	99	93	105	100	102	97
Product 4	103	94	108	100	106	97
Product 5	103	98	103	100	103	99
Product 6	102	97	104	100	103	99
Total	103%	95%	106%	101%	105%	98%

are 103 percent of last year and 95 percent of the plan. However, the forecast revenue for the remainder of the year is 106 percent of last year and 101 percent of the plan. There may be some very good reasons for this inconsistency. I sure would like to hear and evaluate them!

Revenue Change Analysis A useful way to evaluate revenue projections is to compare them to the prior year and identify significant changes. Each source of significant change can be evaluated and tested. There is a tendency to project future revenues by identifying future sources of revenue growth and adding these increments to existing revenue levels. For example, additional revenues may result from new product introductions or geographic expansion. It is also important to identify factors that will decrease revenues. For example, many industries will experience decreases in average selling prices (ASPs) over time. In addition all products are subject to life cycles with the eventuality of declining sales levels at some point. Figure 6.2 provides a good visual summary of significant changes in sales from 2005 to 2006.

Market Size and Share Summary Another view that is useful for evaluating revenue projections is to consider them in the context of the overall market size and growth, as well as market share. Table 6.3 presents the market for Simple Co. For each year, the size of the market is estimated and the growth rate is provided. Sales for each competitor are also estimated, forcing a consideration of competitive dynamics and identification of share gains. In this case, we see that Simple Co.'s 8 percent growth projected for each year is higher than the market growth. Who will the company take market share from? Why? Is 8 percent growth each year possible? Is it consistent with the real-life market dynamics such as product introductions and life cycles, economic factors, and competitive factors?

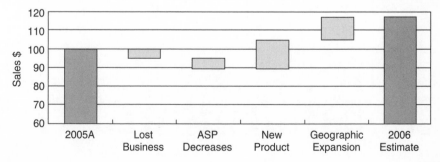

FIGURE 6.2 Revenue Change Analysis

TABLE 6.3 Market Size and Share Analysis

	2006	2007	2008	2009	2010	2011	2012	2013	2014	CAGR 2006–2014
Market Size	$1,500	$1,550	$1,600	$1,650	$1,710	$1,770	$1,825	$1,900	$1,975	3.5%
Growth Rate	4.0%	3.3%	3.2%	3.1%	3.6%	3.5%	3.1%	4.1%	3.9%	
Sales										
BigandSlo Co.	$ 700	$ 705	$710	$712	$705	$700	$680	$660	$640	-1.1%
Complex Co.	390	400	420	430	450	475	480	500	510	3.4
Simple Co.	100	108	117	126	136	147	159	171	185	8.0
Fast Co.	10	30	50	100	150	200	250	300	370	57.0
Other	300	307	303	282	269	248	256	269	270	-1.3
Total	$1,500	$1,550	$1,600	$1,650	$1,710	$1,770	$1,825	$1,900	$1,975	3.5%
Market Share										
BigandSlo Co.	46.7%	45.5%	44.4%	43.2%	41.2%	39.5%	37.3%	34.7%	32.4%	
Complex Co.	26.0	25.8	26.3	26.1	26.3	26.8	26.3	26.3	25.8	
Simple Co.	6.7	7.0	7.3	7.6	8.0	8.3	8.7	9.0	9.4	
Fast Co.	0.7	1.9	3.1	6.1	8.8	11.3	13.7	15.8	18.7	
Other	20.0	19.8	18.9	17.1	15.7	14.0	14.0	14.2	13.7	
Total	100%	100%	100%	100%	100%	100%	100%	100%	100%	
Growth Rate										
BigandSlo Co.		0.7%	0.7%	0.3%	-1.0%	-0.7%	-2.9%	-2.9%	-3.0%	
Complex Co.		2.6	5.0	2.4	4.7	5.6	1.1	4.2	2.0	
Simple Co.		8.0	8.0	8.0	8.0	8.0	8.0	8.0	8.0	
Fast Co.		200.0	66.7	100.0	50.0	33.3	25.0	20.0	23.3	
Other		2.3	-1.3	-6.9	-4.6	-7.8	3.2	5.1	0.4	
Total		3.3%	3.2%	3.1%	3.6%	3.5%	3.1%	4.1%	3.9%	

Measure Forecast Effectiveness

A very effective way to improve the forecast accuracy is to monitor and track actual performance against the forecasts. Two examples are provided. Table 6.4 presents the changes made to each quarterly projection over the course of 12 months. It is very effective in identifying biases and forecast gamesmanship. In this example, the analysis surfaces a number of concerns and questions. Note that the actual revenue achieved for each quarter is consistently under the forecast developed at the beginning of that quarter. In addition, shortfalls in one quarter are pushed out into subsequent quarters. However, the team does seem to be able to forecast revenues within one month of the quarter end.

Figure 6.3 tracks the evolution of the total year forecast over a 12-month period. Note that the forecast for the year was not decreased until two quarterly shortfalls were posted.

Deal Effectively with Special Issues

There are a number of special circumstances that present challenges in developing and evaluating revenue projections. These include sales projec-

TABLE 6.4 Revenue Forecast Accuracy

Month Forecast Submitted	Q1	Q2	Q3	Q4	Year
January	$7,500	$8,000	$8,700	$9,200	$33,400
February	7,200	8,300	8,700	9,200	33,400
March	7,000	8,500	8,700	9,200	33,400
April	$7,045	8,400	8,800	9,200	33,445
May		8,400	8,800	9,200	33,445
June		8,000	9,200	9,200	33,445
July		$7,076	9,200	9,200	32,521
August			9,100	9,200	32,421
September			8,700	9,600	32,421
October			$8,725	9,600	32,446
November				9,600	32,446
December				9,200	32,046
January				$9,250	$32,096
Variance, from beginning of quarter ($)	($455)	($1,324)	($475)	($350)	($1,304)
Variance, from beginning of quarter (%)	−6.1%	−15.8%	−5.2%	−3.6%	−4.1%

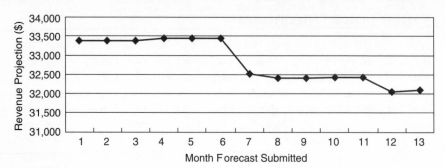

FIGURE 6.3 Forecast Trend Analysis

tions for new products, chunky or lumpy businesses with uneven sales patterns, and large programs.

Sales Projections for New Products   The development and introduction of new products is always a factor in growing or maintaining sales. Revenue plans for new products must be directly linked to new product development schedules. These schedules must be monitored closely and changes reflected in the related revenue projections. A delay in the product schedule will likely delay introduction and the revenue ramp. Product introduction plans must be broad, expanding beyond product development to incorporate key marketing and customer activities. Critical assumptions should be reviewed as well. Any changes in these underlying assumptions should be tested to support revenue plans and even project viability. Examples include changes in key customer performance, economic conditions, and competitor actions.

Chunky and Lumpy Businesses   Some businesses are characterized by large orders resulting in lumpy business patterns from the presence or absence of these orders. These chunks wreak havoc in trend analysis and short-term projections. Depending on the cost structure and degree of operating leverage, these swings in revenue can result in extremely large fluctuations in profits. Care must be taken in setting expense levels in these situations. It may be appropriate to set expectations and expense levels for a base level of revenue and consider these lumps as upsides. Communicating with investors about the business variability and disclosing the inclusion of lumpy business is essential to avoid significant fluctuation in the stock price and loss of management credibility.

Large Programs and Procurements   In many industries, large procurements, programs, or long-term contracts are awarded periodically, for example every three years. Revenue changes in these situations are often binary and significant: if the contract is awarded to your firm, significant sales growth will be achieved for the contract period. If unsuccessful, your firm loses the opportunity to obtain that business for that contract period. If a firm loses that business at the end of the contract period, there is a significant decrease to sales. This presents a number of management, financial planning, and investor communication issues.

When pursuing a large procurement opportunity, it is useful to prepare a base forecast without the inclusion of the large procurement and prepare an upside forecast reflecting the award. If a company's existing contracts are up for grabs, consideration should be given to a downside scenario, reflecting conditions if the contract is lost. Investors should have visibility into the presence and expiration dates of significant contracts.

KEY PERFORMANCE MEASURES: REVENUE GROWTH

A number of key performance measures can provide insight into historical trends and future revenue potential.

Sales Growth: Sequential and Year-over-Year

A critical measure of business performance is simply to measure the rate of growth in sales from one period to another. Table 6.5 illustrates a typical presentation of sales growth rates. Two different measures are frequently used. The first is simply to compute the growth from the previous year. The second measure computes sequential growth rates, that is, from one quarter to another.

While these growth rate measures are important top-level performance measures, they are of limited usefulness without additional analysis. Some

TABLE 6.5   Quarterly Sales Trend ($ Millions)

	Q104	Q204	Q304	Q404	Year 2004	Q105	Q205	Q305	Q405	Year 2005
Sales	62	64	60	75	261	65	70	58	82	275
Year-over-Year Growth	5.1%	6.7%	11.1%	8.7%	7.9%	4.8%	9.4%	−3.3%	9.3%	5.4%
Sequential Growth	−10.1%	3.2%	−6.3%	25.0%		−13.3%	7.7%	−17.1%	41.4%	

managers and investors will extrapolate past sales growth rates into the future. This works in certain circumstances for a period of time; however, it does not take into consideration the underlying dynamics that will drive future revenues. These factors include market forces, competitive position, innovation, and customer satisfaction.

Customer/Competitor Growth Index

The evaluation of a company's performance is best done in the context of competitor, customer, and overall market performance. This is very important in assessing a company's performance in growing sales. For example, if Simple Co. grew 8 percent last year, the market grew by 3 percent, and one of the competitors grew 25 percent, would we consider this acceptable performance?

Comparing growth to rates experienced by key competitors and customers places the company's performance in an appropriate context. It can also be important input to strategic analysis. For example, what are the causes and implications of customer growth exceeding our own? Are we missing potential opportunities to grow with our customers? A summary of comparative growth rates is provided in Figure 6.4. In this case, Simple Co. is growing faster than the market, and at a rate between the company's two largest customers. Simple Co.'s growth rate is ahead of those of two competitors, but is significantly under Fast Co.'s growth rate.

Percentage of Revenue from New Products

Most companies seek to maintain and grow sales by developing and introducing new products. An important indicator of the success of the new product development and introduction activities is the percentage

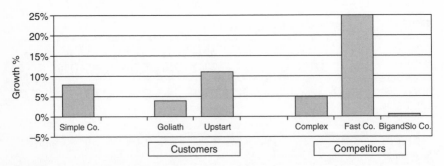

FIGURE 6.4   Year-over-Year Growth

of revenue from products recently introduced. Some companies would define *recently* as two years. Others may shorten the period to reflect shorter product life cycles.

Customer Retention and Lost Customers

Given the cost and difficulty in obtaining new customers, companies must go to great lengths to retain existing customers. Identifying the loss or potential loss of a customer on a timely basis provides immediate visibility into the revenue impact of losing that customer and may afford the company an opportunity to take corrective action. Of course, the reason for losing a customer should be understood, contemplated, and acted upon.

Lost Orders

Companies should track the value and number of orders lost to competitors. Significant trends may signal some change in the competitive environment. Drilling down into lost orders to identify the root cause can also be enlightening. Most companies expect to lose some orders. For example, a high-end equipment supplier expects to lose some orders to a low-end supplier where price is a driving factor in the customer's buy decision. However, if the company began to lose orders based on performance or service, the alarm should sound.

Revenue from New Customers

Companies may expect future growth by acquiring new customers. In these cases it would be useful to track revenue derived from sales to new customers. *New* is defined by individual circumstance, but is frequently defined as revenue derived from customers acquired over the prior 12 months.

Customer Satisfaction

An important factor in maintaining current sales levels and in growing sales is customer satisfaction. An increasing number of companies periodically solicit overall performance ratings from their customers. Many customers have sophisticated supply chain processes that include the evaluation of overall vendor performance. These performance ratings are used as a basis for selecting and retaining vendors.

Key elements of the customer's total experience will include price, quality, delivery performance, and service. Therefore, management should measure these factors frequently. It is important to measure these factors from the customer's viewpoint. For example, the customer may measure quality or service levels differently than the supplier. What matters, of course, is only the customer's perspective.

Past Due Orders

Monitoring the level of past due orders can provide important insight into customer satisfaction. An increase in the level of past due orders may indicate a manufacturing or supply problem that resulted in delayed shipments to customers. In addition to tracking (and attacking) the level of past due orders, much can be learned by identifying and addressing recurring causes of past due orders. Reducing the level of past due sales orders will increase sales and customer satisfaction and reduce inventories and costs.

On-Time Delivery

On-time delivery is a very important determiner of customer satisfaction. Some companies measure delivery to "quoted delivery dates." Progressive companies measure delivery performance against the date the customer originally requested, since that is the date the customer originally wanted the product.

Quality

Measuring the quality of product and other customer-facing activities is an important indicator of customer satisfaction. Examples include: product returns, warranty experience, and the volume of sales credits issued.

Projected Revenue in Product Pipeline

If future growth is highly dependent on new product development and introduction, then management should have a clear view of the revenue potential and project status in each product in the development pipeline. Table 6.6 is an example of a summary of revenue in the product development pipeline.

A key benefit to this summary is that development, marketing, sales, and other personnel involved in the introduction of new products have clear visibility to the linkage of their activities relative to future revenue targets. The impact of any delay or acceleration in the development time line on revenue expectations is easily understood.

TABLE 6.6   Revenue in Product Development Pipeline ($ Millions)

Project Name	2005	2006	2007	2008	Annual Revenue Potential	Status	Comment
Coyote	$ 0	$ 7	$18	$ 24	$ 25	Green	On track, intro 3/06
Fox	0	12	26	30	30	Yellow	2 critical milestones missed
Rabbit	15	15	15	12	15	Red	Technical performance issues
Tortoise	0	20	30	50	60	Green	1st shipments, next week
Total	$15	$54	$89	$116	$130		

Revenue per Transaction

Tracking revenue per transaction can provide important insight into sales trends. Is average transaction or order value increasing or decreasing? Can we capture more revenue per order by selling supplies, related products, service agreements, or consumables? In retail industries, revenue per customer visit is a key revenue driver, and retailers put substantial effort into increasing customers' spending per visit by offering related products, cross merchandising, and impulse buy displays.

Revenue per Customer

Reviewing the revenue per customer in total and for key customers can identify important trends. Identifying and tracking sales to top customers is essential to understanding revenue trends and developing future projections.

Quote Levels

For certain businesses with long purchasing cycles, tracking the level of open quotes over time can be a leading indicator of future revenue levels. Not all quotes are created equal. Some may be for budgetary purposes, indicating a long-term purchase horizon. Others may indicate order potential in the short term. For this reason, quote levels are often summarized by key characteristics to enhance the insight into potential order flow.

Order Backlog Levels

Some businesses have long lead times or order cycles. Customers must place orders well in advance of requested delivery dates. Examples include aircraft, shipbuilding, and large equipment industries. In these industries, the order backlog levels are an important leading indicator of revenue and general business health.

Anecdotal Input

Nothing beats a customer letter or survey response containing specific feedback. Post them with the quantitative measures and watch the reaction of employees. Many include points actionable by employees at various levels in the company. A few examples:

- "Customer service never answers the phone. Voice mail messages are not returned for several days."
- "Service levels have declined. We are contemplating an alternative supplier."
- "The delay in scheduling installation and training is unacceptable."

REVENUE DASHBOARD

Based on the most important drivers and issues impacting current and future revenue growth, a performance dashboard would be created to present these measures to managers (see Figure 6.5). The selection of the individual measures to include in the dashboard is an extremely important process. There should be an emphasis on leading and predictive indicators of revenue growth. The measures should focus on the most important drivers and should be changed over time as appropriate. Properly constructed, this one-page summary of critical factors is sure to focus the team's attention on appropriate issues and opportunities.

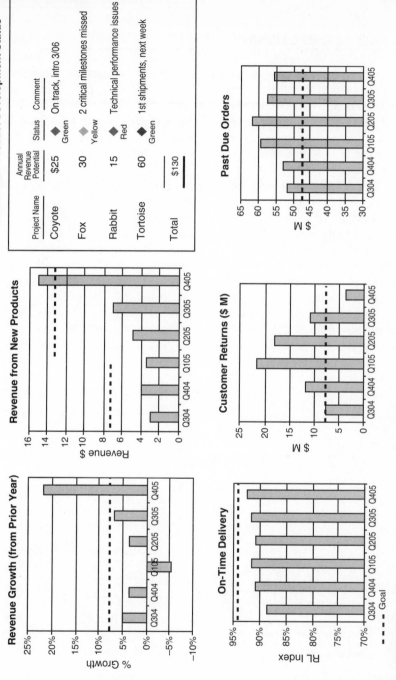

FIGURE 6.5 Revenue: Growth and Innovation Dashboard

RELATIVE PRICING STRENGTH

It is easy to look at a company with high gross margins and profitability and assume that it is highly efficient from an operating perspective. However, a company may be inefficient but still achieve high margins on the basis of a strong competitive advantage that affords it a premium price. This relative pricing advantage can mask operating inefficiencies and high costs, which can be a source of competitive vulnerability. Over time, relative pricing advantages tend to dissipate, leading to margin erosion unless cost and operating efficiencies are achieved. Figure 6.6 charts gross margins and relative pricing strength.

Gross margins are primarily a function of two variables, cost of goods sold and pricing. Pricing will be driven by a combination of cost and market forces. What typically drives relative pricing strength for a company is a unique product/service offering or an offering with significantly higher performance attributes than competitors offer. The leading market indicators for pricing will center around the competitive position and landscape. Factors such as excess industry capacity, aggressive competitor strategies to gain share, and industry health also will play a role.

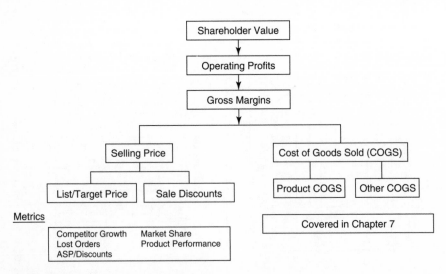

FIGURE 6.6 Gross Margins and Relative Pricing Strength

Cost of Goods Sold

Costs and operating effectiveness are covered in greater depth in Chapter 7. Costs are comprised of direct or product cost of goods sold (COGS) and indirect COGS. Product or service COGS generally include those costs that are directly associated with the product or service. For example, product costs will include the cost of materials, labor, and overhead to assemble or manufacture that product. Other or indirect COGS include items such as warranty, manufacturing variances, and cost overruns.

Gross margin analysis is also impacted by other factors, including changes in product mix and foreign currency fluctuations. Most well-run companies examine gross margin trends carefully and identify the factors accounting for changes between periods, as illustrated in Table 6.7.

MEASURES OF RELATIVE PRICING STRENGTH

A number of measures can provide visibility into a company's pricing strength.

Average Selling Price (ASP)

Tracking and monitoring the ASP of products over time is a good indicator of the relative pricing strength of a product in the market. ASP will decline, often rapidly, in highly competitive situations. In many markets, customers expect lower pricing over time as a result of anticipated efficiencies and savings.

Discounts or Discounts as a Percentage of List Price

Tracking the level of pricing discounts is a useful indicator of pricing strength that also quantifies the magnitude of any pricing erosion.

Lost Orders

This measure provides insight into future revenue and pricing trends. Orders lost on the basis of pricing are of particular concern, since they foreshadow a decrease in both revenue and margins.

TABLE 6.7 Gross Margin Analysis

	2004	2005	Variance	Volume Increase	Pricing Changes	Mix	Cost Increases	Quality Savings	Other	Total
Sales	$125,000	$126,000	$ 1,000	$2,500	$-1,500					$ 1,000
Cost of Sales	78,000	82,000	-4,000	-1,560		$-1,500	$-820	$280	$-400	-4,000
Gross Margin	$ 47,000	$ 44,000	$-3,000	$ 940	$-1,500	$-1,500	$-820	$280	$-400	$-3,000
Gross Margin %	37.6%	34.9%	-2.7%	0.0%	-0.8%	-1.2%	-0.7%	0.2%	-0.3%	-2.7%

Product Competitive Analysis

Capturing and monitoring price and performance characteristics of competitive products is a good way to anticipate changes in relative pricing strength. If a competitor introduces a product with better performance attributes, the pricing dynamics in the market are likely to change in very short order.

Market Share

The pricing and performance measures just described can be combined with the market share analysis and other measures discussed under revenue growth to help form a complete view of the competitive landscape in the context of pricing and gross margins. For example, it is possible that a company is holding firm on pricing but losing market share to lower-priced competitors.

GROSS MARGIN AND PRICING STRENGTH DASHBOARD

Based on the most important drivers and issues impacting current and future pricing and gross margins, a performance dashboard as shown in Figure 6.7 would be created to provide visibility for managers. Again, the selection of the individual measures to include in the dashboard is extremely important. There should be an emphasis on leading and predictive indicators of competitive forces and pricing. The measures should focus on the most important drivers and should be modified over time as appropriate.

SUMMARY

Revenue growth and relative pricing strength are among the most important value drivers. Yet in spite of this importance, managers often do a better job in measuring and managing other value drivers. Revenue planning is inherently difficult due to the complexity of drivers and the impact of external factors. However, managers can greatly increase their ability to build and sustain shareholder value by improving their discipline over projecting, measuring, and growing revenue.

Relative pricing strength is a key driver of value and is realized by holding a strong competitive advantage. Companies that enjoy a strong competitive advantage or have a unique product offering will enjoy strong

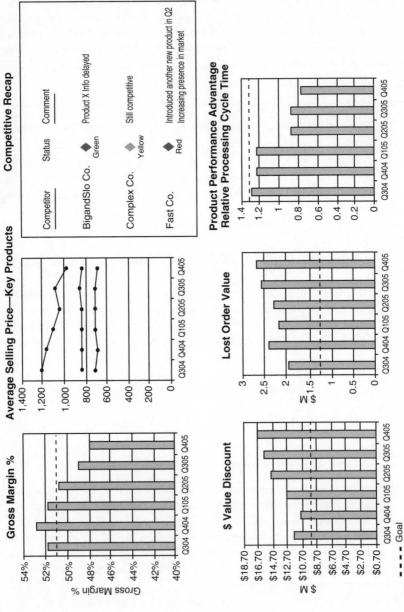

FIGURE 6.7 Dashboard: Gross Margin and Pricing Strength

product margins. It is important to distinguish between strong operating margins resulting from pricing strength and those due to operational efficiency. Over time, competitive advantage and pricing strength often dissipate. This unfavorable impact to margins can be offset by improving operational effectiveness, our topic for Chapter 7.

QUESTIONS FOR CONSIDERATION

1. How important is revenue growth to the value of your firm?
2. How effective is the revenue forecasting process?
3. What are the most important leading indicators of future revenue for your firm?

CHAPTER 7

Operating Effectiveness

In this chapter, we focus on another critical value driver: operating effectiveness. Managers and consultants often debate the relative suitability of the words *effectiveness* and *efficiency* in this context. While effectiveness is often interpreted as doing things well or selecting the right things to address, efficiency connotes doing things faster and cheaper. We will use the term *effectiveness* to encompass both interpretations. Obviously, managers do not want to become highly efficient in unimportant processes or activities; however, improving efficiency by reducing cycle time, costs, and errors can be a tremendous source of value.

Many observers look to profitability as a key indicator of operating effectiveness. It is a good start, but we recognize that it is possible for a highly inefficient organization to post high profit margins if it possesses a strong competitive advantage leading to pricing strength. In this case, it is able to pass along to its customers the high costs arising from inefficiencies. This is rarely a sustainable situation over the long term. Additionally, profitability does not directly reflect the asset levels required to support a business. Return on invested capital (ROIC) and return on equity (ROE) are considered better overall measures of management effectiveness, since they reflect both profitability and asset effectiveness measures.

There is significant crossover between operating effectiveness and capital effectiveness. While accounts receivable and inventory have other critical drivers, they are directly related to the effectiveness of the revenue and supply chain processes, respectively. We discuss these two processes in this chapter and again in more detail in Chapter 8, "Capital Effectiveness: Working Capital."

DRIVERS OF OPERATING EFFECTIVENESS

Operating effectiveness has a significant impact on cost and therefore value. Even a company recording respectable 15 percent operating margins is still "high-cost" since the company incurs costs and expenses equal to 85 percent of the company's revenue. This represents a tremendous pool of opportunity for value creation. (See Figure 7.1.)

A primary driver of operating effectiveness and profit margins is the effectiveness of business processes. Figure 7.2 identifies critical business processes, including supply chain management, revenue process management, and new product development, that will impact key financial factors including costs, revenue levels, working capital requirements, and cash flow.

Typically, a given process will cross a number of functional areas. For example, new product development may start with product managers for concept development, then move to research and development (R&D) for product design. As the product design approaches completion, procurement and manufacturing will begin purchasing materials and developing the manufacturing process for the product. Marketing and sales will become engaged in the promotion and distribution of the product. The effectiveness of this new product development process will impact costs in each of these functional areas. Mistakes made early in the process, in product conceptualization and design, will often have a significant impact on subsequent steps in the process. Further, the new product development process will contribute to sales growth, pricing strength, and working capital re-

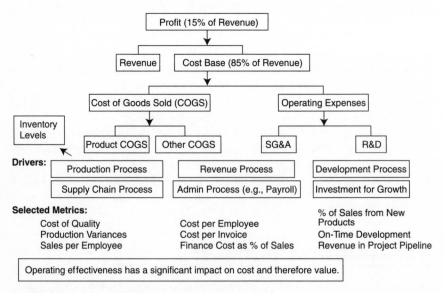

FIGURE 7.1   Operating Effectiveness Overview

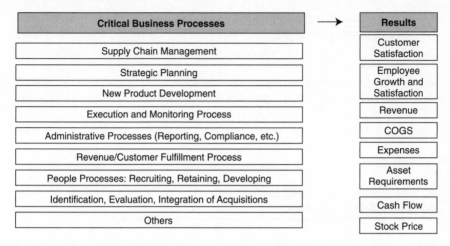

The process view appropriately recognizes cross-functional interaction versus functional silos. In order to improve performance in most critical processes, cross-functional cooperation and teaming are required.

FIGURE 7.2   Process View

quirements. It is typically far more effective to evaluate the performance of a complete process rather than to evaluate by income statement classifications (e.g., SG&A) or functions (e.g., sales).

Another critical driver of operational effectiveness is simply a strong focus on execution and cost management. If the CEO and other senior managers do not have a focus on operational effectiveness, the organization will drift to follow the other priorities. Even organizations with a history of operational effectiveness can regress quickly when a CEO shifts emphasis away from this important driver. Managers must achieve a balance between operating effectiveness and other value drivers in order to be successful over the long run.

The specific industry or market served by a company will also impact operational effectiveness. Mature, highly competitive industries such as automotive must relentlessly pursue cost reductions and operational improvements. Other industries, such as aerospace and medical, place a great deal of emphasis on quality due to the nature of the use of their products. Operational effectiveness may be less important for a technology company with products offering significant performance advantages. However, over time, this advantage is likely to dissipate and operational effectiveness is likely to become more important.

Most businesses must anticipate future demand so that product can be ordered or manufactured and be available for customers at the time of purchase. Ineffective forecasting can increase manufacturing costs, including inventory write-offs, labor, and expediting costs, and impact quality, customer satisfaction, and working capital levels. However, because forecasting involves an attempt to predict the future, it will always be an imperfect activity. Therefore, in addition to improving the forecasting process, managers should also strive to improve flexibility and response times, for example, by reducing lead times. Forecasting future revenue levels was covered in detail in Chapter 6.

KEY PERFORMANCE INDICATORS: OPERATING EFFECTIVENESS

In this section we review selected measures covering a number of areas, including overall effectiveness, the business model, asset utilization, revenue patterns, key business processes, quality, and functional and people management. For additional background and explanation on the financial statement ratios that follow, please refer to Chapter 2, "Fundamentals of Finance."

Overall Measures of Operating Effectiveness

The following measures represent top-level indicators of overall operating effectiveness.

Return on Invested Capital   Return on invested capital (ROIC) is one of the best overall measures of operating effectiveness since it reflects both profitability and investment levels. ROIC is computed as:

$$\text{ROIC} = \frac{\text{Earnings Before Interest After Tax (EBIAT)}}{\text{Invested Capital}}$$

Asset Turnover   This measure reflects the level of investment in all assets, including working capital; property, plant, and equipment; and intangible assets, relative to sales. It reflects each of the individual asset utilization factors discussed in Chapter 2. This measure and underlying drivers are covered in detail in Chapters 8 and 9.

$$\text{Asset Turnover} = \frac{\text{Sales}}{\text{Total Assets}}$$

Profitability: Operating Income % Sales   This is a broad measure of operating performance. In addition to operating effectiveness, it will reflect other factors including pricing strength and the level of investments for future growth. Profitability is computed as follows:

$$\text{Profitability} = \frac{\text{Operating Income}}{\text{Sales}}$$

Gross Margin %   Gross margin % is simply the gross margin as a percentage of total revenues, computed as:

$$\text{Gross Margin \%} = \frac{\text{Gross Margin}}{\text{Sales}}$$

The gross margin % will be impacted by a number of factors and therefore will require comprehensive analysis. The factors affecting gross margin include both operating effectiveness and other factors.

Operational Effectiveness
- Composition of fixed and variable costs.
- Product costs.
- Production variances.
- Material and labor costs.

Other
- Industry.
- Competition and pricing.
- Product mix.

R&D % Sales   R&D as a percentage of sales is computed as follows:

$$\text{R\&D \% Sales} = \frac{\text{R\&D}}{\text{Sales}}$$

This ratio determines the level of investment in research and development compared to the current period sales. The R&D as a percentage of sales ratio will vary significantly from industry to industry and from high-growth to low-growth companies. Objective analysis is required to determine if a high

R&D percentage of sales is due to ineffective processes or large investments to drive future revenues.

Selling, General, and Administrative (SG&A) % Sales   Since this measure compares the level of SG&A spending to sales, it provides a view of spending levels in selling and distributing the firms' products and in supporting the administrative aspects of the business. The measure will reflect the method of distribution, process efficiency, and administrative overhead. Often SG&A will also include costs associated with initiating or introducing new products. Recall that SG&A percent to sales is computed as follows:

$$\text{SG\&A \% Sales} = \frac{\text{SG\&A}}{\text{Sales}}$$

Sales per Employee   This measure is often used as a high-level ratio to measure employee productivity. It is computed as:

$$\text{Sales per Employee} = \frac{\text{Sales}}{\text{Employees}}$$

The problem with sales per employee is that the measure is very dependent on the business model of a company. If a company outsources a substantial part of manufacturing, for example, the revenue per employee may be much higher than for a company that is vertically integrated. This makes it difficult to compare performance to that of other companies or industries. For example, most retail companies have high sales per employee since they typically purchase rather than manufacture all products sold. Certain manufacturing companies purchase a relatively small level of raw materials and manufacture or transform this material with substantial labor or technology into a finished product, resulting in lower sales per employee. Nevertheless, it is useful to look at trends over time and to benchmark performance and business models.

Value Added per Employee   This measure attempts to address the limitation in the sales per employee measure. Instead of computing the sales per employee, we estimate the value added per employee. Value added would be computed by subtracting purchased labor and materials from sales. The example in Table 7.1 illustrates the difference between the two employee productivity methods.

TABLE 7.1 Employee Productivity Measures: Sales and Value Added per Employee

	$ 000s
Sales	$100,000
Purchased or Contract Costs	
Purchased Product	$ 15,000
Purchased Labor	12,000
Outside Processing	5,000
Other	7,000
Total	$ 39,000
Internal Costs	
Salaries	$ 30,000
Labor	10,000
Rent	5,000
Other	2,000
Total	$ 47,000
Operating Profit	$ 14,000
Employees	900
Sales per Employee	$111,111
Value Added per Employee	$ 67,778

Sales per Employee $\left(\dfrac{\$100,000,000}{900}\right)$

Value Added per Employee $\left(\dfrac{\$100,000,000 - 39,000,000}{900}\right)$

Test the Business Model

In Chapter 3, we discussed the importance of a company's business model, including the composition of costs between fixed and variable and the level of sales required to achieve a breakeven level of profits.

Fixed Costs per Week   In Table 4.6 we estimated the annual level of fixed costs. It can be helpful to compute the weekly fixed cost level (divide by 52) and track over time. In doing so, the organization will become sensitive to the level of fixed costs and to any changes in the fixed costs levels on a timely basis. The impact of increasing staffing levels or committing to additional space will be reflected in real time in this measure.

Breakeven Sales Levels per Week or Month   Breakeven sales levels can also be easily estimated and tracked on a weekly or monthly basis. This measure translates any changes to the cost model immediately into required increases in sales to break even. It also tends to subliminally influence the organization to level shipments within a given quarter.

Factory or Asset Utilization

In many businesses, there is a substantial fixed cost in factories, stores, or other assets, including people. The extent to which these assets are utilized in a period is a significant driver of breakeven levels and profitability. Until the facility reaches a breakeven level of utilization, these fixed costs will not be covered. Once production exceeds the breakeven level, there is usually a significant increase in profitability, since a substantial part of the costs are fixed and do not increase with production.

Factory Utilization   Depending on the nature of the business, factory utilization may be measured on the basis of labor hours, material or process throughput, or production output. If a factory has resources in place with a capacity to work a certain number of hours, then you can measure the utilization of these resources based on the amount of time spent working on product as a percentage of total available hours. Similarly, it would be critical to understand the capacity, breakeven, and utilization of a refinery operation on a continuous basis. Actual production levels would be closely monitored since they would be a very significant driver of the operating performance.

Professional Services—People Utilization   A significant driver of revenue and profitability for a professional services firm would be the level of professional staff hours that can be billed to clients. Typically, the total billable hours for a professional would be estimated by taking total available hours for a year (40 hours per week × 52 weeks = 2,080 hours per year), then subtracting time for holidays, vacations, company meetings, and the like. Partners and managers in these firms may also be expected to spend a significant time in business development and administrative activities. The utilization rate would be computed as follows:

$$\text{People Utilization} = \frac{\text{Hours Billed to Clients}}{\text{Billable Hours}}$$

Space Utilization   For businesses that incur significant occupancy costs, measures are often put in place to monitor the utilization of space. These can range from sales per square foot in a retail setting to head count per square foot for manufacturing and office space. Head count per square foot can vary significantly among manufacturing, research, office, and other uses. Standards have been developed that allow companies to compare their density levels to those of other companies.

Head Count Analysis People-related costs are typically a significant percentage of total costs. Tracking head count levels is essential to cost management. Significant changes to the cost model will result from additions or deletions to head count. Tracking head count by department over time can provide significant insight into changes in costs. Some companies include the full-time equivalent (FTE) of part-time, temporary, or contract employees in the analysis to provide a comprehensive view and to prevent gaming the measure by using resources that may fall outside the employee definition. In addition, tracking open employment requisitions, new hires, and terminations provides a leading indicator of future cost levels. An example of a head count analysis is presented in Table 7.2.

Revenue Patterns

Many companies have revenue patterns that are significantly skewed to the end of the quarter or year. Revenue patterns impact a number of areas, including receivables, inventories, costs, and risk. A revenue pattern impacts so many drivers that we consider it a pressure point (addressed in Chapter 13). Some firms are successful in leveling production and revenue evenly throughout a quarter; others ship as much as 60 percent (or more) in the last two weeks of a 13-week quarter. This latter pattern is often described as a "hockey stick" based on the shape of the curve of weekly shipments, shown in Figure 7.3.

These graphs are presentations of revenue patterns within a quarter. The revenue linearity index can be used to track revenue patterns over time, computed as follows:

$$\text{Revenue Linearity Index} = \frac{\text{Shipments First 45 Days}}{\text{Shipments Last 45 Days}}$$

Hockey stick:

$$\frac{\$28.0 \text{ million}}{\$140.5 \text{ million}} = 19.9\%$$

TABLE 7.2 Head Count Analysis

Department	Q404	Q105	Q205	Q305	Q405	Q106	Q206	Q306	Q406	Increase (Decrease) Q405–Q406
Operations										
Manufacturing	125	123	126	135	126	127	125	140	132	6
Quality Control	7	7	7	7	7	7	7	7	7	0
Inspection	3	3	3	3	3	3	3	3	3	0
Procurement	8	8	8	8	8	8	8	8	8	0
Other	9	9	9	9	9	9	9	9	9	0
Total	152	150	153	162	153	154	152	167	159	6
R&D										
Hardware Engineering	15	15	15	15	15	15	15	15	15	0
Software Engineering	17	17	17	17	17	19	23	25	30	13
Other	2	2	2	2	2	2	2	2	2	0
Total	34	34	34	34	34	36	40	42	47	13
SG&A										
Management	7	7	7	7	7	7	7	7	7	0
Sales	15	15	15	15	15	15	15	15	15	0
Finance	11	11	12	12	14	14	14	14	14	0
Human Resources	4	4	4	4	4	4	4	4	4	0
Total	37	37	38	38	40	40	40	40	40	0
Company Total	223	221	225	234	227	230	232	249	246	19
Increase (Decrease)		−2	4	9	−7	3	2	17	−3	

Open Requisitions	Number	Annual Cost (000s)
Operations	3	$ 150
R&D	6	750
Finance	1	95
Human Resources	1	75
Total	11	$1,070

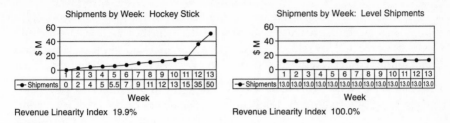

FIGURE 7.3 Quarterly Revenue Patterns

Level shipments:

$$\frac{\$84.25 \text{ million}}{\$84.25 \text{ million}} = 100\%$$

Revenue patterns can have a significant impact on cost, quality, and risk. Revenue patterns that are skewed to the end of a quarter result in higher costs, since overtime and other costs to match product with demand are likely to be incurred. Quality may suffer because the flurry at the end of a quarter can lead to errors in building, testing, documenting, and shipping product. Hockey sticks increase the risk that a problem or event may lead to a significant shortfall in revenue for a given period. Revenue patterns also have a significant impact on working capital levels, specifically accounts receivable and inventory. This aspect is addressed in detail in Chapter 8.

Forecast Accuracy

Measuring and improving the accuracy of sales forecasts compared to actual demand levels will provide visibility into a key performance driver and serve to establish accountability for sales projections. Inaccurate forecasts lead to operating inefficiencies and higher levels of working capital. The measurements presented in Chapter 6 for measuring revenue forecast accuracy can easily be adapted to other variables, including costs, expenses, and profits.

Revenue Process

The revenue process covers all activities around a customer order, from the presales activities to order entry, shipping, invoicing, and collections. This process is covered in detail in Chapter 8. A few additional measures that focus on efficiency of the revenue process are covered next.

Cost per Revenue Transaction   What is the total cost to process a revenue transaction, including order processing, shipping and handling, billing, and collections? This measure can be computed by estimating the cost incurred in each department and dividing by the number of transactions. The cost is typically higher than expected and may lead to further analysis to identify process or technology issues. This measure may also lead to the consideration of minimum order levels necessary to cover the cost of transaction processing.

Invoice Error Rate   Invoicing errors can result in a number of problems. They are costly to correct, requiring the issuance of credit memos or additional invoices. They impact customer satisfaction, since the customers must also address invoicing errors in their systems. Invoicing errors will delay collection, resulting in higher levels of accounts receivable. They may also go undetected, likely impacting margins and profitability.

New Product Development Process

Key elements of R&D performance include innovation, cost and time to develop, and impact of design on downstream process activities, for example manufacturing. Measuring R&D effectiveness presents a number of challenges. New product development often involves planning for new projects that contain tasks that haven't been performed before. Another challenge is that some engineering professionals resist performance measures in a creative environment. However, there are many aspects of the process that are repeatable and for which feedback on past projects can be extremely useful in planning and managing future projects. In addition, some aspects may be compared to the performance at other companies, for example the time and cost to develop a printed circuit board with certain characteristics.

Key performance indicators for new product development are also discussed in Chapter 6, "Revenue Growth and Pricing Strength," and include percentage of revenue from new products and projected revenue in the R&D project pipeline. Additional measures that should be considered to evaluate the effectiveness of the new product development process are actual performance versus target development schedule and cost, and target product cost. To measure the broad effectiveness of new product development, other measures should also be considered, including production yields, engineering change notices (ECNs) or orders, and warranty costs for new products.

Actual versus Target Development Costs   The comparison of actual costs incurred to the costs estimated for each project can be done at the conclusion of the project, but the measure is more useful if it is also examined periodically during the project. Underspending is not necessarily a good thing if it is the result or cause of delays in the development process. This issue can be addressed by combining the cost evaluation with a measure of project progress, which requires disciplined project planning that details key project phases and checkpoints in addition to cost. This type of discipline could result in the analysis shown in Table 7.3.

TABLE 7.3 Critical New Product Development Status

Project Name	Costs			Status (% Completion)[a]			Annual Revenue Potential	Status	Comment
	Actual	Projected	%	Actual	Projected	%			
Coyote	$0.7	$0.8	88%	95%	93%	102%	$ 25	Green	On track, intro 3/06
Fox	2.8	2.5	112	60	80	75	30	Yellow	2 critical milestones missed
Rabbit	1.4	1.3	108	40	50	80	15	Red	Technical performance issues
Tortoise	1.8	2	90	100	100	100	60	Green	1st shipments, next week
Total	$6.7	$6.6	102%	74%	81%	89%	$130		

[a]Based on project milestones planned and achieved.

Actual Product Costs versus Target Costs   Even if the product is developed on time and within the development cost estimate, it is unlikely to be a successful project unless the product can be manufactured at a cost approximating the cost target developed in the project proposal. Adopting this measure will help to ensure that the product managers and development team will be attentive to estimating and achieving target costs.

Production Yields on New Products   It is understandable that a new product may incur some problems in the first few production runs. The learning curve and process efficiencies will typically kick in over time. However, if manufacturing incurs large cost overruns, rework, or excessive production variances on new products, this may be an indication of design problems or a failure to design the product for manufacturability.

Engineering Change Notices/Orders on New Products   After a product is designed and released to manufacturing for production, any subsequent changes to the design or manufacturing process are initiated by ECNs. These orders are very expensive in terms of time, rework, and inventory costs. An excessive level of ECNs on new products may indicate process issues or premature release to manufacturing.

Warranty and Return Levels   The new product development process has a significant impact on downstream activities in manufacturing and in quality and customer service levels. These measures are typically tracked for other reasons, but should be included in the new product development dashboard, since these measures will be impacted by the development process.

Supply Chain Management and Production

Supply chain management is covered in detail in Chapter 8, since it is a critical driver of inventory. Additional measures related directly to operating effectiveness are discussed here.

Cycle Time   A very effective measure of supply chain and inventory management is the amount of time required to produce a unit of inventory. The shorter the cycle time for a product, the less time the product spends in the factory. Reducing cycle times typically leads to lower manufacturing costs, lower inventory balances, and increased flexibility. Cycle time can be estimated by using the days in inventory for the company in total or by looking at days in inventory for specific products or processes. Specific cycle times can be measured by tracking the flow of material through the factory until completion. This detail method is likely to identify opportunities to reduce the cycle time by exposing bottlenecks and dead time in the process.

First-Time Production Yield   During most manufacturing or process activities, there are critical steps where the product must be tested for conformity to specifications, including performance, appearance, and other characteristics. Significant costs will be incurred if a large percentage of product must be scrapped or reworked. Measuring the yield rate of product that passes inspection and reviewing the root causes of failures will provide good visibility into critical production processes.

Number of Vendors   There is a significant cost in dealing with vendors. Each buyer can deal with only a certain number of vendors. Contracts must be negotiated. Vendor performance must be assessed. Many companies have reduced procurement and overhead costs and inventory levels by reducing the number of vendors, subject to good business sense on maintaining alternative suppliers.

Number of Unique Parts   The number of unique parts a company carries in inventory is a significant driver of both costs and inventories. Each part number must be ordered, received, stored, and counted. Each part is susceptible to obsolescence and forecasting errors. Companies with a focus on supply chain management attempt to reduce the number of parts. They often start by identifying low-volume or redundant parts. This may lead to decisions to prune the product line of old or low-volume products and drive the development team to use common components where possible.

Vendor Performance Assessment   Companies with an effective supply chain management process will monitor vendor performance and typically evaluate performance formally at least once per year. Underperforming vendors may be counseled or terminated in favor of suppliers that consistently meet or exceed pricing, delivery, and quality expectations.

Quality

Quality is an important factor in business performance. It will impact costs and expenses, revenues, receivables, inventories, and customer satisfaction. Corporations have focused significant attention on quality over the past 20 years. A few additional measures not covered in other areas are described next.

Cost of Quality (or Cost of Quality Failures) This measure can be a very effective way to estimate the cost of quality issues across the organization. Variations of the measure became widely used beginning in the 1980s during the quality movement. Typical costs that should be considered for inclusion in this measure include:

- *Manufacturing.* Any costs arising from quality problems or that are incurred because of the need to test for frequent quality lapses should be included. Examples include:
  - Warranty costs.
  - Rework.
  - Scrap.
  - Inventory write-offs.
  - Customer returns.
  - Inspection.
  - Quality control.
- *Back office.* The quality of back office activities should also be considered. Examples include:
  - Accounts receivable problem resolution.
  - Cost of issuing credit memos.
  - Cost of journal entries to correct mistakes.
- *Revenue.* Quality issues can have a significant impact on customer satisfaction and may result in lost customers and revenue.

These costs can be aggregated and used to track the dollar level of quality failures and the cost of quality measure as a percentage of sales:

$$\text{Cost of Quality \% Sales} = \frac{\text{Total Cost of Quality Failures}}{\text{Sales}}$$

Defined broadly, the cost of quality failures can easily exceed 10 percent for many companies. The measure will typically identify a significant opportunity to address the root cause of these failures and can lead to improved profitability, inventory, receivables, and customer satisfaction.

Error or Defect Rates We have covered error rates in a number of areas, including invoicing errors and production failures. Many companies have achieved great success with initiatives to measure error rates, including six sigma. This program has an objective of decreasing error or failure rates to an extremely low level. Care must be exercised to select and focus on critical activities and processes so that the level of effort in driving to six sigma performance will impact important performance drivers.

People and People Management

Many CEOs are quoted as saying that people are the company's greatest asset and resource. Progressive companies treat these assets well and measure the effectiveness of people-related processes.

Employee Satisfaction Many companies survey employee satisfaction annually or on a rotating basis. These surveys test overall satisfaction as well as specific areas including compensation, perceived growth opportunities, communication, level of engagement, and management effectiveness. Another good way to get a pulse on employee satisfaction and underlying causes is for senior managers to meet with small groups of employees without other managers and supervisors present. Some companies refer to these as "skip level" meetings, since several levels of managers may be skipped in the sessions. Employees are incredibly candid, especially when the process gains credibility by providing anonymity of comments and action on issues they raise. The effectiveness of surveys and skip level meetings are highly dependent on how employees perceive management's commitment to address the findings. If the findings are not communicated to employees or acted upon, the process will lose employee participation and engagement.

Employee Turnover Employee turnover is very costly. Significant time and costs are incurred in recruiting, hiring, training, and terminating employees. Some level of turnover may be good. If employees are leaving for great opportunities, the turnover can be a reflection of a strong company that is developing talent. A variation of this measure is to split this between involuntary and voluntary turnover. What are the root causes of each? Is the turnover due to employee dissatisfaction, low compensation levels, poor hiring practices, incompatible culture, or lack of growth?

Benefits per Employee Employee benefits are a significant cost. Some of these costs, including health care premiums, have risen significantly in recent years. The benefits per employee measure is more meaningful than benefits as a percentage of payroll, since payroll can be skewed by the inclusion of highly compensated managers and executives. Note that reducing the cost of employee benefits by reducing the benefits themselves may have implications on retaining and attracting talent.

Average Training Hours per Employee This measure provides a good indicator of the level of training and learning within the organization. Since training needs may vary across the organization depending on the level and function of employees, this measure is often tracked separately for engineers, managers, technicians, and so forth.

Percentage of Openings Filled Internally   Some companies have a philosophy of promoting internally. Others prefer a mix of internal promotions and hiring from the outside. This measure captures the actual mix of hiring and provides an indication of the effectiveness of the organization in developing talent for internal growth and promotion.

Percentage of Offers Accepted   Another way to assess the recruiting and hiring process is to track offers accepted as a percentage of offers extended. A low acceptance percentage may indicate a problem in assessing the potential fit of applicants or an unfavorable perception of the company developed by the candidates during the recruiting process. This measure will also reflect the conditions in the job market.

Functional Perspective

While it is better to look at process measures in general, some measures of functional performance are useful, particularly where an entire process falls within that function; for example, closing the books of the company is primarily an accounting activity. Functional managers should strive to ensure that their organizations are competitive and incorporate best practices in key activities. Consulting firms, including the Hackett Group, developed comprehensive benchmarks and identified best practices for certain functions for this purpose in the 1990s. Here are some examples of measures that are widely used to evaluate performance of functional areas.

Financial Function

Budget Cycle   Preparing the annual operating plan or budget can be a time-consuming and inefficient process in many organizations. The cost and time involved in preparing the budget go well beyond the finance department, since nearly every function in the organization is involved in the process. The budget cycle can be measured in terms of days, from initial planning through management or board approval. Many organizations have reduced the budget cycle by implementing process changes and technology solutions.

Financial Closing Cycle   The closing cycle can be a time when accounting folks work excessive hours and are unavailable to support the business. The closing cycle begins sometime before the end of the accounting period (e.g., quarter end) and ends with the review of financials with the CEO, audit committee, or with publishing or filing financial statements. Many organizations have reduced this cycle significantly while maintaining or improving quality by implementing process and technology improvements. This reduces time spent in this activity and provides the management team with critical business information sooner.

Finance: Percentage of Time Spent in Transaction Processing and Compliance Activities   During the 1990s many finance organizations began to measure the percentage of time spent on transaction and compliance versus value-added activities such as decision support and financial analysis. The objective was to become more efficient (but not less effective) in the areas of compliance and processing in order to devote more time to business support.

Human Resources

HR: Costs per Employee   How efficient is the human resources (HR) department? What are the costs incurred in recruiting, providing benefits, employee development, and evaluating performance? How do these costs compare to those of other companies in our industry? To best-practice companies?

HR: Average Days to Fill Open Positions   This measure captures the speed in filling vacant positions. This is a good productivity measure so long as it is balanced by a measure of hiring effectiveness.

HR: Successful Hire Rate Percentage   While it is important to fill open positions on a timely basis, it is obviously more important to fill the positions with capable people who will be compatible with the organization. This measure tracks the success rate in hiring new employees or managers. The percentage of new employees retained for certain periods or achieving a performance rating above a certain level is a good indication of the effectiveness of the recruiting and hiring process.

Information Technology

IT: Costs as a Percentage of Sales   Information technology (IT) has become both a significant asset and cost to most businesses. Measures should be used to monitor both effectiveness and efficiency of this critical function. IT costs as a percentage of sales have risen sharply over the past 10 years. Capturing this spending rate and evaluating benefits is a necessity.

IT: Network Uptime   Nearly all business functions are dependent on the reliability of the IT network. Measuring the percentage of time that the network is up and running is an important indicator of service levels and performance.

IT Help Desk: Request Levels and Response Times   How many requests are received by the help desk for application or desktop support? What are the root causes of these requests? They may be due to inadequate training, software problems, user errors, or equipment problems that indicate required action. How fast and effective are we in responding to help desk requests?

Other Measures

Over time there may be certain specific issues or challenges that warrant special consideration and visibility. These may be due to a dramatic shift in the market or increased regulatory pressure, for example the costs associated with being a public company.

Costs Associated with Being a Public Company   There has always been a focus on the cost of public versus private ownership of a firm. With the enactment of Sarbanes-Oxley and subsequent attempts to comply with the new requirements implied in the legislation, the cost of compliance has risen significantly. These costs should be captured and should be part of an overall evaluation of whether a company should be taken public or remain public. The costs of being a public company fall into two categories: obvious and subtle.

Obvious
- Investor relations program.
- Professional fees (legal and audit) associated with public company filings and compliance.
- Cost of annual reports and meetings.
- Increased directors' and officers' insurance premiums.
- Cost of evaluating and certifying internal controls.

Subtle
- Cost of maintaining a public company board.
- Executive time in communicating with investors.
- Compensation consultants for proxy documentation.
- The cost and impact of the focus on short-term and quarterly performance.

TOOLS FOR ASSESSING AND IMPROVING OPERATING EFFECTIVENESS

In addition to the performance measures covering operating effectiveness, two other tools may be used to understand costs and business processes: natural expense code analysis and business process assessment.

Natural Expense Code Analysis

While it is generally better to focus on costs and efficiency from a process perspective, another essential view is what accountants call the natural expense accounts. Instead of looking at expenses based on the typical income statement classifications such as R&D or SG&A, we look at the type of spending—for example, salaries and wages or fringe benefits—across the entire company. A top-level summary of natural expense codes is presented in Table 7.4. Note that it is essentially a roll-up of information typically presented on a department or cost center report.

This view provides a great way to examine costs. If we are attempting to control or reduce costs, it is important to understand the largest cost categories. The 80/20 rule typically applies here: A small number of expense categories are likely to account for 80 percent of the total cost. For example, if people and related costs approximate 40 percent of the total cost base, then these expenses would likely have to be addressed in order to have an impact on total costs. If purchased materials are significant, then we must look at our procurement practices, vendor pricing, and perhaps alternative sources. Can we attack the cost of health care premiums? Can we negotiate better terms with travel vendors to reduce costs? These opportunities do not come into sharp focus if expense analysis is limited to either income statement classification or process view. The results of the natural expense code analysis can then be graphically presented as in Figure 7.4. This analysis is at a summary level. Each of the categories can be broken down into more detail. For example, fringe benefits can be further broken down into medical costs, retirement contributions, and payroll taxes.

Process Evaluation

Each significant business process can be reviewed to assess the effectiveness and the efficiency of the process. The following critical business processes are likely to have a significant impact on overall business performance, and therefore should be assessed periodically:

- New product development.
- Supply chain management.

TABLE 7.4 Natural Expense Code Analysis ($ Millions)

	Cost of Sales		R&D	Selling	Marketing	General	Other	Total	%
	Product	Other							
Salaries and Wages	$175.0	$10.0	$15.0	$10.0	$6.0	$15.0	$2.0	$233.0	32%
Fringe Benefits	35.0	2.0	3.0	2.0	1.2	3.0	0.4	46.6	6
Travel	4.0	0.5	0.8	2.0	1.5	2.0		10.8	1
Telecommunications	4.0	0.5	1.0	2.0	1.5	3.0		12.0	2
Rent	15.0	1.0	1.0	1.4	0.5	0.7		19.6	3
Depreciation	15.0	1.0	3.0	2.0	3.0	4.0		28.0	4
Purchased Materials	275.0	4.0	2.0		1.0			282.0	39
Purchased Labor	55.0	3.0	4.0	1.0				63.0	9
Consultants	3.0		2.0		1.0	6.0		12.0	2
Other	4.0	1.0	3.0	2.0	4.0	3.0	1.0	18.0	2
Total	$585.0	$23.0	$34.8	$22.4	$19.7	$36.7	$3.4	$725.0	100%

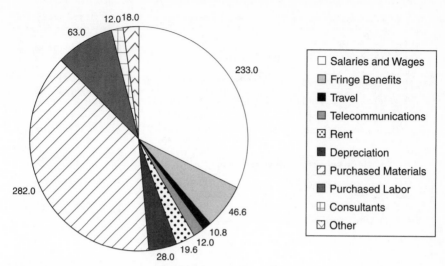

FIGURE 7.4   Natural Expense Code Analysis Pie Chart

- Revenue/customer fulfillment.
- Strategic and operational planning.
- Mergers and acquisitions.

Examples of process assessment tools for the revenue process and supply chain management processes are reviewed in Chapter 8.

OPERATING EFFECTIVENESS DASHBOARDS

Sample dashboards are shown for overall operating effectiveness (Figure 7.5) and new product development (Figure 7.6). The measures selected by an individual company should be based on its specific circumstances and priorities.

SUMMARY

Operating effectiveness is a tremendous source of potential shareholder value. Operating effectiveness impacts profitability, sales growth, and asset requirements. There are hundreds of potential measures to choose

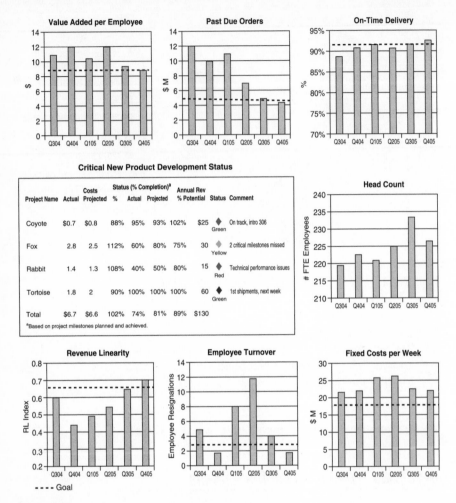

FIGURE 7.5   Overall Operating Effectiveness

from to measure different aspects of operating effectiveness. Great care must be exercised in selecting the measures that are most appropriate to a firm at a specific point in time. The performance dashboards must reflect key business priorities. The measures should be evaluated periodically and revised to reflect ever-changing priorities and conditions. It is also critical to provide balance to ensure that a focus on efficiency is not achieved at the expense of quality, customer satisfaction, or growth.

Critical New Product Development Status

Project Name	Costs			Status (% Completion)[a]			Annual Revenue % Potential	Status	Comment
	Actual	Projected	%	Actual	Projected	%			
Coyote	$0.7	$0.8	88%	95%	93%	102%	$25	◆ Green	On track, info 3/06
Fox	2.8	2.5	112	60	80	75	30	◆ Yellow	2 critical milestones missed
Rabbit	1.4	1.3	108	40	50	80	15	◆ Red	Technical performance issues
Tortoise	1.8	2	90	100	100	100	6 0	◆ Green	1st shipments, next week
Total	$6.7	$6.6	102%	74%	81%	89%	$130		

[a]Based on project milestones planned and achieved.

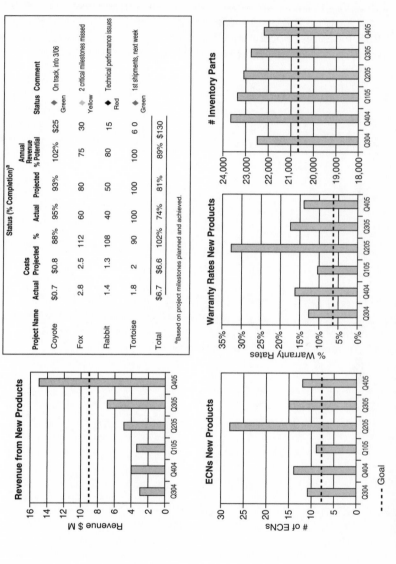

Revenue from New Products

Warranty Rates New Products

Inventory Parts

ECNs New Products

- - - - Goal

FIGURE 7.6 New Product Development Process

143

QUESTIONS FOR CONSIDERATION

1. Is operating effectiveness a priority for your company? For your competitors or customers?
2. How do you rate your performance on operating effectiveness? What is the basis for this assessment?
3. What measures of operating effectiveness does your organization track? Are they covering the most important elements of your business?

CHAPTER 8

Capital Effectiveness: Working Capital

Capital efficiency is a critical driver of shareholder value. Improving the management and turnover of assets can significantly improve cash flow and returns. Unfortunately, due to the emphasis on sales and earnings per share growth at many companies, capital management often doesn't get the attention it deserves. Managers and investors who understand the importance of working capital in cash flow appreciate the role that effective capital management plays in value creation. Figure 8.1 provides an overview of the key drivers of capital efficiency and asset management and highlights the major components of capital employed in a typical business:

- Operating capital (OC).
- Capital assets, including property, plant, and equipment.
- Intangible assets, including goodwill.

The balance sheet is a snapshot of transactions in process. Therefore, it stands to reason that a company with greater process efficiency will have a leaner balance sheet than a company that is less efficient. This leaner balance sheet is evidenced by better measures of asset utilization and turnover including accounts receivable days sales outstanding (DSO), inventory turns, and asset turnover. In addition to eroding returns and decreasing cash flow, companies that have bloated balance sheets (i.e., excessive inventories or receivables) are also inherently more risky than their leaner counterparts. A company with excess inventory or slow-paying customers is more likely to have future write-offs. A wise CFO once told me, "There are only two things that happen to inventory; you either sell it to a customer or write it off." A rising DSO may indicate a number of problems, including potential collection problems, aggressive revenue recognition policies, or a delay of shipments to the end of the quarter. Key asset utilization and

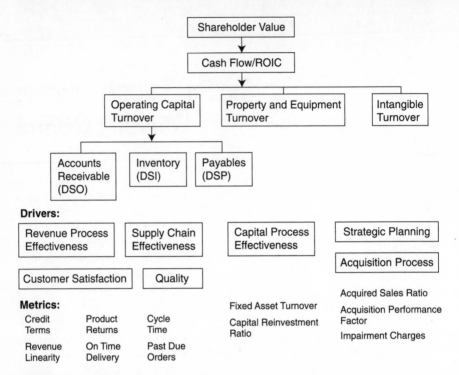

FIGURE 8.1 Drill-Down: Capital Efficiency and Asset Management

turnover measures described later in the chapter can also be used to identify potential risks due to excessive asset levels.

In Chapter 4, we noted that different businesses will have distinct operating models. Among other differences, capital requirements and asset
turnover will vary significantly across businesses. Some will require large
capital outlays for manufacturing plants; others will require little capital
for this purpose. For example, a consulting firm typically requires little in
the way of capital assets, since people are the firm's primary assets. These
firms do not require large expenditures for plants, warehouses, and the like
that other firms may need. Some businesses will sell products or services on
credit and will carry large accounts receivables. Others will collect the
money up front in cash or credit card sales. Each of these extremes must be
considered in developing the overall business model in order to earn an acceptable to superior return for shareholders. Within specific industries,
there is also a wide range of asset and turnover levels. Effective operating
capital management is driven by several factors, including management attention and process efficiency.

CRITICAL SUCCESS FACTORS

There are a number of critical success factors in achieving improved capital management. They include management attention, performance visibility, process efficiency, context, and accountability.

Management Attention

The extent to which managers emphasize and attend to any specific process, project, or measure will have a large impact on the effort and result of that endeavor. This is very true in capital management. If a manager is only sales or earnings driven, it will follow that operating capital levels will be higher. Conversely, if a manager recognizes the importance of working capital and actively drives and monitors performance, operating capital levels will be lower. In addition, a well-designed management compensation plan that includes capital utilization or uses a broad measure such as return on invested capital (ROIC) that reflects capital will ensure focus in this important area.

Performance Visibility

Capital management will be improved if managers have appropriate visibility into key performance indicators on a timely basis. Well-designed performance dashboards provide managers with key process measures and leading indicators of capital performance.

Process Efficiency

Capital requirements are very closely associated with process efficiency. Companies that have well-established process and quality programs will typically require less capital to support the business. Conversely, a manufacturing process that is not efficient and has a high level of rejected product will result in high inventories (and costs).

Creating Context: Understanding the Importance of Capital Management

When managers and employees fully understand the dynamic impact of capital in creating value, more attention is paid to this driver and related processes. However, organizations with an exclusive focus on sales or earnings growth will often view capital as free, with the result of higher than required asset levels.

Accountability

Assigning appropriate accountability for assets, including inventory and receivables, is a difficult objective. Out of convenience, many companies look at the functional area responsible for the last step in the related process. For example, manufacturing is often held responsible for inventory, and finance is held responsible for receivables levels since finance is typically involved in collections. However, most financial measures and other outcomes are the result of a business process that crosses a number of functional areas. For example, inventory levels are certainly related to manufacturing activities. But they are also a result of the design of products and the product demand forecasts typically furnished by sales or marketing management. Each driver must be disaggregated and key activities must be assigned to the appropriate process team and leader.

The remainder of this chapter focuses on measuring and improving the management of operating capital. We explore the other components of capital investment, fixed assets, and intangibles in Chapter 9.

OPERATING CAPITAL MANAGEMENT

In this section we focus on measuring and improving the operating components of working capital, primarily accounts receivable, inventories, and accounts payable. We are treating the remaining components of working capital—cash and short-term debt—as nonoperating or financing accounts. Table 8.1 presents the major components of operating capital and includes key activity measures for these accounts. Operating capital assets such as receivables and inventories represent a past investment in cash or a future claim to cash. Reducing either of these balances will increase cash and improve returns.

Accounts payable and accrued liabilities offset these investments and reduce the total cash required to support the business. Although increasing accounts payable by delaying payments to vendors will reduce the total investment and improve returns, caution must be exercised with this tactic. It runs counter to developing a partnership with vendors and is inconsistent with driving vendors to higher performance and service levels. Vendors

TABLE 8.1 Operating Capital (Working Capital Less Cash and Debt)

Simple Co. Component	2006	Measure Description	Measure Result	% of Sales	Sales Turnover
Receivables	$ 20,000	DSO	73.0	20%	5.0
Inventory	18,000	Inventory Turns	2.5	18	5.6
Other	900			1	111.1
Payables	–4,500	DSP	–16.4	–5	–22.2
Accrued Liabilities	–5,000			–5	–20.0
Operating Capital (OC)	$ 29,400	OC Turnover	3.4	29%	3.4
Sales	$100,000				
COGS	$ 45,000				

may seek compensation for the delayed payment in the form of higher prices or in other subtle ways.

UNDERSTANDING THE DYNAMICS OF OPERATING CAPITAL

In order to understand the dynamics of working capital and to be able to predict future levels of operating capital and cash flows, managers should employ the operating capital budget, illustrated in Table 8.2. This tool is very helpful in understanding the inputs and outputs to receivables and inventories. The basic idea is to start with a projected profit and loss statement by month. Then, based on past experience and management practices, receivables, inventories, and payables can be projected. Let's take a look at the projected levels and activity for accounts payable. We will discuss receivables and inventories in each respective section later in the chapter.

Payables represent amounts due vendors. When inventory is delivered to a company, an addition to inventory and payables is recorded. When the invoice is paid, the payment is subtracted from the balance. In Table 8.2, payables will increase by the amount of inventory purchases each month. In January, the company received $84 million worth of inventory and typically pays vendors in 30 days. This transaction will increase both inventory and payables by $84 million. Payables will be reduced in February when we pay vendors $84 million for deliveries received in the prior month.

TABLE 8.2 Operating Capital Budget ($ Millions)

	History			Projections			
	Oct.	Nov.	Dec.	Jan.	Feb.	March	April
Income Statement							
Sales	$600.0	$660.0	$1,000.0	$400.0	$500.0	$550.0	$600.0
COGS	420.0	462.0	700.0	280.0	350.0	385.0	420.0
Gross Margin	$180.0	$198.0	$ 300.0	$120.0	$150.0	$165.0	$180.0
GM % Sales	30.0%	30.0%	30.0%	30.0%	30.0%	30.0%	30.0%
Operating Expenses	165.0	174.0	225.0	135.0	150.0	157.5	165.0
Operating Profit	15.0	24.0	75.0	−15.0	0.0	7.5	15.0
Tax Expense	6.0	9.6	30.0	−6.0	0.0	3.0	6.0
Net Income	9.0	14.4	45.0	−9.0	0.0	4.5	9.0
Accounts Receivable							
Beginning Balance	$ 950	$1,150	$1,310	$1,810	$1,452	$1,310	$1,285
Sales	600	660	1000	400	500	550	600
Collections	−400	−500	−500	−758	−642	−575	−510
Other							
Ending Balance	$1,150	$1,310	$1,810	$1,452	$1,310	$1,285	$1,375
DSO	57.5	59.5	54.3	108.9	78.6	70.1	68.8
% Sales (Annualized)	16.0%	16.5%	15.1%	30.3%	21.8%	19.5%	19.1%
Collections	CM	M+1	M+2	M+3			
Assumptions	10.0%	40.0%	30.0%	20.0%			
Inventories							
Beginning Balance	$1,300	$1,220	$1,112	$ 832	$ 762	$ 902	$1,077
Purchases	140	154	168	84	196	224	280
Labor	100	100	168	84	196	224	280
OH	100	100	84	42	98	112	140
COGS	−420	−462	−700	−280	−350	−385	−420
Ending Balance	$1,220	$1,112	$ 832	$ 762	$ 902	$1,077	$1,357
Inventory Turns	4.1	5.0	10.1	4.4	4.7	4.3	3.7
DSI	87.1	72.2	35.7	81.6	77.3	83.9	96.9
% Sales	16.9%	14.0%	6.9%	15.9%	15.0%	16.3%	18.8%
Accounts Payable							
Beginning Balance	$160	$170	$184	$198	$114	$226	$254
Purchases	140	154	168	84	196	224	280
Payments	−130	−140	−154	−168	−84	−196	−224
Other							
Ending Balance	$170	$184	$198	$114	$226	$254	$310
% of Annualized Sales	2.4%	2.3%	1.7%	2.4%	3.8%	3.8%	4.3%

UNLEASHING THE VALUE TRAPPED IN OPERATING CAPITAL

It is not uncommon to find companies that have operating capital levels between 20 and 30 percent of annual sales levels. Many managers have been able to improve on these levels and achieve ratios of 5 to 10 and, in some cases, negative operating capital. In other words, companies, including Dell, have created business models that provide for payables and accrued liabilities that exceed accounts receivable and inventory levels. The potential value associated with dramatic improvements is significant. Table 8.3 presents a summary of the benefits of a company reducing operating capital levels by 10, 20, and 30 percent. An income statement, balance sheet, and key activity ratios are presented. To fully understand the benefits, key measures of operating and financial performance are also shown on the analysis, including earnings per share, asset turnover, return on equity (ROE), and economic profit.

Most attention should be focused on reducing receivables and inventory rather than increasing accounts payable or other liabilities. A focus on receivables and inventories will reduce investment levels and can lead to improvements in the revenue and supply chain management processes, customer service, and profitability.

The base case presents a company with $1,200 million in sales and net income of $135.6 million. The company has accounts receivable of $250 million (76 DSO) and inventories of $200 million (3.0 turns). Let's look at the 20 percent improvement scenario. What would be the benefit of reducing receivables to $200 million (60.8 DSO) and inventories to $160 million (3.8 turns)? The following changes would result:

- Some $90 million additional cash is generated.
- The additional cash could be used to repurchase shares, pay down debt, or make strategic investments, including acquisitions. In this case, we paid down debt from $200 million to $110 million.
- Reducing debt also reduces annual interest expense from $14.0 million to $7.7 million. Net income increases from $135.6 million to $139.4 million.
- Asset turnover increases from 1.85 to 2.14.
- ROIC increases from 27.4 percent to 33.1 percent.

TABLE 8.3 Working Capital Improvement Illustration

| | Base | | Improvement Scenario | | | | | |
| | | | 10% | | 20% | | 30% | |
	$ M	% Sales	$ M	% Sales	$ M	% Sales	$ M	% Sales
P&L								
Sales	$1,200	100.0%	$1,200	100%	$1,200	100%	$1,200	100%
COGS	600	50.0	600	50	600	50	600	50
Operating Profit	240	20.0	240	20	240	20	240	20
Interest Expense	14.0	1.2	10.9	1	7.7	1	4.6	0
Profit Before Taxes	226.0	18.8	229.2	19	232.3	19	235.5	20
Taxes 40%	90.4	7.5	91.7	8	92.9	8	94.2	8
Net Income	135.6	11.3	137.5	11	139.4	12	141.3	12
Balance Sheet								
Cash	$ 100	8.3%	$ 100	8%	$ 100	8%	$ 100	8%
Accounts Receivable	250	20.8	225	19	200	17	175	15
Inventory	200	16.7	180	15	160	13	140	12
Net Fixed Assets	100	8.3	100	8	100	8	100	8
Total Assets	650	54.2	605	50	560	47	515	43
Accounts Payable	$ 75	6.3%	$ 75	6%	$ 75	6%	$ 75	6%
Accrued	50	4.2	50	4	50	4	50	4
Debt	200	16.7	155	13	110	9	65	5
Equity	325	27.1	325	27	325	27	325	27
Total Liabilities & Equity	650	54.2	605	50	560	47	515	43

Cost of Capital	12.0%							
Interest Rate	7.0%							
Key Measures								
DSO	76.0		68.4		60.8		53.2	
Inventory Turns	3.0		3.3		3.8		4.3	
Asset Turnover	1.8		2.0		2.1		2.3	
Working Capital	425	35.4%	380	32%	335	28%	290	24%
Net Operating Assets	525	43.8	480	40	435	36	390	33
Invested Capital	525	43.8	480	40	435	36	390	33
ROE Analysis	41.7%		42.3%		42.9%		43.5%	
Profitability	11.3%		11.5%		11.6%		11.8%	
Asset Turnover	1.85		1.98		2.14		2.33	
Leverage	2.00		1.86		1.72		1.58	
ROIC	27.4%		30.0%		33.1%		36.9%	
Additional Cash Generated			$45		$90		$135	
Earnings			1.9	1%	3.8	3%	5.7	4%

ACCOUNTS RECEIVABLE

Figure 8.2 drills down into the drivers and critical measures for accounts receivable. Key among these drivers are credit terms, quality of products and paperwork, the effectiveness of the revenue process, and revenue patterns.

Customer Credit Terms

A significant determiner of a company's actual DSOs is the credit terms extended to customers. There tends to be wide variation in credit terms by industry, country, and competitive situation. Even within a company, it is fairly typical to see a wide range of terms extended to customers for different products, channels, and regions. A useful way to evaluate receivables management is to compare an actual DSO to the best possible DSO. This computation estimates the DSO level if all customers paid invoices on the contractually agreed date. It is computed by weighting the credit terms for each type of customer, region, or business line by annual sales and is illustrated later in this chapter in Table 8.5. Companies should also consider the possibility and merits of reducing credit terms to customers, resulting in a reduction to best possible DSO.

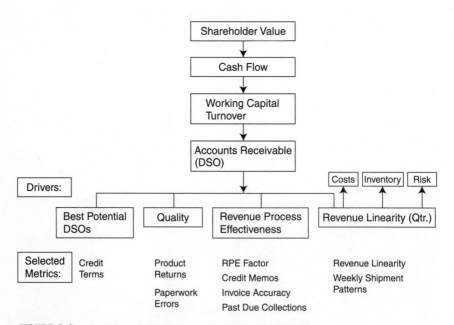

FIGURE 8.2   Drill-Down Illustration: Accounts Receivable

Quality

It stands to reason that receivables collections will be impacted by the quality of products and services and customer-facing processes such as billing. The typical customer is not anxious to part with cash in the first place. Obviously, if the product is not performing, the customer will not pay. The same is true for nonconforming or incomplete paperwork. If the invoice does not match the customer purchase order or does not provide required supplemental information, the payment cannot be processed without additional action.

We all recognize that the impact of quality problems goes far beyond slow collections. It reduces customer satisfaction and loyalty, increases costs for both you and your customer, and may jeopardize future sales. By examining slow-paying accounts and identifying underlying reasons, managers can learn a great deal about any customer dissatisfaction and take steps to deal with underlying product or process problems.

Effectiveness of the Revenue Process

The effectiveness of the revenue process is a key driver of accounts receivable. The time line of the revenue process for a typical company is summarized in Figure 8.3. The process starts long before a product is shipped, when the company is engaged in the product design and preselling activities with the customer.

Other activities preceding shipment include order processing, manufacturing, and quality control. Imagine the downstream process implications of botching the order entry step by entering an incorrect part number or shipping address. The wrong product will be shipped to the customer, or the product will be shipped to an incorrect location. The ability to reduce defects at this stage in the process can save a great deal of time, money, and customer goodwill.

When available, the product is shipped, an invoice is generated, and delivery is made to the customer by post or electronic means. Understanding what happens at the customer to process purchases and payments is essential to speed collections. What process and system does the customer employ to receive the product, test that it works properly, review the transaction, and initiate payment? Do they require special paperwork to facilitate processing? How do they identify and resolve problems and discrepancies? Do they pay on negotiated terms or do they routinely delay payment to help their own cash flow, often called the cash management lag (CML)?

A best practice is for customer service to contact the customer shortly after delivery to ensure that they have received and are satisfied with the

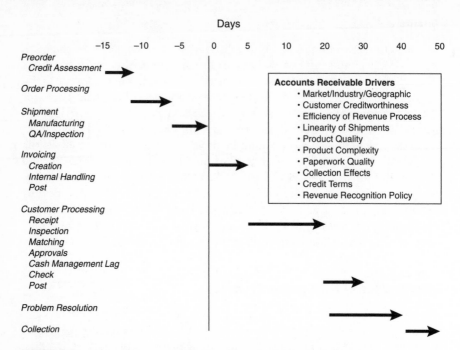

FIGURE 8.3   Revenue Process Time Line from Order to Collection

product and have everything necessary to pay the invoice. If any issues exist, they are identified early and can be addressed at this time. Unfortunately, many companies wait until the receivable is past due to contact the customer. They may be unaware that there is a problem with the product or paperwork, preventing payment. Under the best of circumstances, this situation results in an unsatisfied customer and delayed payment for 40 days or more.

Key Performance Indicators for the Revenue Process and Accounts Receivable

The specific measures utilized will vary based on the individual circumstances. However, some common measures that are useful in evaluating and measuring improvements in this area include the following.

Days Sales Outstanding   Days sales outstanding (DSO) is a measure of the length of time it takes to collect from customers. It will be impacted by the industry in which the firm participates, the creditworthiness of customers, and even the countries in which the firm does business. In addition, DSO is affected by the efficiency and effectiveness of the revenue process (billing and collection), product quality, and even by the pattern of shipments within the quarter or the year.

The basic DSO formula is:

$$DSO = \frac{Receivables \times 365}{Sales}$$

In Chapter 2, we computed the DSO for Simple Co. as follows:

$$DSO = \frac{\$20,000 \times 365}{\$100,000}$$
$$= 73 \text{ days}$$

The basic formula can be adjusted for use as a quarter or monthly measure by annualizing sales for the period. For example, DSO for a quarter would be computed as follows:

$$DSO = \frac{Receivables \times 365}{Quarterly\ Sales \times 4}$$

Assuming that Q4 sales for Simple Co. were $35 million, the quarterly DSO would be computed as follows:

$$DSO = \frac{\$20,000 \times 365}{\$35,000 \times 4} = 52.1 \text{ days}$$

Many financial and operating managers prefer to examine DSOs based on average levels of receivables throughout the year:

$$DSO = \frac{Average\ Monthly\ Receivables \times 365}{Annual\ Sales}$$

DSO Count-Back Method This measure is a terrific variation of the basic DSO concept that considers variations in shipment patterns. The traditional DSO measure just described can be significantly impacted by shipment patterns during a period. For example, if a disproportionate level of shipments is made at the end of the quarter, DSO will rise since it is very unlikely that these invoices will be collected in 0 to 15 days from shipment.

The DSO count-back method accumulates sales starting with the last day of the quarter and continuing backwards until the total equals the receivables balance as illustrated in Table 8.4.

The count-back method results in a DSO of 35 days, approximately 17 days lower than the traditional DSO computation. The difference is a good estimate of the impact of a nonlinear revenue pattern during the quarter.

Best Potential DSO A useful way to evaluate the actual DSO performance is to compute the best possible DSO (Table 8.5). This computation estimates the DSO level if all customers paid invoices on the contractually agreed date. It is computed by weighting the credit terms for each type of customer, region or business line by annual sales. This is a key step in understanding an important variable in receivables management and in setting realistic targets for DSO levels.

TABLE 8.4 DSO Count-Back Illustration

	Sales	Cumulative Count-Back	Days
October			
Week 1	$ 700.0	$35,000.0	
Week 2	900.0	34,300.0	
Week 3	1,200.0	33,400.0	
Week 4	2,000.0	32,200.0	
November			
Week 1	2,200.0	30,200.0	
Week 2	2,300.0	28,000.0	
Week 3	2,700.0	25,700.0	
Week 4	3,000.0	23,000.0	
December			
Week 1	3,800.0	20,000.0	7.0
Week 2	3,200.0	16,200.0	7.0
Week 3	3,700.0	13,000.0	7.0
Week 4	3,800.0	9,300.0	7.0
Week 5	5,500.0	5,500.0	7.0
Total Sales	$35,000.0		
Ending Accounts Receivable	$20,000.0		
	Quarterly		**Count-Back**
DSO	52.1		35.0

TABLE 8.5 Best Possible DSO Estimate: Simple Co.

Geography/Channel	Credit Terms	Estimated Revenue ($ M)	% of Total	Weighting[a]
Product Line 1 Direct	30	$ 30.5	30.5%	9.2
Product Line 1 Distributor	45	7.5	7.5	3.4
Product Line 1 Export	60	15.0	15.0	9.0
Product Line 2 Direct	30	30.0	30.0	9.0
Product Line 2 Distributor	50	5.0	5.0	2.5
Product Line 2 Export	60	12.0	12.0	7.2
Total		$100.0	100%	40.2
				Best Possible DSO

[a]Weighting is computed as: credit terms × % of total.

Past Due Collections   Receivables that are not collected in a reasonable period (e.g., 10 days past terms) will obviously have a significant impact on DSOs. Tracking this level of past due receivables on a monthly, weekly, and even daily basis allows for timely identification and faster resolution of emerging problems and is a leading indicator of accounts receivable performance.

Returns   Product that is returned by customers represents a costly transaction on a number of fronts. Performance problems culminating in product returns are likely to have a significant negative impact on customer satisfaction. Process failures and problems can be identified and addressed by determining the root cause of these returns. There is also a significant transaction cost of shipping, receiving, and carrying the returned product. Depending on the specific circumstance, some companies choose to track the dollar value of returns; others prefer to measure the number of transactions.

Revenue Patterns   In Chapter 7, the impact of revenue patterns on operating efficiency was discussed. Revenue patterns, especially those with revenue skewed toward the end of the quarter, also impact working capital requirements. As evident in the count-back method, accounts receivable will be higher if the revenue pattern is a "hockey stick" since a greater percentage of revenue will be uncollected at the end of the period. Inventories will likely be higher since more inventory must be carried to meet last-minute orders.

Revenue patterns within a quarter can be plotted as shown in Figure 7.3 in Chapter 7. The revenue linearity index is a useful measure to track revenue patterns over time.

Revenue Process and Accounts Receivable Dashboard

Depending on the specific facts and circumstances, several of these measures should be selected and combined to create a dashboard for the revenue process and accounts receivable, illustrated in Figure 8.4.

Tools for Assessing and Improving Revenue Process and Accounts Receivable

A number of tools can be employed to help in assessing and improving the revenue process and accounts receivable management.

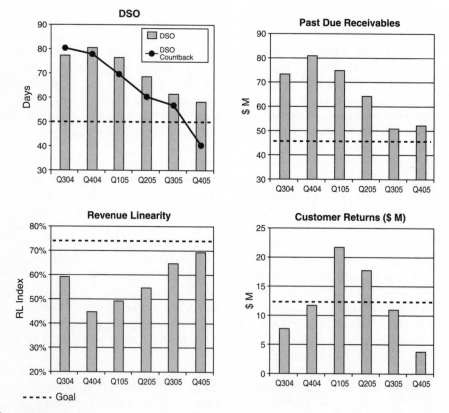

FIGURE 8.4 Revenue Process and Accounts Receivable Dashboard

Accounts Receivable—DSO Driver Chart   The chart in Figure 8.5 presents a high-impact visual summary of DSOs. We begin with the best possible DSO (BPDSO) of 40 days and then identify the number of days associated with significant factors resulting in an actual DSO of 64 days. In this illustration, three factors account for most of the 24 day difference: customer cash management lag (CML), revenue linearity, and past due collections. Each of these items represents a high-leverage improvement opportunity for managers to address.

Accounts Receivable Aging Schedule   A useful tool for managing accounts receivable, customer satisfaction, and the revenue process is the standard accounts receivable aging report. An example of an accounts receivable aging report is shown in Table 8.6. This report simply details the accounts receivable balance for each customer by age of invoice. Invoices issued in the prior 30 days would be included in the 0–30 days column. Invoices issued in the previous month would be reported in the 31–60 days column, and so on. This report allows you to identify macro payment patterns, such as slow-to-pay customers, but will also identify specific overdue invoices for review and follow-up. The report is used by accounts receivable and collections staff but is so rich in information about customers and payment delays that it may also be useful for managers to review from time to time.

Root Cause Analysis: Past Due Collections   A very effective way of assessing key aspects of the revenue process and accounts receivable management is to perform a root cause analysis of any invoice exceeding a certain dollar level and past due for a certain period of time. This also serves as an

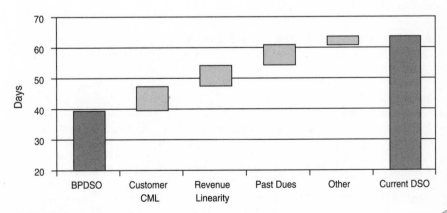

FIGURE 8.5   DSO Drivers

TABLE 8.6 Accounts Receivable Aging Schedule for ABC Company

Customer	Total	0–30 (Current)	31–60	61–90	91–120	>120
A	$ 83,000	$ 50,000	$20,000	$10,000	—	$3,000
B	54,000	20,000	20,000	10,000	$2,000	2,000
C	40,000	10,000	20,000	10,000	—	—
Others	50,000	30,000	20,000			
Total	$ 227,000	$110,000	$80,000	$30,000	$2,000	$5,000
Sales	$1,500,000					
DSO Impact	55.2	26.8	19.4	7.3	0.5	1.2
Aging % of Total Balance						
%	100.0%	48.5%	35.2%	13.2%	0.9%	2.2%
Last Month %	100.0%	60.0%	30.0%	5.0%	5.0%	0.0%

extremely useful tool to identify customer service problems, since an unsatisfied customer will not pay the invoice. Once identified, overdue invoices can be reviewed to determine the root cause for the delay. Overdue receivables generally fall into one of several root causes categories. For example, key process problems such as invoicing errors or poor quality associated with a particular product may be contributing to overdue receivables. An example of a simple root cause analysis is shown in Table 8.7.

The analysis can then be summarized to provide useful insight to the root cause of problems that can lead to the development of a corrective action plan, as shown in Figure 8.6.

Accounts Receivable Roll-Forward Summary This analysis, illustrated in Table 8.8, is a subset of the operating capital budget tool discussed earlier

TABLE 8.7 Accounts Receivable Past Due Analysis

Invoice	Date	Division	Customer	Product	Amount	Root Cause
220921	11/3/05	A	XYZ	M-1	$ 22,000	Dead on arrival
230073	10/4/05	B	LMN	B-1	$ 15,000	Installation problem
223578	9/30/05	B	CDE	C-1	$140,000	Paperwork discrepancy

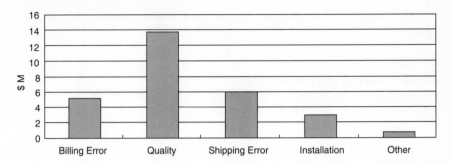

FIGURE 8.6 Past Due by Root Cause

TABLE 8.8 Accounts Receivable Roll-Forward Summary

	History			Projections			
Accounts Receivable	Oct.	Nov.	Dec.	Jan.	Feb.	March	April
Beginning Balance	$ 950	$1,150	$1,310	$1,810	$1,452	$1,310	$1,285
Sales	600	660	1000	400	500	550	600
Collections	–400	–500	–500	–758	–642	–575	–510
Other							
Ending Balance	$1,150	$1,310	$1,810	$1,452	$1,310	$1,285	$1,375
DSO	57.5	59.5	54.3	108.9	78.6	70.1	68.8
% Sales (Annualized)	16.0%	16.5%	15.1%	30.3%	21.8%	19.5%	19.1%
Collections	**CM**	**M+1**	**M+2**	**M+3**			
Assumptions	10.0%	40.0%	30.0%	20.0%			

in the chapter. It is a great tool to understand and communicate the dynamics of accounts receivable. Accounts receivable represent amounts due from customers for product delivered or services rendered. Receivables are increased by sales and reduced by amounts collected from customers. Sales for each month are taken from the P&L forecast. Collections are estimated based on past and projected payment patterns. In this example, it is estimated that 10 percent of sales are collected in the current month, 40 percent in the next month, then 30 percent and 20 percent in months 2 and 3, respectively.

For example, collections in January of $758 million are estimated as follows:

January shipments: 10% of $400 million	$ 40 million
December shipments: 40% of $1,000 million	400 million
November shipments: 30% of $660 million	198 million
October shipments: 20% of $600 million	120 million
Total	$758 million

Assess Effectiveness of Revenue Process　Before embarking on a project to establish measures and improve the revenue process and accounts receivable, many companies first assess the effectiveness of the process by evaluating each segment of the process and identifying high-leverage improvement opportunities. Using tool kits or best-practice surveys for the revenue process, a rating (on a scale of 1 to 5) can be assigned to each stage:

Preorder	3.0
Credit assessment	4.0
Manufacturing	4.0
Quality	4.5
Invoicing	2.5
Follow-up	2.0
Problem resolution	4.0
Visibility: metrics and reporting	1.5

This evaluation will set the focus on weak segments of the process, in this case invoicing, follow-up, and visibility.

INVENTORIES

Many businesses must build, manufacture, or hold product for resale to customers. Inventory levels are the result of a number of drivers and the effectiveness of the procurement and conversion process, as shown in Figure 8.7.

Drivers of Inventory Levels

There are a number of drivers of inventory levels. These include the market and industry, process effectiveness, product life cycles, quality, and forecasting accuracy.

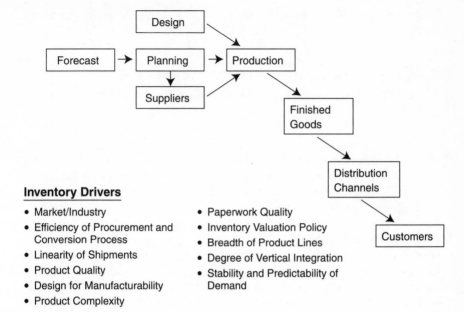

Inventory Drivers

- Market/Industry
- Efficiency of Procurement and Conversion Process
- Linearity of Shipments
- Product Quality
- Design for Manufacturability
- Product Complexity

- Paperwork Quality
- Inventory Valuation Policy
- Breadth of Product Lines
- Degree of Vertical Integration
- Stability and Predictability of Demand

FIGURE 8.7 Procurement and Conversion Processes

Market and Industry The very nature of certain businesses and industries often determines the level of inventory required. For example, retailers must purchase and hold inventories for resale to consumers. Manufacturing companies must acquire materials, assemble product, and distribute finished goods to their customers. By contrast, service companies, including consulting firms, do not have to hold significant levels of inventory.

Effectiveness of Procurement and Conversion Processes Inventories as well as manufacturing costs can be reduced by improving procurement and manufacturing or conversion processes. By evaluating and then improving vendor quality and delivery performance, for example, the company can reduce lead times and inventory levels. Over the past 15 years, tremendous improvements have been made by many companies in improving the flow and efficiency of the manufacturing process.

Product Life Cycle Issues The evolution of a product from conception to full-scale production to end of life has significant impact on inventory levels. Two critical phases in the product life cycle are new product intro-duction and the end of the product's life.

1. *New product introduction.* Many companies carry high inventory levels associated with problems in the design and introduction of new prod-ucts. If a new product is transferred to manufacturing before all design issues are resolved, high inventory levels are likely to be associated with the product. In addition to tying up excess capital, this inventory may be at risk for obsolescence if the design of the product is changed.
2. *End of life.* The company must carefully plan and manage the end of a product's life cycle. If this is not done effectively, the company may carry and ultimately write off inventories that are no longer salable to customers.

Design for Manufacturability   Many companies have reduced costs and in-ventory requirements by designing products that are easier to manufacture. Examples include using common components and requiring fewer complex assembly steps. These types of improvements reduce costs and inventories, improve quality, and help prevent delays associated with introducing prod-ucts to market.

Product Quality   If a company manufactures a quality product, inventory levels will be lower than for a similar product with quality problems. A firm with high-quality manufacturing processes will require lower levels of material input; less time and inventory in test, repair, and rework; and lower levels of inventory returned from customers.

Breadth of Product Line   The company that offers a broad selection of products will typically require higher inventory levels. Conversely, a firm with limited product alternatives will typically have less inventory. Many firms have reduced inventory levels by limiting product variety to fewer op-tions and choices, for example color, size, configurations, and power.

Vertical Integration   Companies that are vertically integrated will carry higher inventory balances than a firm that outsources a substantial part of the manufacturing process to other firms.

Forecasting   In Chapter 6 we discussed that most businesses must antici-pate future demand for their products so that product can be ordered or manufactured and be available for customers at the time of purchase. The revenue forecast typically drives procurement and manufacturing schedules and activities. The accuracy of forecasts has a significant impact on inventory levels. If demand is overestimated, excess inventory will result. Even if the total revenue forecast is accurate but the mix of product is different than projected, the company may miss sales and build product that was not ordered, leading to an increase in inventory. In Chapter 7, we outlined several measures that can be taken to improve the forecasting process. In addition to improving the forecasting process, managers should also strive to improve flexibility and response times, for example by reducing lead times. Forecasting is a very important activity within most companies and is included in our list of pressure points addressed in Chapter 13.

Key Performance Indicators for Supply Chain Management and Inventory

There are a number of performance measures that can be developed and tracked to provide visibility into key drivers of supply chain and inventory management.

Inventory Turns   In Chapter 2, we computed inventory turns and days sales in inventory (DSI) for Simple Co., as follows:

$$\text{Inventory Turns} = \frac{\text{Cost of Goods Sold (COGS)}}{\text{Inventory}}$$
$$= \frac{\$45,000}{\$18,000}$$
$$= 2.5 \text{ times (turns)}$$

Inventory turns measure how much inventory a firm carries compared to sales levels. Factors that will affect this measure include: effectiveness of supply chain management and production processes, product quality, breadth of product line, degree of vertical integration, and predictability of sales.

Days Sales in Inventory   The DSI measure is a derivative of inventory turns and is computed as follows:

$$\text{DSI} = \frac{365}{\text{Inventory Turns}}$$
$$= \frac{365}{2.5}$$
$$= 146 \text{ days}$$

This measure is impacted by the same factors as inventory turns. The advantage to this measure is that it can be easier for people to relate to the number of days sales in inventory. As a result, it may be easier to conceptualize the appropriateness (or potential improvement opportunity) of carrying 146 days' worth of sales in inventory than 2.5 inventory turns.

Slow-Moving and Obsolete Inventory Levels It is important to identify and manage excess and obsolete (E&O) inventory. Excess inventory is the inventory on hand in excess of foreseeable demand over a defined period such as 12 months. Excess inventory results from overestimating demand or from radical changes in demand patterns. Obsolete inventory results from holding inventory that is no longer salable or usable in the ordinary course of business. A useful summary of excess and obsolete inventory is illustrated in Figure 8.8. A good first step in managing excess and obsolete inventory is to trend the levels over time. Measuring levels of E&O will provide visibility and identify trends. This measure is complemented by a root cause analysis that provides insight into the underlying causes of excess and obsolete inventory. Typical causes include product life cycle issues (end of life issues, new product introductions) and forecasting errors.

Number of Unique Inventory Parts Tracking the number of unique inventoried parts may provide insight into a key driver of inventory management. The company may be able to reduce inventory levels by reducing the number of unique inventory parts. This objective may take time to achieve and must consider supplier, customer, and manufacturing issues.

Past Due Customer Orders If customer orders are delayed past the requested delivery date, the inventory must be carried until the order can be completed. Perhaps the inventory for an order is completed except for a single, integral part that is out of stock. Obviously, past due orders are likely to negatively impact customer satisfaction as well.

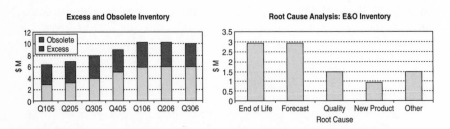

FIGURE 8.8 Excess and Obsolete Inventory Summary

Supplier Performance Companies should measure the quality of parts supplied by vendors. Poor quality of incoming parts will delay internal processes and result in higher inventories. Late deliveries from suppliers will also wreak havoc with production schedules, resulting in higher inventories and potential delays in shipments to customers.

Forecast Accuracy Measuring the accuracy of sales forecasts compared to actual demand levels will help to explain inventory shortages and excesses. It will also provide visibility into a key performance driver and serve to establish accountability for sales projections. Measures of forecast accuracy were presented in Chapter 6.

Cycle Time A very effective measure of supply chain management and inventories is the amount of time required to produce a unit of inventory. The shorter the cycle time for a product, the less time the product spends in the factory. Reducing cycle times typically leads to lower manufacturing costs, lower inventory balances, and increased flexibility. It can also lead to higher levels of customer satisfaction.

Additional measures for supply chain management are discussed in Chapter 7.

Supply Chain Management and Inventory Dashboard

Several of these measures can be selected and combined to create a dashboard for supply chain management and inventory. See Figure 8.9.

Tools for Understanding and Assessing Inventory and Related Processes

Assessment-Related Business Process Similar to the approach suggested for accounts receivable earlier in the chapter, it may be helpful to assess the supply chain and related processes before selecting performance measures. Using tool kits or best-practice surveys for the supply chain management process, a rating (on a scale of 1 to 5) can be assigned to each stage:

Product design and new product introduction	2.0
Forecasting and production planning	3.0
Manufacturing	3.5
Quality	4.5
Management of end of life, excess, and slow-moving inventories	2.5
Visibility: metrics and reporting	3.5

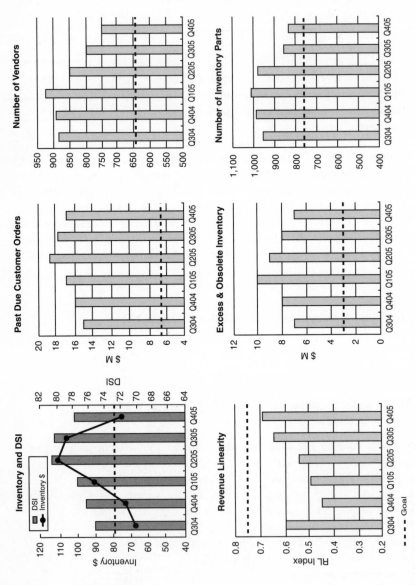

FIGURE 8.9 Supply Chain and Inventory Dashboard

This assessment will focus attention on weak segments of the process, in this case product design and new product introduction, forecasting, and management of excess and obsolete inventory.

Improving Visibility: Useful Analytical Reports

In addition to the dashboard and assessment, there are a number of reports and tools that are very useful in identifying trends and providing visibility into key drivers of inventory.

Inventory Trend Schedule by Major Category Much can be learned by drilling down into the major components of inventory and tracking trends in each over time. It is also useful to compute turnover for each significant category of inventory.

The schedule in Table 8.9 includes outstanding purchase commitments to provide visibility into the inventory that the company has ordered and is contractually obliged to take in the near term. Tracking and managing the purchase commitments and the total inventory commitments provides a leading indicator of future inventory levels.

Inventory Roll-Forward Summary Similar to the schedule we presented for receivables, the inventory roll-forward summary shown in Table 8.10 displays the transactions projected for each month that will increase or decrease the inventory balance. Inventory will be increased by purchases, manufacturing labor, and overhead applied to inventory. It will be reduced by cost of goods sold (COGS), including cost of product sold, write-offs, and so on.

This schedule is a great tool for tracking and communicating the key variables that impact inventories. It also allows us to understand why inventories are higher or lower than we projected they would be. Did we purchase more material than projected? If so, inventories will be higher than expected. Did we sell less product, resulting in lower cost of sales relief from inventory? If so, then inventories would also be higher.

Tracking the Top 20 to 50 Inventory Items Focusing attention on the inventory items that have the greatest value can provide insight into inventory performance and allow managers to focus on specific items that account for the lion's share of the inventory value. It is fairly typical for the top 20 to 50 line items to account for 50 to 70 percent of the total inventory value.

TABLE 8.9 Inventory Trend Schedule by Category ($ Millions)

	Jan.	Feb.	Mar.	April	May
Raw Material					
Incoming Inspection	$ 2	$ 2	$ 5	$ 7	$ 7
Supplies	6	6	6	6	6
Electronic Components	22	25	27	22	22
Total	$30	$33	$38	$35	$35
Work in Process					
Fabrication	$ 4	$ 4	$ 4	$ 4	$ 4
Assembly	12	13	14	18	18
Burn In	1	1	1	1	1
Rework	3	3	3	3	3
Test	1	1	1	1	1
Final Inspection	4	4	4	4	4
Total	$25	$26	$27	$31	$31
Finished Goods					
Manufacturing Plants	$ 5	$ 4	$ 6	$ 4	$ 5
Warehouse	7	7	7	7	7
International Locations	12	12	13	12	10
Sales Offices	6	6	6	6	6
Total	$30	$29	$32	$29	$28
Total Gross Inventory	85	88	97	95	94
Less: Inventory Reserves	−15	−15	−16	−16	−17
Net Inventory	70	73	81	79	77
Purchase Commitments	15	17	22	25	30
Total Inventory Commitments	85	90	103	104	107
Key Performance Indicators					
Inventory Turns	2.9	2.7	2.5	2.5	2.6
Days Inventory	127.8	133.2	147.8	144.2	140.5
% of Total					
Raw Materials	35.3%	37.5%	39.2%	36.8%	37.2%
Work in Process	29.4	29.5	27.8	32.6	33.0
Finished Goods	35.3	33.0	33.0	30.5	29.8
Inventory Reserves % of Total	17.6%	17.0%	16.5%	16.8%	18.1%
Committed Inventory % Cost of Sales	43%	45%	52%	52%	54%
Cost of Sales (Annual)	$200				

TABLE 8.10 Inventory Roll-Forward Summary

Inventories	History			Projections			
	Oct.	Nov.	Dec.	Jan.	Feb.	March	April
Beginning Balance	$1,300	$1,220	$1,112	$832	$762	$ 902	$1,077
Purchases	140	154	168	84	196	224	280
Labor	100	100	168	84	196	224	280
Overhead	100	100	84	42	98	112	140
COGS	–420	–462	–700	–280	–350	–385	–420
Ending Balance	$1,220	$1,112	$ 832	$762	$902	$1,077	$1,357
Inventory Turns	4.1	5.0	10.1	4.4	4.7	4.3	3.7
DSI	87.1	72.2	35.7	81.6	77.3	83.9	96.9
% Sales	16.9%	14.0%	6.9%	15.9%	15.0%	16.3%	18.8%

SUMMARY

The capital required to support a business and the effectiveness of management in managing capital assets are significant drivers of performance and value. Major components of capital include operating capital; property, plant, and equipment; and intangible assets. The level of assets required to support a business is driven by a number of factors, including the nature of the industry, the business model, and the level of efficiency in key business processes such as supply chain management and revenue processes. Significant improvement in asset utilization is possible by improving the effectiveness of the related business processes.

QUESTIONS FOR CONSIDERATION

1. How much attention is paid to operating capital management in your company?
2. Has the linkage between working capital and related processes been established?
3. How much profit, cash, and value would be generated by improving operating capital by 20 percent?
4. Are managers evaluated and compensated on measures that reflect the level of capital employed in the business (e.g., ROIC)?

CHAPTER 9

Capital Effectiveness: Long-Term Assets

In Chapter 8, we introduced capital efficiency as a key value driver and explored operating capital in detail. This chapter examines the remaining components of capital effectiveness, including property, plant, and equipment, and intangible assets. Figure 9.1 drills down into the components of capital effectiveness and asset management.

CAPITAL INTENSITY

The term *capital intensity* is used to describe the level of property, plant, and equipment (also known as fixed assets) that is required to support a business. Capital intensity will vary significantly from firm to firm, and from industry to industry. Key among the drivers of capital intensity are the nature of the industry, the effectiveness of capital processes, and the degree of vertical integration.

Nature of Industry

Certain industries, such as automotive manufacturing, refining, and transportation, require high levels of capital assets. Others, such as consulting, require very little in the way of capital assets. Other industries fall somewhere between these two extremes.

Effectiveness of Capital Process

Companies that require substantial investments in capital assets must develop effective decision and control processes over capital spending and asset management. Key process controls include review of proposed expenditures

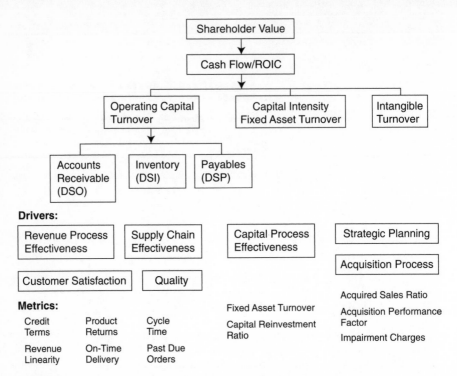

FIGURE 9.1   Drill-Down: Capital Effectiveness and Asset Management

to ensure business and economic justification, reviews to monitor project implementation, postaudits, physical control over existing assets, and identification and disposal of underutilized assets. The capital process is discussed in detail later in the chapter.

Vertical Integration

Vertical integration refers to the extent to which a company directly owns supply chain activities and resources. A company that is considered vertically integrated will produce a substantial part of the final product. An example of a vertically integrated organization would be a company engaged in growing, harvesting, processing, and distribution of food products. Other companies purchase or acquire a substantial part of their products from third parties, commonly referred to as outsourcing. In recent years, there has been a strong movement toward outsourcing activities such as manufacturing, so that the enterprise can focus attention and resources on "core" activities such as product design and marketing. A company that outsources a substantial part of its manufacturing will require substantially less plant and equipment (and of course inventory) than a company that is vertically integrated.

Depreciation Policy

Capital assets are defined as assets with a utility greater than one year. Accounting practices require that these investments be capitalized (recorded as assets) and depreciated over an estimated useful life. While there are general guidelines for depreciation methods and periods for each type of asset, companies can adopt either a conservative or an aggressive practice within the acceptable range. Companies that use shorter lives and faster depreciation methods will depreciate assets faster, resulting in higher depreciation expense and lower book values for these assets on the balance sheet.

TOOLS FOR IMPROVING THE MANAGEMENT OF LONG-TERM CAPITAL

There are a number of tools and best practices to improve the utilization and effectiveness of long-term assets. These include developing an effective capital investment process, monitoring projects, and postimplementation reviews.

Effective Capital Review and Approval Process

A fundamental driver of effective utilization of capital is the strength of the capital investment process. Figure 9.2 recaps key steps in an effective capital investment process.

Companies should identify significant capital requirements as part of their strategic and annual operating planning activities. The capital budget will be an important element of each plan. For strategic plans, the managers should look out three to five years and anticipate significant capital expenditures to support growth, strategic initiatives, and other requirements. Integrating the capital plan into the financial projections will afford the opportunity to review cash flow projections and determine the adequacy of returns over the strategic planning horizon.

For significant expenditures, a capital investment proposal (CIP) should be prepared to document key aspects of the project, including business justification, economic case, alternatives, and implementation plan.

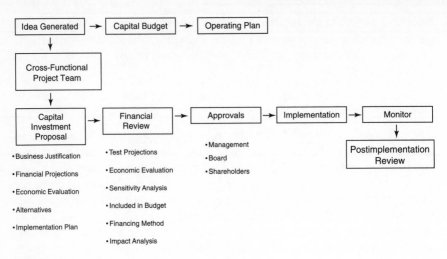

FIGURE 9.2   Capital Investment Process Overview

The scope of the CIP and the management approval level should scale with the size and importance of the project.

Business Case   The business case should define the strategic and business objectives that will be achieved or supported with this use of capital. In addition to passing certain economic tests, the project must be clearly linked to a strategic or operational objective. Some projects may make economic sense, but are outside, or even inconsistent with, the strategic direction of the company.

Economic Case   All capital investment projects should be supported by financial projections and an economic evaluation. The financial projections should be based on the business case and implementation plan and include the following:

- Estimated costs to purchase and start up the project.
- Incremental revenues, costs, and capital requirements that result from undertaking the project.
- Estimated salvage or terminal value at the end of the project life.

TABLE 9.1 Capital Investment Evaluation

	Year 0	Year 1	Year 2	Year 3
Sales	$ 0	$15,000	$20,000	$18,000
COGS	0	(10,000)	(13,400)	(12,060)
Gross Margin	0	5,000	6,600	5,940
%		33.3%	33.0%	33.0%
–Expenses	(1,000)	(2,500)	(2,600)	(3,000)
–Depreciation		(1,650)	(1,650)	(1,650)
Profit Before Taxes	(1,000)	850	2,350	1,290
–Taxes 34.0%	340	(289)	(799)	(439)
Profit After Taxes	(660)	561	1,551	851
+Depreciation	0	1,650	1,650	1,650
–Capital Expenditures	(5,000)	0	0	0
(Increase) Decrease in Operating Capital	0	(750)	(250)	1,000
Free Cash Flows	(5,660)	1,461	2,951	3,501
+Salvage/Terminal Value				330
Net Cash Flow	(5,660)	1,461	2,951	3,831
Cumulative Cash Flow	$(5,660)	$(4,199)	$(1,248)	$2,583
Present Value Factor	1.000	0.893	0.797	0.712
Present Value of Cash Flow	$(5,660)	$1,304	$2,353	$2,727
Cumulative Present Value Cash Flow	$(5,660)	$(4,356)	$(2,003)	$ 724
Discount Rate 12.0%				

Economic Tests	
NPV	$724
IRR	18.28%
Payback	2.33

A simple illustration is presented in Table 9.1 for an investment with the following characteristics:

Project life   3 years

Implementation costs:

Capital $5,000
Operating expenses   1,000

Projected results:

	Sales	Expenses
Year 1	$15,000	$2,500
Year 2	20,000	2,600
Year 3	18,000	3,000

Gross margin	33% of sales
Working capital requirements	5% of sales
Tax rate	34%
Discount rate	12%

Project terminates at end of year 3:

Net salvage value of capital	$330
Working capital is reduced to zero.	

Most economic evaluations should be based on projected cash flows. The first step will be to estimate the incremental profit and loss on the project and then estimate cash flows, reflecting the capital investment, depreciation, and working capital requirements. Note that our example indicates that cash flow will be negative in year 0, the year we make the investment. Cash flow turns positive in years 1 through 3.

A variety of measures or decision criteria are used to evaluate the economic characteristics of the investment. In addition to satisfying these economic tests, the project must also be justified on a business and strategic basis. The three most common measures are net present value (NPV), internal rate of return (IRR), and payback:

1. *Net present value (NPV)*. Net present value utilizes the discounted cash flow (DCF) methodology described in Chapter 2 to account for the time value of money and project risk. The cash flow for each year is discounted back to the equivalent value today (year 0). Net present value is the sum of all discounted cash inflows and outflows. A positive NPV indicates that the project has a return in excess of the discount rate used, and therefore should be approved. A negative NPV indicates that the project has a return under the discount rate, and should not be undertaken.

   The economic evaluation of our example is presented in Table 9.1. The NPV for this project is $724. Since the NPV is greater than zero, the project passes this economic test.

2. *Internal rate of return (IRR)*. The IRR of a project is the actual rate of return implied in the project's cash flows. If the IRR exceeds the discount rate (DR), the project should be approved. If the IRR is less than the dis-

count rate, the project should be rejected. The project in this example has an IRR of 18.28 percent, which is above the 12 percent discount rate used for the project. Note that IRR and NPV are consistent decision criteria, using estimated cash flows and the discount rate as key inputs. The use of IRR and NPV will result in consistent decisions in most cases:

IRR	NPV	Result
IRR > DR	NPV > 0	Approve
IRR < DR	NPV < 0	Reject

3. *Payback.* Payback is a simple rule-of-thumb measure that determines the number of years until the cash investment is recovered. Investments with shorter payback periods are typically viewed as positive; investments with longer payback periods may be rejected or require additional review. Payback is criticized because it does not directly take into account the time value of money in an investment. Despite this criticism, it is one of the most common methods used in practice.

In this example the cumulative cash flow for the project becomes positive in year 3. We estimate the payback in Table 9.1 as follows:

Number of years prior to breakeven   2.00 years

$$\frac{\text{Unrecovered cash end of year 2}}{\text{Total cash flow in year 3}} = \frac{1,248}{3,831} = .33$$

Total estimated payback   2.33 years

All three methods illustrated in Table 9.1 should be utilized, since they each provide a different view into the economic dynamics of the project. While NPV indicates whether the project should be undertaken based on a given discount rate, IRR provides the precise rate of return on the project. By comparing the internal rate to the discount rate, you can get a sense of the return slack. Payback complements these measures by estimating the number of years until cash outlays are fully recovered. For example, a project may have a positive NPV and a high rate of return but the bulk of the cash may be recovered late in the project life, or even in the terminal or salvage value. This long payback should be evaluated in the context of project risks.

We used a discount rate of 12 percent in the example. The discount rate for each project should be based on the level of risk associated with the project. For practical reasons, companies often set a hurdle rate well above the company's cost of capital (covered in Chapter 10) to ensure that projects will earn an acceptable return. If individual projects are perceived as having very low or high risk, the discount rate may be adjusted accordingly.

Alternatives   Most projects have a number of alternatives. These should be explored as part of the capital investment decision and documented in the capital investment proposal. Reviewers should test the basis for selecting the recommended plan to ensure that this alternative provides the best balance of technical, business, and economic performance.

Implementation Plan   Execution and implementation are always a critical success factor for any project. Capital projects should be supported with a detailed implementation plan. This plan will provide a road map to achieve the objectives of the capital investment. A good implementation plan is a strong indication that the project is well planned, including identification of resource requirements, risks, and alternatives. The implementation plan also provides a basis for monitoring and reviewing progress of the project. Identifying key assumptions, checkpoints, and go-no-go decision points will also allow managers to consider redirecting or terminating projects that may be at risk. The characteristics of a good implementation plan are detailed in the sidebar.

CHARACTERISTICS OF GOOD IMPLEMENTATION PLANS

- Identify and address obstacles and barriers.
- Identify critical success factors.
- Identify resource requirements and key assumptions.
- Assign responsibility.
- Include sufficient detail:
    - Specific tasks: What should I be doing today?
    - Interdependencies/critical path.
    - Monitoring and communication value.
- Identify measurable objectives and targets:
    - Make sure these link to and support financial targets.
    - Key performance indicators.

EXECUTIVE REVIEW OF CAPITAL PROJECTS

Key points:
- Consistency with mission/strategy.
- Strategic and business case.
- Economic case:
  - Projections: market, market share, adoption rate, business model, investment requirements.
- Identify and test assumptions.
  - Review scenario and sensitivity analysis: Can we live with downside scenarios?
- Project management and ownership:
  - Experience/knowledge.
  - Track record.
  - Passion for program.
- Implementation plan: human and financial resource requirements.
- Risk identification and mitigation plans.

Executive Review of Capital Investment Projects

Most companies require management approval for investments over a certain limit. Approval requirements typically escalate to higher levels of management, the board, or even shareholders based on the nature and size of the investment. The sidebar ("Executive Review of Capital Projects") highlights key points that executives should consider in their evaluation of significant investments.

Evaluating Projections Understanding and evaluating the financial projections in a capital decision are always two of the most important and difficult aspects in the review process. For large projects, it may be appropriate to look at a series of projections and analyses, including:

1. *Base case.* The DCF analysis using the most likely estimates for all variables represents a single outcome from a range of potential outcomes.

2. *Sensitivity analysis.* This technique determines the sensitivity of the decision criteria (e.g., NPV) to changes in the assumptions used in the base case.
3. *Breakeven analysis.* At what point does the change in an estimated variable result in a zero NPV?
4. *Scenario analysis.* This tool determines NPV of the project under specified scenarios, for example recession, best case, competitive reaction.
5. *Simulations.* Information across an entire probability distribution for key variables is utilized in developing NPV (e.g., Monte Carlo simulation).
6. *Decision trees.* A decision tree presents decisions and probable outcomes at each stage of a project.

Project Monitoring and Postimplementation Review

If a capital project has been supported by a well-documented proposal, including a detailed implementation plan, managers can review the progress of the project at various points. Is the project on schedule? If not, why? Have the underlying assumptions changed? If so, is the project still worth doing?

A terrific way to improve the utilization of capital and the capital investment process is to review the actual performance of capital investments compared to the original CIP (see sidebar, "Postaudit Review of Projects"). While this can be a difficult exercise for many projects, there is great value in the effort. First, if managers know in advance that the project results will be formally evaluated, this will encourage well-thought-out and realistic plans. Second, even where the results may be difficult to measure, much can be learned about the project results as well as lessons learned for the future. Third, the review can identify improvement opportunities in the capital investment process or management issues such as unrealistic projections or inadequate project oversight.

My first attempt at postimplementation review of capital projects was both difficult and modest. Managers complained that they didn't have adequate systems to measure the incremental savings for many projects. So we simply met to discuss the project and physically inspected the asset, where appropriate. On one occasion, we discovered that a substantial piece of equipment had been essentially abandoned shortly after purchase. We were able to sell the equipment, generating cash and reducing asset and depreciation levels. We also worked with the managers to ensure that the process

POSTAUDIT REVIEW OF PROJECTS

Objectives:
- Hold managers accountable.
- Identify indicated actions (project specific), for example dispose/ shut down/stay course.
- Global feedback on process and execution.

Feedback:
- How many projects have met or exceeded planned results?
- Identify and address estimation bias.
- What are the root causes of underperforming projects?
- What are the key ingredients in successful projects?
- What should we do differently on future projects?

Postaudit reviews are sometimes difficult to perform:
- Results are not always easily identifiable.
- Process is worth the effort.

to develop capital project proposals was improved to decrease the chances of this occurring in the future.

Asset Inventory and Utilization Review

Periodically, companies should perform a physical inventory of fixed assets and compare this to accounting records. This process should be part of a company's internal control framework. The inventory can easily be expanded to review the estimated utilization of significant assets. If certain assets are not utilized, these assets may be sold or disposed of, which will generate cash; reduce associated expenses including taxes, depreciation, maintenance, and insurance; and increase asset turnover.

In some cases, an asset's fair value may appreciate significantly over the value carried in the accounting records. This occurs frequently with real estate assets. Management should consider if the potential value realized by liquidating that asset may exceed the value of continuing to hold and operate that asset.

Expand Key Business Decisions to Include Capital Requirements

Frequently, capital requirements are not fully considered in business decisions. This may occur in companies with a narrow focus on sales and earnings per share (EPS) growth and in companies with cash surpluses. Capital is sometimes viewed as "free" in these situations because of the muted effect of capital on EPS (depreciation expense is spread out over years) and limited alternatives for utilizing excess cash.

KEY PERFORMANCE INDICATORS FOR CAPITAL INTENSITY

Managers can utilize a number of performance measures to provide visibility into drivers of capital intensity and the effectiveness of capital management.

Capital Asset Intensity (Fixed Asset Turnover)

Capital asset intensity, or fixed asset turnover, is computed as follows:

$$\text{Capital Asset Intensity} = \frac{\text{Sales}}{\text{Net Fixed Assets}}$$

For Simple Co. in 2006,

$$\text{Capital Asset Intensity} = \frac{\$100,000}{\$20,000}$$
$$= 5 \text{ turns per year}$$

This measure reflects the level of investment in property, plant, and equipment relative to sales. Some businesses are very capital intensive (that is, they require a substantial investment in capital) whereas others have modest requirements. For example, electric utility and transportation industries typically require high capital investments. On the other end of the spectrum, software development companies would usually require minimal levels of capital.

Capital Asset Intensity—at Cost (Fixed Asset Turnover—at Cost)

This variation of the preceding formula uses the original cost of the assets instead of the net book or depreciated value. It may be more useful in those situations where capital remains employed far beyond the original depreciation period or when making comparisons across companies with different depreciation policies.

$$\text{Capital Asset Intensity—at Cost} = \frac{\text{Sales}}{\text{Fixed Assets}}$$
$$= \frac{\$100,000}{\$50,000}$$
$$= 2 \text{ turns per year}$$

Capital Reinvestment Rate

One way of measuring the rate of investment in capital is to compute the ratio of capital spending to depreciation.

$$\text{Capital Reinvestment Rate} = \frac{\text{Capital Expenditures}}{\text{Depreciation}}$$

For Simple Co. in 2006,

$$\frac{\$5,000}{\$3,750} = 1.33$$

Changes in depreciation levels lag capital investment because assets are depreciated over a number of years. For businesses with little or modest top-line growth, a reinvestment index of 1 or lower may be appropriate. For high-growth businesses, capital expenditures will typically exceed depreciation for a period of time, resulting in a high capital reinvestment rate.

Asset Write-Offs and Impairment History

Significant charges to write off or write down assets may indicate an ineffective decision or implementation process for capital investment. Companies that have frequent asset write-offs and impairment charges (and other nonrecurring charges) likely have an opportunity to improve capital investment, strategic, and related processes.

INTANGIBLE ASSETS

Unlike tangible fixed assets, intangible assets are not associated with a specific identifiable asset like property or equipment. Intangible assets typically arise from acquisitions, where the purchase price of an acquisition target exceeds the fair market value of tangible assets. The excess of the purchase price is recorded as goodwill or assigned to other intangible assets as shown in Table 9.2.

A company that has made one or several acquisitions is likely to have a substantial balance in goodwill and intangible assets. Companies that focus exclusively on internal growth will not have goodwill or related intangibles, although they may have such intangibles as patents, trademarks, and customer lists.

Companies that have done a poor job in evaluating, valuing, and integrating acquisitions will likely have been forced to write off or write down goodwill arising from failed acquisitions. Companies that are successful with M&A will continue to carry the goodwill as an asset. Under accounting rules effective in 2001, goodwill and certain acquisition intangibles must be evaluated each year to determine whether the assets are impaired. Stated simply, the performance of acquisitions is monitored to determine if the purchase price paid and resulting assets on the balance sheet are supported by current performance expectations.

The level of goodwill and related intangibles for firms that have completed acquisitions must be evaluated in the context of other value drivers,

TABLE 9.2   Acquisition Purchase Price Allocation

Purchase Price	$100,000
Assigned to Tangible Assets	
Accounts Receivable	15,000
Inventories	12,000
Property, Plant, and Equipment	17,000
Other Assets	2,000
Accounts Payable	(4,000)
Accrued Liabilities	(6,000)
Net Tangible Assets	$ 36,000
Excess of Purchase Price over Tangible Assets	$ 64,000
Value of Identifiable Intangibles[a]	15,000
Remainder (Goodwill)	$ 49,000

[a]Includes patents, trademarks, customer lists, and so on.

including sales growth and ROIC. Refer to the economics of M&A in Chapter 12 for additional discussion of acquisitions.

KEY PERFORMANCE INDICATORS: GOODWILL AND INTANGIBLE ASSETS

There are several performance measures that will provide insight and visibility into the level and management of intangible assets and related processes.

Intangible Asset Turnover

This turnover ratio helps explain the overall measure of asset turnover. Companies that have made significant acquisitions will have a large intangible balance and lower asset turnover than a company that has grown organically. The measure provides an indication of how significant acquisition activity has been relative to sales levels, and is computed as:

$$\text{Intangible Asset Turnover} = \frac{\text{Annual Sales}}{\substack{\text{Intangible Assets} \\ (\text{Goodwill} + \text{Other Intangibles})}}$$

For Simple Co., the intangible asset turnover is:

$$\frac{\$100,000}{\$11,000} = 9.1 \text{ times}$$

Goodwill Impairment Charges

Goodwill impairment charges result from acquisitions failing to achieve performance expectations that supported the original purchase price. Significant charges to write off or write down assets may indicate an ineffective decision or implementation process for business acquisitions. Companies that have recorded impairment (and other nonrecurring) charges likely have an opportunity to improve acquisition and strategic processes.

Performance of Acquisitions: Synergies and Strategic Objectives

A current way to determine if the intangibles related to an acquisition will be substantiated or required to be written down in the future is to track key performance indicators on the value drivers that are critical to the success of the acquisition. Examples include key integration milestones such as sales force consolidation, the introduction of new products based on combined technologies, sales growth resulting from distribution synergies, and head count reductions. Achieving these objectives, as set out in the acquisition plan and reflected in the acquisition pricing, should result in a favorable impairment test result.

EXCESS CASH BALANCES

In Chapter 8, we indicated that we would exclude financing accounts from our discussion of capital efficiency. However, we do need to address the impact of holding excessive levels of cash or short-term investments. What is excess cash? Most businesses need a minimum level of cash to operate. The minimum level of cash to operate will be a function of several factors, including business seasonality, cash generation and requirements, life cycle stage, and management preference. This minimum level may be reduced if the company has ready access to a short-term credit facility. Many companies hold cash well in excess of any amount necessary to support operations. Typically this occurs in profitable firms with good returns where investment opportunities for future growth have declined. Many firms retain excess cash as a cushion against unforeseen challenges or as a war chest to allow the company to pursue large investments, including acquisitions. Some of these firms hold on to the excess cash, year after year, despite their stated intention to invest the cash.

Maintaining this flexibility by holding excess cash dilutes shareholder returns. The interest earned (after tax) on cash and short-term investments is typically much lower than the firm's cost of capital. Table 9.3 illustrates the impact of retaining excess cash. Retainage Inc. has a $600 million cash balance, of which $100 million is required to support the business. The firm has net income of $150 million and total assets of $1,500 million. The cash earns 6 percent and is taxed at 30 percent. The firm's cost of capital is 15 percent.

The analysis estimates that retaining excess cash reduces economic profit by $54 million and reduces return on assets by 29 percent.

Managers and boards should carefully evaluate the trade-off involved in retaining excess cash. In some situations, some or all of the excess cash should be returned to shareholders in the form of dividends or share repurchases. This methodology can also be used to estimate the economic impact of retaining other underperforming assets, for example a unit with low profitability or returns.

TABLE 9.3 Estimating the Economic Cost (Penalty) of Retaining Excess Cash: Retainage Inc. ($ Millions)

Estimate of Excess Cash				
Year-End Cash Balance			$600.0	
Assume $100M Required to Support Business			−100.0	
Excess Cash			$500.0	
Estimate of Impact on Economic Profit				
Earnings (6 Percent Interest Rate, 30% Tax Rate)				
After-Tax Interest Rate of			4.2%	
Profit After Tax			$ 21.0	
Cost of Capital: WACC		15.0%		
Excess Cash		$500.0	−75.0	
Economic Profit or Loss on Excess Cash			$−54.0	

Estimated Impact on ROA

	Including Cash	Excess Cash	Excluding Cash	% Change
Net Income	$ 150.0	$ −21.0	$ 129.0	−14.0%
Assets	$1,500.0	$−500.0	$1,000.0	−33.3%
ROA	10.0%	4.2%	12.9%	29.0%

LONG-TERM CAPITAL DASHBOARD

Based on the specific facts and circumstances, managers can combine several key performance measures into a dashboard to monitor key drivers of long-term capital assets (Figure 9.3).

SUMMARY

The capital required to support a business and the effectiveness of management in managing capital assets are significant drivers of performance and value. Major components of capital include operating capital; property, plant, and equipment; and intangible assets. The level of assets required to support a business is driven by a number of factors, including the nature of the industry, the business model, and the level of efficiency in key business processes. Improvements to the capital investment process such as postimplementation and utilization reviews can lead to improved cash flow, prof-

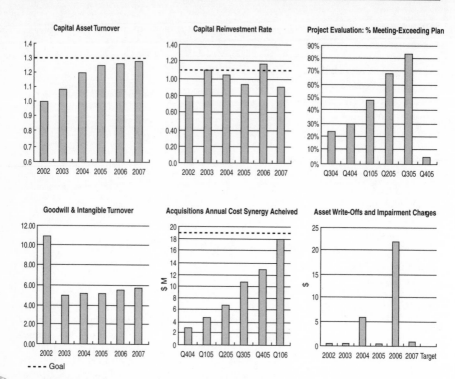

FIGURE 9.3 Long-Term Capital Dashboard

itability, asset turnover, and return on equity. Goodwill and intangibles are largely a function of acquisition activity and the effectiveness of the acquisition process, including the evaluation, valuation, and integration of acquisitions. Companies should estimate the economic impact of retaining excess levels of cash and other underperforming assets and consider this in their evaluation of these assets.

QUESTIONS FOR CONSIDERATION

1. Does your company have an effective process for evaluating and monitoring capital investments?
2. Does your company retain excess cash? What is the estimated economic cost of this policy?
3. How have acquisitions impacted asset levels and key measures, including asset turnover, ROA, and ROIC?

CHAPTER 10

Cost of Capital and the Intangibles

The cost of capital is a significant determinant of shareholder value. It is the rate used by investors to discount future cash flows, as shown in Figure 10.1. For investors who value companies using multiples of earnings or sales, it is one of the implicit assumptions made in selecting the multiple to use. Value is inversely related to the cost of capital. As the cost of capital declines the value of the firm will increase, and vice versa.

Cost of capital can have a significant impact on the value of a firm. Figure 10.2 plots the relationship between cost of capital and enterprise value for Simple Co. based on the DCF model used in Chapter 3.

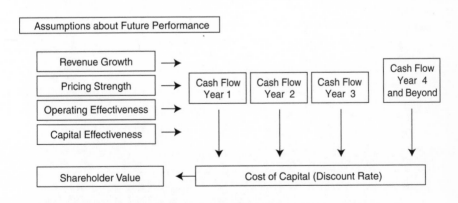

FIGURE 10.1 Discounted Cash Flow (DCF)

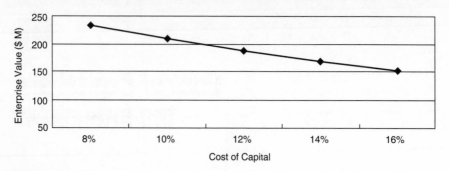

FIGURE 10.2   Cost of Capital—Value Sensitivity

A key concept underlying the cost of capital is the relationship be-tween risk and return. We all recognize that unless a riskier investment was expected to have a higher potential return than a safer one, we would sim-ply invest in the safer investment. For example, few sensible people would invest in a start-up company that was expected to return a rate close to the risk-free rate on U.S. Treasury bonds. Most would invest in the much safer investment providing a similar return. We all would expect a risk premium for the higher-risk start-up investment. This risk-return trade-off is pic-tured in Figure 10.3.

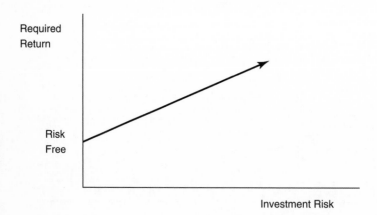

FIGURE 10.3   Risk and Return

COST OF CAPITAL DRIVERS

The cost of capital for a firm is driven by a number of factors, as illustrated in Figure 10.4, including interest rates, equity or market premium, financial and operating leverage, volatility, and risk.

Market Interest Rates

The starting point in determining the cost of capital is typically the risk-free rate of return. Investors have the opportunity to invest in an essentially risk-free investment, U.S. Treasury notes. This risk-free rate will form the baseline for setting required rates of return for alternative investments with progressively higher risks.

Market Premium

Equity investors expect to earn a premium over the risk-free rate to compensate for the additional risk inherent in all stocks. This is commonly referred to as the market premium or market risk premium.

Cost of capital is the rate used to discount estimated future cash flows.
Shareholder value can be increased by reducing the cost of capital.

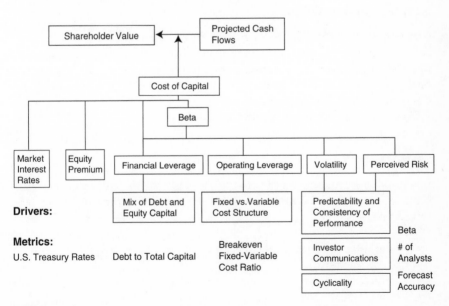

FIGURE 10.4 Cost of Capital Drivers

Financial Leverage

Another significant driver of the cost of capital for a firm is the mix of capital used to run the business. Typically, the cost of debt is lower than the cost of equity, as interest rates are generally well below expected rates of return on equity investments. In addition, the cost of debt is reduced by the related tax savings, since interest expense is a deduction in computing taxable income for corporations.

Operating Leverage

Operating leverage refers to the composition of costs and expenses for a company and was covered in detail in Chapter 4. A firm that has most of its costs fixed in the short term is said to have a high degree of operating leverage. A change in sales levels will have a dramatic effect on profits for this firm, since most of its costs are fixed. By contrast, a company with lower operating leverage has a greater portion of its cost structure as variable. That is, if sales decline, the variable costs will also be reduced. The firm with high operating leverage will experience greater fluctuations in profits and cash flows for a given change in sales, leading to a higher level of volatility and perceived risk.

Volatility and Variability

Companies that have unpredictable or inconsistent business results typically are valued at a discount to companies with predictable and consistent operating performance. Investors using multiples to value a highly volatile business will use a lower multiple of sales or earnings. Investors who use discounted cash flow will use a higher weighted average cost of capital (WACC) to discount future projected cash flows.

Perceived Risk

Investors will demand returns commensurate with the risk level they perceive in a business. Examples of additional factors leading to higher perceived risk:

- Geographical, for example developing countries or unstable regions.
- Currency exposure.
- Competitive pressure.
- Technological obsolescence.
- Management departures.

ESTIMATING THE COST OF CAPITAL

The most common method used to estimate the cost of capital is the weighted average cost of capital (WACC) method. This method is also known as the capital asset pricing model (CAPM). The WACC methodology computes a blended or weighted cost of capital, considering that capital is often supplied to the firm in various forms. The most common are equity, provided by shareholders, and debt, provided by bondholders. In addition, there are many other forms that combine elements of both debt and equity. Examples of these hybrid securities include preferred stock and convertible bonds. It is important to emphasize that the cost of capital represents an estimate or approximation. Recognizing this, we should test the inputs to the WACC formula and use sensitivity analysis to understand the impact of these assumptions on the valuation of a company.

WACC Computation

The steps to compute the weighted average cost of capital (WACC) are:

1. Estimate the cost of equity.
2. Estimate the cost of debt.
3. Weight the cost of equity and debt to compute the WACC.

The following information will be used to illustrate the WACC computation:

Current risk-free rate on U.S. Treasury notes	4.0%
Historical market premium for stocks (over risk-free rate)	5.5%
Beta	1.09
Market value of debt	$10.0 million
Market value of equity	$90.0 million
Yield to maturity on debt	6%
Tax rate	40%

Step 1: Estimate the Cost of Equity   The cost of equity represents the estimated return expected by shareholders and potential shareholders. Three components are considered: the risk-free rate, the premium expected for equity investments (market premium), and risk attributable to the specific

company (beta). The cost of equity for this firm would be computed as follows:

$$\text{Cost of Equity} = \text{Risk-Free Rate} + (\text{Beta} \times \text{Market Premium})$$
$$= 4.0\% + (1.09 \times 5.5\%) = 10.0\%$$

Step 2: Estimate the Cost of Debt Since interest expense is generally tax deductible, the cost of debt is reduced by the tax savings and is computed as follows:

$$\text{Cost of Debt} = \text{Yield to Maturity} \times (1 - \text{Tax Rate})$$
$$= 6\% \times (1 - 40\%)$$
$$= 3.6\%$$

Step 3: Weight the Cost of Equity and Debt to Compute WACC

	Cost	Market Value	%	Weighting
Debt	3.6%	$ 10,000	10%	.0036
Equity	10.0%	$ 90,000	90%	.0900
		$100,000	100%	.0936

$$\text{WACC} = 9.36\%$$

Figure 10.5 provides a visual of how these elements come together in the WACC computation. Investors who purchase equity securities expect a premium over returns obtainable from risk-free securities (U.S. Treasury notes). This market premium results in an expected return for the market (e.g., S&P 500) in Figure 10.5 just above 10 percent. The cost of capital for a particular

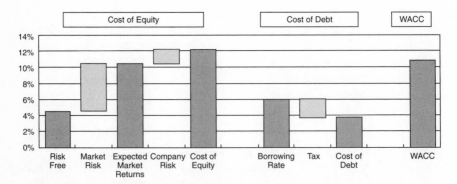

FIGURE 10.5 WACC Visual Summary

security is then computed by adding a premium for the risk of investing in an individual security. The cost of equity is then blended with the after-tax cost of debt to estimate the weighted average cost of capital.

Since the cost of debt is typically lower than the cost of equity, it is easy to conclude that some blend of debt and equity would result in a lower cost of capital than all equity. The combination of debt and equity that results in the lowest cost of capital is called the optimal capital structure. This concept is illustrated in Figure 10.6. A firm with no debt will have a WACC equal to the cost of equity. As the firm adds debt to the mix, the WACC will be reduced to a point. At some point the increased risk associated with high borrowings will increase the required interest rates and will also increase the required cost of equity. The combined effects will increase the WACC above the minimum level projected at the optimal capital structure.

Most firms do not operate at or near the optimal capital structure, however. There are a number of reasons for this. First, some managers do not fully accept the concept of discounted cash flow/cost of capital or WACC. Others are very conservative and are opposed to the risk introduced by using or increasing debt. Even some managers who accept the basic concept nevertheless choose not to add leverage, or will add reasonable levels of debt that leave them far short of the theoretical optimal capital structure. Typically companies will set a target capital structure, expressed as a range of debt to total capital, for example 30 to 40 percent. Figure 10.7

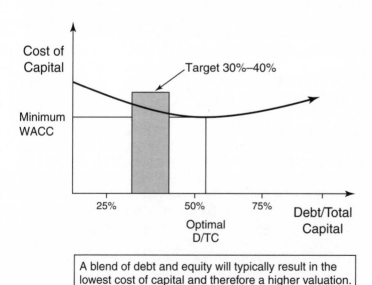

A blend of debt and equity will typically result in the lowest cost of capital and therefore a higher valuation.

FIGURE 10.6 Optimal Cost of Capital and Capital Structure

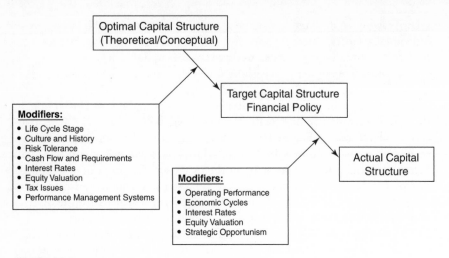

FIGURE 10.7 Capital Structure and Financial Policy

captures some of the factors that influence decision makers in setting a target capital structure. Tolerance for risk, life cycle stage, and cash flow requirements are a few examples. Firms will then often deviate from this target capital structure for several reasons. For example, they may choose to exceed the target range to finance a strategic opportunity such as an acquisition. Typically, the corporation would plan to return to the target range within a couple of years or reset the range to a higher level.

KEY WAYS MANAGERS CAN REDUCE THE COST OF CAPITAL

Some of the factors that determine cost of capital are out of the firm's control. For example, market interest rates are the foundation for estimating cost of capital. Unless you have influence over the general economy or inflation or are the chairman of the Federal Reserve Board, there is little managers can do about interest rates. Managers can influence a number of other factors. Here are some specific actions managers can take to reduce the cost of capital (see also sidebar, "Key Ways Operating Managers Can Influence Perceived Risk"):

- First, managers can reduce surprises and volatility, which will result in a lower beta and cost of capital and therefore higher valuation. Managers should strive to improve the predictability and consistency of business performance for several reasons. In addition to reducing surprises and volatility that affect the cost of capital, improvements in this area will result in lower working capital requirements and operating costs.

- Second, managers can consider using a reasonable level of debt in the capital structure. Utilizing a sensible level of debt provides leverage to equity investors and reduces the cost of capital. The level of debt should be lower than theoretical borrowing capacity, to provide for a cushion to service this debt during a business downturn or unforeseen future challenges.
- Third, managers can improve communications with investors. To the extent that investors have a full understanding of the business performance and potential they will likely have a better perspective on the business. This better understanding and perspective will result in reducing potential overreactions to expected variations in business performance.

THE INTANGIBLES

The term *intangibles* describes two sets of factors or issues. The first is the accounting definition, which is discussed in detail in Chapter 9. The accounting definition refers to intangible assets recorded on the balance sheet. These assets typically include trademarks, patents, and goodwill arising from acquisitions. These assets are valued using a number of different methods. In the case of goodwill, it simply represents the excess of the purchase price over the estimated value of tangible assets of an acquired company. Intangibles arising from acquisition accounting are discussed in Chapter 12.

The second use of the term *intangibles* refers to certain factors or assets that impact the performance and value of the firm, but may be very difficult to directly account for or value. Examples include the reputation, abilities, and experience of management; brand names; and the strength of

---

KEY WAYS OPERATING MANAGERS CAN INFLUENCE PERCEIVED RISK

- Utilize a reasonable level of debt in the capital structure.
- Reduce surprises and volatility:
  - Improve predictability and consistency of performance.
  - Reduce operating leverage by having a greater portion of variable costs.
- Improve communications with investors.

key management processes such as strategic and operational planning and people development. Many of these soft, intangible factors are considered by investors in estimating the cost of capital for DCF valuations. These factors also play a significant role in determining the multiple to be applied to sales or earnings.

Many of these factors should be considered directly in the valuation process. For example, a strong brand name certainly has value. But this value will be realized only if the company uses the brand name to sustain and grow sales, profits, and cash flow in the future. Strong brand names and market reputation should be one of many factors considered in estimating future sales levels.

Management

The depth and quality of management has a significant effect on the performance and value of the company. Key factors include integrity, experience, strategic thinking, a sense of urgency, focus on execution, ability to communicate effectively with customers and investors, and ability to recruit and retain a management team.

This is often very evident when a company announces the appointment of a new CEO. It is not uncommon for the price of a stock to soar 5 to 10 percent on the announcement that a prominent CEO with a strong track record is joining the company. This increase may translate to hundreds or even billions of dollars of market value. Is there a valid justification for the increase in value in these cases? The market anticipates that, based on the past track record of the manager, significant changes will be implemented that will result in improved financial performance. Could we test the reasonableness of the market reaction? Think of the key drivers of long-term value and the explicit assumptions required for the DCF model. Will the new CEO increase the estimated growth rates? Improve margins and working capital management? Reduce perceived risk? Utilize or return excess cash to shareholders? Do these potential changes support the increase in the stock price by increasing cash flows and the resultant DCF valuation?

Business Processes

Some business processes, such as supply chain management, have a direct impact on operating performance, including profitability and working capital requirements. Many others have an indirect impact on performance and value. Examples include the management and development of people, strategic and operational planning, corporate governance, and investor relations.

People and Organization Many successful companies have very effective processes to develop managers and build strong organizations. Key elements typically include effective recruitment, training, developmental assignments and rotations, performance evaluation, and succession planning. Companies that are effective in this area have a cadre of managers who are fully committed and capable of executing the firm's strategic and operational objectives.

Planning Developing effective strategic and operational planning processes provides a framework for decision making and management. An effective strategic planning process will assist managers in identifying threats and opportunities and ensure broad strategic goals are translated into implementation plans that can be acted upon and monitored. A strong operational planning process will provide a basis for monitoring key trends, developing appropriate business forecasts, and monitoring business performance.

Corporate Governance By establishing effective corporate governance practices, a firm can promote an environment with a focus on aligning the interests of the firm, managers, customers, and shareholders and provide assurance to key stakeholders that these practices are in place. A strong and independent board of directors, for example, will likely lead to the selection of an effective executive team, successor planning, and compensation practices. These in turn are likely to lead to appropriate motivation, behavior, and oversight in the development of strategy, management, and financial reporting practices. Conversely, a board of directors that does not have the appropriate independence or experience may provide less value to the firm and fail to create confidence among investors.

Investor Relations The investor relations activity is a critical function in all companies, whether informal in private companies or formal in publicly traded firms. Providing investors with historical financial results, analysis, and credible expectations for the future is essential for them to evaluate the performance of the company and their investment. Managers who communicate openly with investors about both challenges and opportunities build credibility with the "street" or private investors.

PERFORMANCE MEASURES

A number of measures can be tracked to provide insight into the firm's WACC and identify potential opportunities to reduce the cost of capital.

Financial Leverage: Debt to Total Capital

In Chapter 2, we reviewed key financial ratios that measure financial leverage and capital structure. The mix of debt and equity in the capital structure is an important variable in the cost of capital and valuation. For evaluating financial leverage, the measure is usually computed using book values:

$$\text{Debt to Total Capital} = \frac{\text{Interest-Bearing Debt}}{\text{Total of Interest-Bearing Debt and Equity}}$$

Stock Volatility/Beta

For a public company, the volatility of the company's stock price is an important indicator of the level of risk perceived by investors. Investors attempt to estimate the risk inherent in future performance and cash flows by looking at historical measures of stock volatility or beta. Stock volatility compares the change in the firm's stock price to the change in a broad market measure. Beta, which measures the correlation of an individual stock to the market as a whole, is available in many financial reporting services. Services use different time horizons to calculate beta and stock volatility, often going back several years. Since we want to track beta or stock volatility for the purpose of estimating a cost of capital for *future* performance, we must ensure that the historical measure is indicative of future performance. Care should be exercised in circumstances where significant changes have recently occurred, or are anticipated, in the company's market, strategic direction, or competitive environment. In these cases, managers and investors may focus on recent history or expected future stock price volatility or beta as a better indicator of current investor confidence and perceived risk.

Operating Leverage

In Chapter 4 we concluded that the mix of variable and fixed cost components has a significant impact on the earnings and cash flow of a firm as sales levels vary. Where sales volatility is likely, for example in cyclical businesses, managers should closely monitor and evaluate the cost structure of the company. Fixed cost levels or breakeven sales levels should be measured and evaluated periodically.

Forecast Accuracy

Preparing business forecasts is an important activity for most companies. These forecasts will be the basis for making important decisions and in investor communications. For many firms, future estimates of revenue are typically the most important and difficult operating variable to forecast. In Chapters 6 and 7, we presented a number of tools to monitor and evaluate the accuracy and effectiveness of forecasts. Forecast accuracy should also be reviewed in the context of the firm's cost of capital, since the predictability and consistency of operating performance will impact stock volatility.

DASHBOARD: COST OF CAPITAL AND INTANGIBLES

A dashboard for the cost of capital should be utilized, incorporating key performance indicators appropriate to the specific issues and priorities for each company. An illustrative cost of capital dashboard is presented in Figure 10.8.

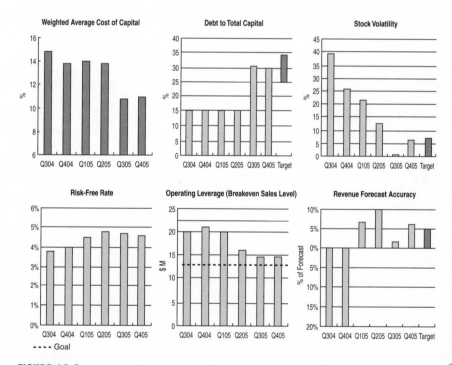

FIGURE 10.8 Cost of Capital Dashboard

SUMMARY

The cost of capital for a firm is a significant value driver. Cost of capital is inversely related to the firm's value. Managers should be aware of the sensitivity of the company's valuation to the cost of capital. Management can reduce the cost of capital, thereby increasing value, by reducing risk and volatility and by using an appropriate mix of debt and equity. Key factors impacting the firm's cost of capital should be identified and measured.

QUESTIONS FOR CONSIDERATION

1. What is the cost of capital for your company? How was it estimated? How sensitive is the company's valuation to estimated changes in the cost of capital?
2. Do your investors (public or private) perceive the company as a risky investment?
3. Have you considered potential actions to reduce the cost of capital?

Driving Performance and Value

CHAPTER 11

Building a Performance Management Framework

I n Chapters 1 through 4, we built a foundation for establishing key elements of a value-oriented performance management framework (PMF). In Chapter 5, we introduced the Value Performance Framework (VPF) and the concept of creating performance dashboards and identifying opportunities to build shareholder value. In Chapters 6 through 10, we reviewed each value driver in detail, exploring the link between each value driver and critical business processes and identifying measures that would provide objective visibility into performance in each of these areas.

In this chapter, we return to the subject of establishing a performance management framework to create shareholder value. Topics include guidance for implementing a performance management framework and identifying best practices and mistakes to avoid.

OBJECTIVE OF A PERFORMANCE MANAGEMENT FRAMEWORK

The objective of a performance management framework is to provide a systematic way of measuring progress on strategic initiatives and performance on key value drivers. A successful PMF will increase visibility into critical areas of business performance and allow managers to assign and enforce accountability for performance. With an effective framework, managers and employees will understand how their activities relate to operating and financial performance, and ultimately, the value of the company. It should also provide early detection of unfavorable events and trends, such as manufacturing problems, competitive threats, and product performance issues.

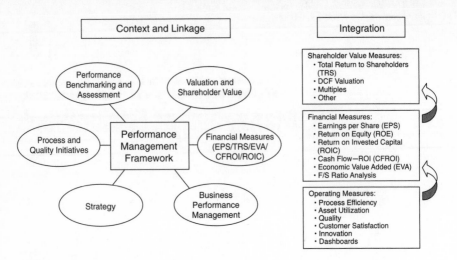

FIGURE 11.1 The Measurement Challenge: Creating Context and Effectively Integrating Value, Financial, and Operational Measures

THE MEASUREMENT CHALLENGE

Figure 11.1 highlights the key challenges that managers encounter when implementing performance measures. The single most important factor for achieving success with a PMF is to create context for the measurement system. This is achieved by creating linkage among strategy, performance management, process and quality initiatives, financial performance, and shareholder value. It is also critical to integrate and link operating measures to financial measures and then ultimately to drivers of shareholder value. Too often, these measures are viewed as unrelated or even conflicting variables. The time spent in establishing this linkage will improve understanding and ultimately the effectiveness of the PMF.

Creating the proper context and integration with other elements of the management system will also ensure that managers and employees will not view this project as just another "flavor of the month." This is not a short-term initiative; instead it will be integrated into the core of the company's management systems.

THE IMPLEMENTATION PROCESS

Most companies use performance measures. However, in many cases, measures are put in place without developing the appropriate context.

Figure 11.2 highlights a four-step, systematic process for building an effective performance management framework leading to the maximization of shareholder value.

Step 1: Create Context: Determine Strategic Initiatives, Identify Value Drivers, and Assess Performance

Strategic Initiatives Effective managers have a short list of essential projects and programs that are critical to executing the strategic plan and achieving the long-term goals of the company. Examples of key strategic initiatives may be the introduction of a series of new products, the establishment of a distribution channel, or significant reduction of manufacturing costs for improving profitability and price competitiveness. These strategic initiatives should be documented and fully integrated into the development of a performance management system.

Assess Performance Before proceeding with the selection of performance measures it is important to complement the strategic focus with an objective

Steps

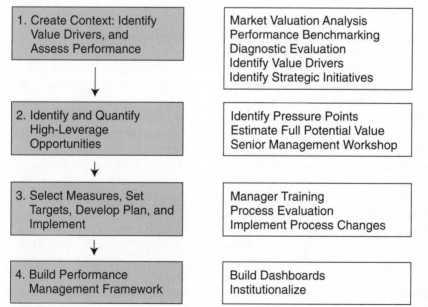

FIGURE 11.2 VPF Implementation Overview

assessment of the company's performance. The assessment can begin with the performance evaluation introduced in Chapter 2. It should include a review of financial performance and recent trends as illustrated for Simple Co. in Table 2.7. While this analysis contains a great deal of useful information on the financial performance of the company, it will be more useful if key elements are summarized in graphical form as shown in Figure 2.3. The evaluation should also include benchmarking key elements of operating, financial, and value measures against a peer group and to best-practice companies.

Benchmarking Performance   In Chapter 4, we discussed important elements of benchmarking, including the selection of companies to include in the benchmark group. The selection of companies to be included in the benchmark group is very important. Many managers limit benchmarking to a peer group of similar companies or competitors. The potential for learning can be greatly increased if the universe of companies in the benchmark is expanded as shown in Figure 4.1, "Expanded Benchmark View." A one-page summary of benchmark results is illustrated in Figure 5.6, providing managers the ability to compare critical elements of their company's financial performance and valuation to competitors, customers, as well as most-admired and best-practice companies.

However, limiting the benchmarking to top-level measures has a number of shortcomings. While it does identify gaps and differences, it stops short of providing insight behind the numbers. Without an understanding of the business practices and other factors, it provides limited benefit. For example, it is useful to observe that Dell Inc. turns inventory nearly 100 times per year. But just how does Dell do that? Are there best practices here that can be considered for use in your company?

Two additional steps will greatly enhance the value of benchmarking performance. The first is to climb under the numbers to understand the practices and drivers of firms included in the benchmark. This requires a detailed knowledge of the market, business model, processes, and practices of the firm. For example, Dell's performance in inventory management is a result of creating a breakthrough business model with significant attention to managing the supply chain, order fulfillment, and distribution processes. Much has been written and published about best practices at Dell and other companies. Many best-practice companies have been open about sharing the methods they employ to achieve breakthrough performance in a particular area. In addition, numerous consulting firms have developed practices in this area or offer training courses in implementing best practices in various business processes, including supply chain and revenue processes. Various trade and professional associations also sponsor benchmarking studies. By comparing your performance to that of competitors as well as best-practice companies, it is possible to identify gaps in your performance that represent significant opportunities to increase shareholder value. Understanding the best practices that lead to extraordinary performance provides a road map to closing these performance gaps.

The second way to enhance the value of the benchmarking assessment is to collect operating and process measures for your firm that provide insight into high-level financial and operating measures. For example, to better understand sales growth relative to competitors, it would be helpful to examine key performance indicators for this driver. These measures, covered in Chapter 6, will frame the assessment of performance and identify specific opportunities for actionable improvement. A sample collection sheet for selected measures relating to revenue growth is shown in Table 11.1. Preliminary dashboards and analysis can then be created from this data to assist with understanding the performance on each driver.

Drilling down into the performance of each value driver will assist the team in understanding and evaluating current financial performance and in establishing the preliminary performance targets. It is also important to recognize that each variable is not independent of the others. For example, increasing the growth rate in revenues may require increased spending in R&D and selling expense, which may impact profitability. It may not be desirable (or possible) to achieve top-quartile performance on each variable. The key focus should be on long-term shareholder value and key metrics such as growth and return on invested capital (ROIC). The targets for each variable (e.g., sales growth, margins, etc.) should be developed in the context of an overall target business model.

Market Valuation Analysis   In Chapter 3, we described the process for fully understanding and analyzing the recent valuation history of the company. In order to create a linkage between the day-to-day activities of the employees of the company and the company's share value, we created a discounted cash flow (DCF) model for the company in Table 3.1. We first input several years of historical performance as a baseline, and then projected future performance. The projections should be realistic and should be reviewed against the recent historical trends experienced by the firm.

If the firm is publicly traded, the preliminary valuation can be tested against the current stock price. If the value indicated by the DCF model is significantly different from the recent trading range of the stock, one or more of your assumptions may be inconsistent with the assumptions in the investing marketplace. Identifying and testing the critical assumptions made by investors in valuing the firm's stock can be very enlightening. Are assumptions made by investors consistent with your own targets for

TABLE 11.1 Performance Measure Collection Worksheets: Revenue Growth

Simple Co.	2003		2004				2005			
	Q3	Q4	Q1	Q2	Q3	Q4	Q1	Q2	Q3	Q4
Revenue $	21	26	18	18.7	21	28	20	20	22	30.6
Seq growth		24%	-31%	4%	12%	33%	-29%	0%	10%	39%
Y/Y Growth					0%	8%	11%	7%	5%	9%
Year		79.4				85.7				92.6
Y/Y Growth						8%				8%
Lost Orders										
#	15	16	14	12	11	15	11	7	6	5
$	1.2	1.5	2	1.5	1.7	1.8	0.5	0.9	1.5	1.2
% of Sales	5.7%	5.8%	11.1%	8.0%	8.1%	6.4%	2.5%	4.5%	6.8%	3.9%
Lost Customers										
#	15	16	14	12	11	15	11	7	6	5
$	1.3	1.7	2	1	4	2	3	1.5	0.8	1.8
% of Sales	6.2%	6.5%	11.1%	5.3%	19.0%	7.1%	15.0%	7.5%	3.6%	5.9%
New Product Sales	3	2	2	2	2	3.5	3.8	3.9	4.5	4.7
% of Total	14%	8%	11%	11%	10%	13%	19%	20%	20%	15%
New Customer Sales	2	2.5	3	3.2	3	3.5	3.6	3.8	2.2	0.5
% of Total	10%	10%	17%	17%	14%	13%	18%	19%	10%	2%
On-Time Delivery %	88%	75%	89%	91%	84%	87%	91%	92%	91%	89%
Past Due Orders $	1.7	2.2	3.2	2.8	2.7	2.5	2.6	2.3	2.1	1.9

Customer Concentration Trend

	2003		2004		2005	
	Customer	**$**	**Customer**	**$**	**Customer**	**$**
1	Goliath	11.0	Goliath	12.0	Goliath	12.6
2	DEG	10.5	DEG	11.0	DEG	12.0
3	XYZ	5.6	XYZ	7.0	XYZ	9.0
4	PQR	4.8	PQR	5.0	PQR	8.0
5	MNO	2.2	MNO	3.0	MNO	7.0
6	Upstart	1.1	Upstart	1.2	Upstart	1.3
7	HIJ	0.8	HIJ	0.9	HIJ	4.0
8	TUV	0.7	TUV	0.8	TUV	3.0
9	RST	0.6	RST	0.8	RST	2.0
10	ZAB	0.5	ZAB	0.7	ZAB	1.0
Total	0	37.8	0	42.3	0	59.9
% Total Revenue		47.6%		49.4%		64.7%

Historical Revenue

1995	1996	1997	1998	1999	2000	2001	2002	2003	2004	2005
57	58	60	62	63	64	68	73.5	79.4	85.7	92.6

CAGR

2-Year	8.0%
3-Year	8.0%
5-Year	7.7%
10-Year	5.0%

performance? Why or why not? The DCF model will also allow you to eas-ily change key assumptions and observe the potential impact on the value of the stock. It is useful to iterate key assumptions until you can achieve a valuation consistent with recent market values for your company. For firms that are not publicly traded, this process can be performed for comparable firms that are in the same industry. Growth rates, other key drivers, and valuation metrics can then be applied to the private firm.

Since there are a number of critical assumptions, for example revenue growth and profitability, you may want to create multiple projection sce-narios that result in the current value of the company. A very useful tool for representing the outcomes of this analysis is a sensitivity chart, such as the example shown in Table 11.2. This particular chart estimates the stock price at various combinations of assumptions for profitability and sales growth.

Identify Key Value Drivers   Prior to selecting measures to include on per-formance dashboards, we need to identify key value drivers. Once the DCF model and sensitivity analysis have been completed, the relative impor-tance of each driver can be determined. Is increasing sales growth more im-portant to value than improving profitability or working capital? This insight can be integrated with the findings from the performance assess-ment described above.

The DCF model allows managers to evaluate potential improvement projects and other high-leverage opportunities to increase value. Too often, companies or functional managers embark on initiatives to improve certain aspects of the business without fully considering their impact on value cre-ation. Will these projects be worth the investment of time and financial

TABLE 11.2   DCF Value Sensitivity Analysis: Simple Co. Stock Price

| Operating Income | Sales Growth Rate | | | | |
	4%	6%	8%	10%	12%
20.0%	$12.11	$13.49	$15.04	$16.80	$18.77
17.5	10.52	11.68	13.00	14.49	16.17
15.0	8.92	9.88	10.96	12.18	13.56
12.5	7.33	8.08	8.92	9.87	10.95
10.0	5.74	6.27	6.88	7.57	8.34

resources? This framework allows managers to estimate the impact of various programs on shareholder value.

Step 2: Identify and Value (Quantify) High-Leverage Improvement Opportunities

After validating and revising performance targets based on preliminary assessments of operating activities and processes, the team should then consider the targets in the context of shareholder value. By entering key performance targets into our discounted cash flow (DCF) model, we can estimate the market value of the company if these targets are achieved and maintained. The relative significance of each variable can be estimated by changing each variable in the DCF model individually and recording the increase in value.

Based on the performance assessment described earlier, the management team can begin to set preliminary goals and targets. Table 11.3 provides a simple but effective benchmark summary and target-setting worksheet. In this summary, key elements of Simple Co.'s financial performance are compared to benchmark results, including average, top quartile, and best in class. It may also be useful to include, as done here, a column for best practice or wild card to highlight exceptional performance in each measure. This analysis can lead to productive discussions to evaluate the company's performance on an objective basis and provide a basis for establishing credible targets for future performance.

TABLE 11.3 Benchmarking Summary and Target Worksheet

	Simple Co.	Median	Top Quartile	Best in Class	Best Practice	Performance Target
Revenue Growth	8.0%	8.0%	12.0%	15.0%	25.0%	12.0%
Gross Margin %	55.0%	52.0%	56.0%	60.0%		56.0%
Operating Expenses	40.0%	40.0%	38.0%	35.0%		38.0%
Operating Margins	15.0%	12.0%	18.0%	20.0%	25.0%	18.0%
Tax Rate	34.0%	30.0%	25.0%	15.0%	10.0%	25.0%
Operating Capital % Sales	30.0%	25.0%	15.0%	10.0%	15.0%	15.0%
WACC	11.99%	10.59%	10.13%	9.77%	9.07%	10.0%
Cost of Equity	12.4%	11.3%	11.0%	10.7%	9.8%	11.0%
Beta	1.24	1.05	1.00	0.95	0.80	1.00
Debt to Total Capital						
Book	15.3%	30.0%	40.0%	50.0%	50.0%	50.0%
Market	5.3%	10.0%	13.3%	16.7%	16.7%	16.7%

Utilizing the input from the business process assessment and benchmarking comparisons, managers can estimate the potential improvements in the value drivers and quantify the potential value of the firm if the targeted performance is achieved, as illustrated in Table 11.4.

In this case, Simple Co. has set preliminary performance targets to achieve top-quartile performance in each key measure. This may be a good place to start, but requires additional vetting. The targets should be refined by evaluating processes and operating effectiveness and testing the relative impact on value creation to develop a target business model. This exercise is not meaningful unless the team has a plan for how these improvements will be achieved.

A graphic presentation of this analysis is shown in Figure 11.3. Note

TABLE 11.4   Summary of Full Potential Value ($ Millions)

Simple Co.	From	To	Enterprise Value	Increment	How?
Current Value			$196.4		Current performance expectations
Increase Sales Growth Rate	8%	12%	241.0	$44.6	Improve quality and on-time delivery
Improve Gross Margin %	55	56	259.0	18.0	Reduce material costs
Reduce Operating Expenses	40	38	294.0	35.0	Process initiatives
Reduce Tax Rate	34	25	338.0	44.0	Tax benefits from new manufacturing facility
Reduce Operating Capital %	30	15	352.0	14.0	Improve supply chain and revenue process
Reduce WACC	12%	10%	389.0	37.0	Improve forecasting and change capital structure

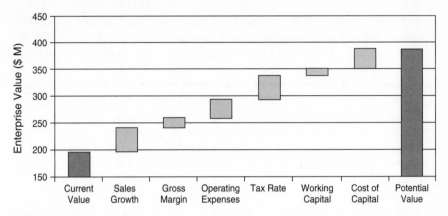

FIGURE 11.3   Full Potential Enterprise Value: Simple Co.

the significant increase in enterprise value from a current level of $196 million to a full potential value of approximately $389 million.

Step 3: Develop Key Measures, Set Targets, and Develop Improvement Programs

Projecting improved performance on spreadsheets is very easy. Achieving these improvements in actual results requires substantial planning, effort, and follow-through. Central to achieving these performance goals is the selection and development of effective performance measures.

Develop Appropriate Measures   After documenting the key strategic issues and initiatives, assessing performance, and setting improvement goals in the context of value creation, we can begin to select the measures that will be important for monitoring performance and progress across the company. What measures will track our progress in achieving strategic objectives and goals for value creation? What are the critical elements of my business that I want to see on a daily, weekly, monthly, or quarterly basis? What measures will serve as leading indicators to alert us to potential problems in time to make meaningful adjustments? Guidelines for selecting and developing performance measures include:

- *Objectivity*. To the extent possible, performance measures should be quantifiable and objective. Qualitative assessments are necessary in certain cases. However, care must be taken to promote objectivity and to complement qualitative assessments with quantitative measures.

- *Measurement definitions.* Specific definitions must be developed and documented for each measure. For example, what is the definition of on-time delivery to customers? Is it the date that *we committed* to delivery or the date the *customer originally requested*? Since this measure is an important part of customer satisfaction, we should view this measure through the eyes of the customer. Definition of performance measures is important and must be consistent with the objective of the measure. These definitions should be documented and approved by management.
- *Data integrity.* Implementing a PMF without having the ability to generate performance measures and dashboards that present accurate data may be worse than not having a PMF at all. It is fairly typical for a company to encounter problems with data accuracy as it begins to use performance measures. In fact, this is a side benefit of the process, improving the accuracy of reported data. Each measure should be defined and approved by the appropriate managers. Data entry and processing codes can be improved over time. It is a good idea to have performance measures reviewed by internal audit teams or the controller's staff to ensure the integrity of the measurement system.
- *Balance.* Performance measures should be balanced to reduce the risk of optimizing performance in one area at the expense of the long-term health and value of the organization. For example, if inventory turnover is selected as a key performance measure without a balancing measure such as on-time deliveries, it may result in reductions in inventory at the expense of customer satisfaction. By balancing the two measures, the company will promote the development of healthy process improvements that lead to improvement in both measures.
- *Timeliness.* Performance measures and dashboards must be available on a timely basis. This requires that systems and databases be maintained and updated on a current basis. This is generally not a problem for the primary business systems, but can be a problem in areas such as entering or updating sales leads or warranty experience.
- *Emphasis on leading indicators of performance.* The systematic approach outlined in this chapter will provide confidence that the performance measures will be predictive of future operating and financial performance. More attention should be paid to measuring and improving the leading indicators of performance. For example, if a company sets a target of improving DSO from 75 to 55 days, it must develop targets and measure performance on leading indicators such as revenue linearity, quality, and collections.

Enable Managers and Employees   After selecting and developing the performance measures, it is important to provide managers and employees with appropriate training and other tools to use the measures and make performance improvements.

Training The effectiveness of a performance management system and related initiatives will be greatly enhanced if accompanied by manager and employee training. The value in the Value Performance Framework is in connecting the dots between operating performance, financial performance, and value creation. A comprehensive training program for managers and executives should include the following topics:

- Fundamentals of finance.
- Valuation and value drivers.
- Linking value to performance.
- Building shareholder value.
- Effective use of performance measures.

The training should be tailored to various levels within the organization. The core concepts can be modified to be appropriate to the executive team, midlevel managers, and other employees.

Process Improvement Tools In order to achieve improvements in performance in critical areas and measures, managers and employees must be provided with tools to evaluate and improve key business processes. In Chapter 8, we reviewed examples of process evaluation tools for the revenue and supply chain management processes. In addition, there are a number of very useful process evaluation and quality management tools that work across all business processes, including six sigma and Total Quality Management (TQM).

Delivery Mechanism Many software vendors have developed and are refining products that will deliver key performance indicators and financial results in real time to designated managers throughout the organization. These are effective long-term solutions in many cases. However, companies sometimes become bogged down in attempting to use these technology tools. Often, the introduction of the software solution is done without the process outlined in steps 1 and 2. The performance measures and dashboards that are developed in this way often fail to fully achieve the objectives of implementing a PMF. In addition, the implementation is often delayed until the technology is procured and installed. In some cases, valuable time is lost in critical performance areas.

While generally not a good long-term solution, many companies begin producing dashboards on spreadsheet tools such as Microsoft Excel. The advantage in this approach is that a few key dashboards can be produced in days, rather than weeks or months. This can be a good way to get started, especially in situations where improving business performance is a matter of urgency, for example in a business turnaround situation. Long-term technology solutions can then be put in place as time permits.

Setting Targets   Realistic performance targets should be set for each measure that will lead to the achievement of strategic objectives and goals for value creation. This should be done by cascading the broad goals for value creation and performance down to the value drivers and individual process and activity measures. Setting targets must also consider the improvement opportunities identified in the process assessments.

Step 4: Build the Performance Management Framework

After evaluating performance, identifying value drivers, and selecting appropriate measures, management can develop performance dashboards and integrate or institutionalize these with existing management processes.

Create Performance Dashboards   Having provided managers with an understanding of the key value drivers for the firm and having identified the key processes and activities that are vital to improving business performance, we must build a reporting mechanism to provide insight into these critical activities. It is essential to provide managers and all employees with critical information about the health of the business and the effectiveness of the activities in which they participate. And if performance improvement is to be achieved, information must be provided consistently and in a timely manner relative to the activity.

Managers have two key decisions to address in implementing dashboards across the organization. The first issue is to determine what dashboards should be developed. Beyond the corporate-level dashboard, it will also be appropriate to have dashboards for various processes, divisions, functions, and departments. Many managers and employees also develop their own personal dashboards. The second issue is to determine the frequency for each dashboard. In some cases, for example at the corporate level, it may be appropriate to establish annual, quarterly, monthly, and weekly dashboards. Each of these dashboards would contain different measures appropriate to the measurement intervals.

Corporate or Division Summary   The corporate dashboard, introduced in Chapter 5, is the most critical dashboard. Figure 11.4 illustrates a quarterly

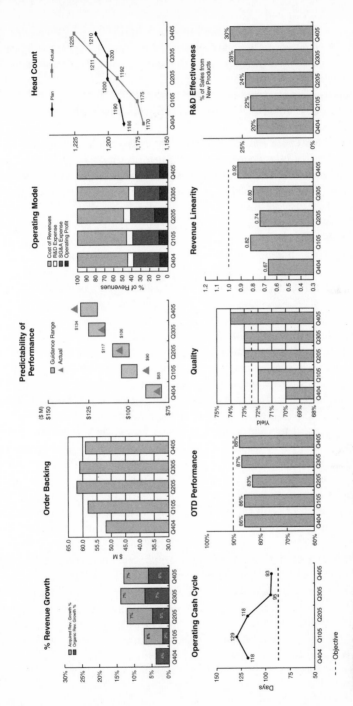

FIGURE 11.4 Quarterly Corporate Dashboard

corporate dashboard. Selecting the most important 8 to 12 measures that capture the key performance variables for the company is both important and difficult. Managers must ensure that all key value drivers are represented. All other dashboards should be developed to support the corporate-level summary. The corporate dashboard should be supported at the functional or department level, process level, and even individual level.

Function or Department Dashboard   Dashboards should be developed for functional areas and departments such as information technology, finance, and human resources. These dashboards must support the corporate objectives and be consistent with the dashboards established for processes that the function leads or serves.

Process Dashboard   Process dashboards were introduced in Chapters 6 through 9. Since business performance and financial performance are largely the result of critical business processes, these are the most critical supporting dashboards. Examples of key business processes include:

- Revenue process.
- Supply chain management.
- New product development.
- Mergers and acquisitions.

Individual Dashboards   In some cases, an individual's dashboard may correspond to a process, functional, or corporate dashboard. For example, the CEO can look at the corporate dashboard as his or her personal dashboard. Similarly, a vice president of R&D may choose the new product development dashboard. Other individuals may develop dashboards that include performance measures that cover critical activities within their responsibility. Care must be exercised to ensure that these individual dashboards are consistent with the objectives and measures of the company and with the function or process to which the individual contributes.

Measurement Frequency   An important design consideration for any dashboard is to consider the optimum frequency for measuring performance and refreshing the dashboard contents. Some process and activity measures need to be monitored daily or continuously. Examples may include product yields from production processing in refinery or fabricating operations, order levels, or weather conditions. Other measures such as ROIC are typically measured at quarterly and annual intervals. Selecting the appropriate frequency for each measure is nearly as important as selecting the right measures.

Institutionalize: Integrate into Core Management Processes

In order to be effective, the performance measurement framework must be integrated with other key management processes and activities, including meetings, performance reviews, reporting, and planning.

Monthly and Quarterly Meetings Discussions at monthly and quarterly management meetings should center around the performance dashboards. All too often, these meetings drift away from critical performance objectives aided by long discussions around lengthy slide show presentations. If the team has developed the PMF by creating context and linking to strategic initiatives and value drivers, then the dashboards will provide visibility into performance in critical areas and programs. Managers can easily be held accountable to the performance tracked by these objective measures.

Manager Evaluation and Compensation Programs It is very unlikely that any performance management system will be completely successful unless it is integrated into the manager evaluation and compensation program. Performance objectives should be established for each manager that are consistent with achieving the company's goals for value creation and strategic and operational objectives. Incorporating the principles from the PMF into the evaluation of manager's performance will increase the effectiveness of the performance reviews and underscore the organization's commitment to performance management.

Management Reporting Monthly financial and management reports should be modified to focus on the key performance indicators selected in the PMF. Typical monthly reports include traditional financial statements, supporting schedules, and spreadsheets that are easily understood by accountants but are difficult for most nonfinancial managers and employees to understand and digest. Key trends or exceptions may be buried in the statements and are extremely difficult to identify or act on. More visual content (graphs) should replace pages of financial tables and reports. Focus should shift away from lagging financial results toward providing crisp, predictive indicators of future performance. The reports should also focus more attention on revenue drivers and analysis of external factors rather than the traditional measures of internal financial performance.

Annual and Strategic Planning Process Most companies develop strategic and annual operating plans each year. These activities will be greatly enhanced by incorporating the key elements of the VPF. What level of shareholder value is likely if the planned results are achieved? The financials included in the plan should not be a spreadsheet exercise, but rather they must be grounded by execution plans and projected levels of performance on key operating measures. For example, if a company plans to achieve improved inventory turnover in the future, this goal should be supported by a detailed plan and targets for key performance indicators that impact inventory levels, such as revenue linearity, production cycle times, past due deliveries, and forecasting accuracy. Each plan or alternative should be valued; that is, the team should estimate what the likely market value of the company will be if the plan is achieved. Is this an acceptable return to shareholders? Can we identify other actions that will enhance value?

Forecasting   Most companies spend a great deal of time forecasting business performance. In a successful PMF, companies place more emphasis on forecasting and tracking key performance measures that will result in achieving the financial projections. These managers recognize that it is easier to track progress and drive improvement to performance measures that will impact financial results rather than attempt to drive improvement directly to financial results.

Investor Communication   For both publicly traded and privately owned firms, communication with investors is a very important activity. Investors are intensely focused on company performance and the potential to create shareholder value. Investors appreciate managers who recognize that a broad set of drivers factors into long-term value creation. They fully understand that successful execution on key strategic initiatives and improvement on value drivers will lead to long-term shareholder returns. Investors applaud managers who are focused on execution and performance management, since they know that these are essential to value creation.

Executives running publicly traded companies should communicate the performance on key value drivers and related performance measures, not just focus on sales or EPS. Investors who use economic valuation methods such as DCF need inputs for sales and earnings growth as well as capital requirements and cost of capital. Even those investors using multiples of revenue or earnings must consider these factors in selecting an appropriate price-earnings (P/E) or revenue multiple to value the company. Presenting and emphasizing the long-term value drivers also encourages investors to focus less attention on short-term quarterly financial results.

Corporate Development   The corporate development function is typically responsible for mergers and acquisitions (M&A) activity within most companies. The M&A process and resultant deals are an important contributor or detractor to performance and value in many companies. For companies active in mergers and acquisitions, it is important that M&A activity be viewed as a process and that the key elements of the VPF be incorporated into the identification, evaluation, valuation, and integration of acquisitions. The economics of M&A are fully explored in Chapter 12.

Management Support   Few initiatives are successful in a company without the passion and support of the CEO and other members of the senior management team. Managers and employees are very adept at reading the level of commitment of leadership to any new project. Senior managers must support the project, both in word and in action. The CEO will drive the success of the PMF. Is she insisting on a review of dashboards at

PERFORMANCE MANAGEMENT

Critical success factors and best practices:

- Create context:
  - Shareholder value.
  - Strategic initiatives.
  - Evaluation of current performance and setting of rational goals.
  - Visibility into key performance drivers.
- High visual content.
- Performance measures: objective, measurable, predictive.
- Management driven:
  - Incorporated into management processes.
  - Integrate with performance appraisal and compensation systems.
- Provide tools:
  - Training.
  - Process improvement/best practice.
  - Delivery mechanism.

management meetings? Is she using the performance measures as a critical element of evaluating managers' performance?

The sidebar summarizes the critical success factors and best practices in performance management.

AVOIDING COMMON MISTAKES

A number of common mistakes limit or prevent the effectiveness of many performance management systems.

Don't Drive the Car by Staring at the Dashboard

You won't keep the car on the road if you focus only on the car's instrument panel. Look through the front and side windows, and check the rearview mirror. Pay attention to road conditions, traffic patterns, and aggressive drivers, as well as the dashboard. Similarly, pilots don't fly by staring at the instrument panel. They utilize their visual input, but also rely on intuition, feel, conditions, and other inputs. Get out of the office. Talk to employees, customers, and suppliers. Combine this input with your intuition and the objective information from the dashboards. Be prepared to modify the dashboard as business conditions evolve.

Don't Make It a Finance or Information Technology Project

Many projects fail because they are driven exclusively by finance or information technology (IT). In order to be successful, a PMF must be driven from the top and integrated into the fabric of the management systems. Functions such as finance and IT are critical in the development, implementation, and support of a PMF. However, in order to achieve buy-in across the organization, other functions should be active participants in the implementation process, including the selection of measures.

Protect Competitive and Nonpublic Information

Whereas it is generally a good thing to share information with managers and employees, companies must obviously consider the security and sensitivity of information. Not all employees need the same access to information, especially in certain highly sensitive areas such as customers and new products. In addition, publicly traded companies must ensure that "material nonpublic information" is not inadvertently revealed and then used as a basis for trading in the company's securities. Dashboards should be developed after considering relevant information security issues and policies.

Don't Use the Dashboards to Micromanage or Embarrass Employees

New information availability may encourage managers to take a pulse of the business and key activities too often. In addition, visibility into the performance of individuals can be embarrassing and can lead to resentment or undermining the objectives of the PMF. Managers need to strike a balance with regard to the depth and frequency of dashboard reviews and the need for visibility into individual performance versus some aggregated level.

SAMPLE DASHBOARDS FOR SELECTED INDUSTRIES

It is often helpful to think about key performance dashboards for businesses other than our own. What are the key value drivers and performance measures? These sample dashboards (shown in Figures 11.5 and 11.6) are focused on revenue, which is critical to any business. Note how these dashboards focus on leading indicators of performance such as critical assumptions and variables affecting revenue levels. These variables will always include external factors. For example, weather impacts each of these businesses and would be reflected in the revenue dashboard. Generally, lower temperatures and precipitation would have a negative impact on most businesses, but not on a ski resort or a retailer selling snow throwers or winter apparel.

SUMMARY

Many companies use performance measures. Few have achieved the full potential benefits that a well-designed and well-implemented performance

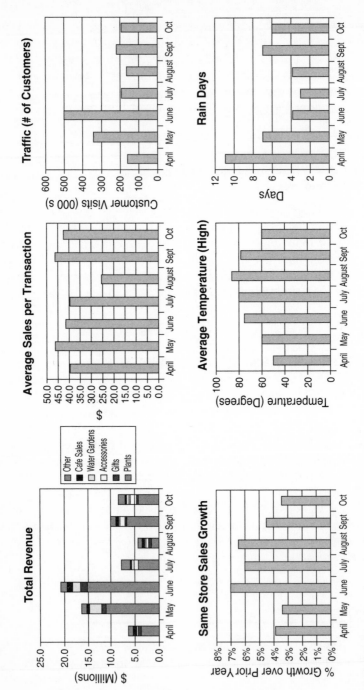

FIGURE 11.5 Dashboard for Specialty Retail: Lawn and Garden

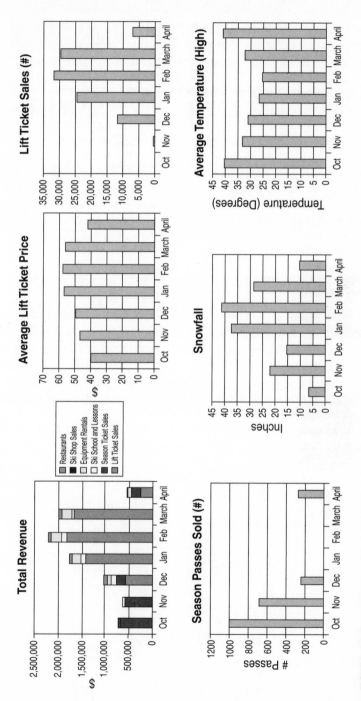

FIGURE 11.6 Dashboard for a Ski Resort

management framework has to offer. The objective of a PMF is to provide a systematic way of measuring progress on strategic initiatives and performance on key value drivers. A successful framework will increase visibility into critical areas of business performance and allow managers to assign and enforce accountability for performance. Managers and employees will understand how their activities relate to operating and financial performance and ultimately the value of the company.

The single most important factor for achieving success with a PMF is to create context for the measurement system. This is achieved by creating linkage among strategy, performance management, process and quality initiatives, financial performance, and shareholder value. It is also critical to integrate and link operating measures to financial measures and then to shareholder value measures. The time spent in establishing this linkage will improve understanding and ultimately the effectiveness of the framework.

QUESTIONS FOR CONSIDERATION

1. Have you assessed the company's performance by benchmarking and evaluating key business processes?
2. Have you identified the key drivers of shareholder value? What performance improvements would have the greatest impact on shareholder value?
3. Have key managers and employees been trained in the basics of finance, valuation, and performance measures?
4. Does the company utilize performance measures that support your strategic objectives and goals for value creation?

CHAPTER 12

The Economics of Mergers and Acquisitions

Managers and boards pursue acquisitions for many reasons. Understanding the rationale for an acquisition is a key element of evaluating a potential deal, assessing the likelihood of success, and determining the reasonableness of the deal price. Successful acquirers have a clear acquisition strategy that flows out of a well-defined corporate strategy. In addition, they typically have competencies in evaluating and valuing potential acquisitions, discipline in pricing deals, and managers with experience in integrating acquisitions. We focus on the economics of mergers and acquisitions (M&A) in this chapter.

THE ACQUISITION CHALLENGE

Many managers, academics, and advisers believe that it is difficult to create value through acquisitions. Research studies over the years consistently report a low percentage of acquisitions that are ultimately successful in creating value for the shareholders of the acquiring firm. The common mistakes that lead to these disappointments are discussed later in this chapter. Many companies do have successful acquisition programs that have resulted in building value for shareholders over a long period of time. The best practices that these companies employ are also discussed later in this chapter.

The stock market's reaction to proposed transactions can be informative. Following the announcement of a proposed transaction the price of the acquirer's stock will typically fall. In contrast, the price of a target's stock will generally rise to a price at or just under the announced acquisition price.

Why does the market react this way? The market typically reacts negatively to the acquiring firm's announcement for several reasons. First, investors recognize that acquirers generally are forced to pay a significant premium and that most deals do not build value for the shareholders of the acquiring firm. Second, they may feel that this specific deal is overpriced. Finally, they recognize that all the risk of implementing the combined strategy and integrating the two organizations is transferred to the acquiring firm. It is interesting to note that the market doesn't always react negatively to acquisition announcements, though. For companies with strong acquisition programs and track records, clear strategic rationale, and a reputation for disciplined pricing, the market price of the acquirer's stock may hold steady or even increase on news of a deal.

The price of the acquired company's stock will rise to approximate the proposed value of the deal. Since there is a good chance that the selling shareholders would receive the deal value at the time of closing, the price trades up toward that level. If, however, the market perceives significant risk that the deal will not be completed, for example due to expected difficulty in obtaining regulatory approvals, then the stock will trade at a discount to the proposed deal price. As impediments to the deal are removed, the stock will trade closer to the deal price. If the market is speculating that another potential buyer may make an offer for the target, the stock price may even rise above the announced deal value anticipating an offer from another bidder.

KEY ELEMENTS IN VALUING AN ACQUISITION

In valuing acquisitions, it is useful to identify and value two components: the value of the company to be acquired (the target) as a stand-alone company and the value of any potential synergies arising from the acquisition.

Stand-Alone Value

The stand-alone value is the worth of a company presuming that it continues to operate on a stand-alone or independent basis. Most publicly traded companies are valued on this basis, unless there are rumors or expectations that the company is a potential acquisition candidate. The stand-alone value is computed using the methodologies described in Chapter 3. We illustrate the M&A valuation concepts in this chapter building on the Simple Co. example. Table 3.1 presented the stand-alone DCF valuation for Simple Co.

Synergies

Synergies are a critical element in valuing acquisitions. Few companies will be sold on the basis of the value of that company on a stand-alone basis. Synergies are generally understood to result when the combined results exceed the sum of the independent parts. For purposes of this discussion, we will use synergies to mean the additional economic benefits that will be achieved by combining two companies. The term *economic benefit* is used here to emphasize that any synergy must be realizable in future cash flows to be relevant in valuation.

Synergies can take many forms. Common types of synergies include higher sales growth, reduced costs and expenses, financial benefits, and improved management practices.

Sales Growth   Sales growth is always an important consideration in valuation. Drivers of sales growth resulting from M&A transactions include:

- *Leverage existing distribution channel.* The sales growth rate of the target may be accelerated if the acquirer can sell the target's products through existing distribution channels (or vice versa). For example, the acquirer may have a strong international distribution organization in a region where the target's presence is weak or nonexistent.
- *Address a new market or develop new products with combined competencies.* The combination of technical competencies from two organizations may result in a new product or technology that will accelerate sales growth.

Reduced Costs   Nearly all acquisitions contemplate some reduction in cost. Common examples include:

- *Eliminate redundant costs and expenses.* The acquirer may not need to maintain the target's procurement or administrative functions. For example, when two publicly traded companies are combined, many of the corporate functions at one of the companies can be eliminated, including the board of directors, investor relations, and financial reporting.
- *Leverage scale and purchasing power.* The combined purchasing power of the two organizations may result in reduced prices for materials or services.

Financial Synergies   Significant value can be created by leveraging the acquirer's lower cost of capital to the target. This is sometimes viewed as financial engineering by operating managers. However, the cost of capital is a significant driver of value, and even a modest reduction can result in a significant increase to value. A great example of the potential power of this synergy is General Electric's (GE) program of acquiring a number of smaller financial services firms. A previously independent firm can realize a substantial increase in earnings power and valuation with GE's borrowing power and low interest rates.

Transfer Best Practices   The acquiring company may have innovative business practices that can be transferred to the target (or vice versa). For example, a highly effective product development process may reduce the product development cycle and time to market, decreasing product development costs and increasing sales. One of the companies may have a highly effective strategic planning framework or experience in improving operations that will lead to tangible improvements in financial performance for its merger partner.

Beware of Vague Synergies

Over time, the word *synergies* has taken on negative connotations because of the loose use of this term in describing benefits from M&A transactions. A number of deals have been justified over time by invoking the *synergy* word, to describe vague or intangible benefits resulting from the transaction. Synergies must be specifically identified, supported by detailed implementation plans, and assigned to managers who will be held accountable for capturing the synergies that result in growth in value for shareholders.

Potential Acquisition Value

The potential economic value resulting from an acquisition is the sum of the stand-alone value and the value of expected synergies, as shown in Figure 12.1.

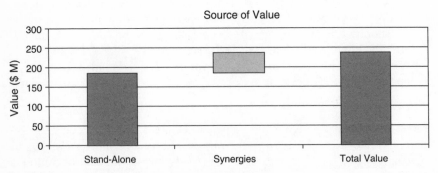

FIGURE 12.1   Stand-Alone Value and Synergy Value

M&A VALUATION METHODS AND METRICS

A variety of valuation methods and metrics are utilized in practice, including:

Accounting and Comparable Methods

- Earnings per share (EPS) accretive/dilutive test.
- Comparable or relative pricing methods: multiples of revenues, earnings, and cash flow.
- Control premium analysis.

Economic Measures and Tests

- Discounted cash flow.
- Economic profit or return on invested capital (ROIC) test.
- Internal rate of return (IRR) and net present value (NPV).

All of the methods have strengths and limitations. Each can play a role in developing a comprehensive view of a potential deal. We illustrate these methods using a proposed acquisition of Simple Co. by Amalgamated Consolidated Inc. (ACI). ACI is offering to acquire all of the outstanding shares of Simple Co. for $233.7 million in cash and will assume the $10 million in debt outstanding. Key assumptions are detailed in Table 12.1.

Accounting and Comparable Methods

Earnings per Share Accretive/Dilutive Test   Since EPS is a critical measure of performance for a company, especially those trading in public capital markets, it is very important to understand the impact of an acquisition on EPS. The basic test is to determine if the acquirer's EPS will increase (accrete) or decrease (dilute) as a result of proceeding with a specific acquisition. A rule of thumb used by many managers, bankers, and investors is that a deal should be accretive within a short period of time, often 12 months. The method involves identifying all of the various ways an acquisition will affect EPS. Examples include:

Favorable to EPS	Unfavorable to EPS
Profits contributed by the acquired firm.	Expenses related to the acquisition.
	Amortization of goodwill (prior to 2001).
Profits from sales synergies.	Amortization of other intangibles.
Reduced costs.	Cost of capital to finance the acquisition:
	▪ Additional shares issued to acquire company.
	▪ Interest expense on debt issued to finance deal.
	▪ Foregone interest on cash utilized.

TABLE 12.1   ACI Acquires Simple Co.: Assumptions ($ Millions)

ACI Forecast	2008E
Sales	$1,000
Profit Before Tax	$ 100
Tax	–34
Profit After Tax	$ 66
Shares	64
EPS	1.03
Price-Earnings Ratio	20.0
Acquisition Financing	
Debt, at interest rate of	6%

Synergies

Revenue: The merger would result in $20 million of additional sales beginning in 2008. The sales are estimated to result in a 55% gross margin and 30% operating expenses. Working capital requirements are estimated at 30% of sales; no additional capital expenditures will be required.

Cost Savings: The merger would result in $6 million of annual savings beginning in 2008 and would cost $2 million in 2007 to implement.

Cost Savings:	
SG&A	$2.0
R&D	1.0
Material Cost Savings	1.0
Plant Closings	2.0
	$6.0

Prior to 2001, acquisitions accounted for under the purchase method of accounting required that goodwill resulting from the transaction be amortized over some future period. Under the rules effective in 2001, goodwill is no longer amortized in the income statement. Now goodwill arising from an acquisition is carried on the balance sheet and evaluated for recoverability on an annual basis. Since goodwill amortization expense is excluded from the income statement, the bar in the accretive/dilutive test has been lowered substantially. Since the EPS test does not fully reflect the true cost of capital for the acquisition, it will result in a positive impact on earnings long before earning an economic return. Table 12.2 illustrates the accretive/dilutive test for the ACI–Simple Co. transaction.

TABLE 12.2 Accretive/Dilutive Test Illustration ($ Millions)

Steady State—First Fiscal Year (2008)

| | ACI | Acquisition | | | | | Debt Combined |
		Simple Co.	Synergies	Financing	Amortization	Total	
Sales	$1,000.0	$116.6	$20.0			$136.6	$1,136.6
PBT	$ 100.0	$ 17.5	$11.0	$-14.6		$ 13.9	$ 113.9
Tax	$ -34.0	$ -5.9	$ -3.7	$ 5.0	$ 0.0	$ -4.7	$ -38.7
PAT	$ 66.0	$ 11.5	$ 7.3	$ -9.7	$ 0.0	$ 9.2	$ 75.2
Shares	64.0	64.0	64.0	64.0	64.0	64.0	64.0
EPS	$ 1.03	$ 0.18	$0.11	$-0.15	$0.00	$ 0.14	$ 1.17
Implied Stock Price	$ 20.63						$ 23.49

This deal as presented would be accretive to (i.e., add to) earnings in the first full year after the acquisition (2008), since the earnings contributed by the target and expected synergies exceed the financing costs. EPS will increase from $1.03 prior to the acquisition to $1.17 reflecting the acquisition. If the investors are focusing on EPS and using a P/E multiple to value the company (and if the P/E multiple remains constant) the price of the acquiring company's stock will rise from $20.63 to $23.49 per share.

What about the economics of the transaction? What is the hurdle rate implied in this EPS analysis (i.e., what is the required rate of return on the capital used to purchase this company to break even on EPS)? The hurdle rate implied in this EPS accretion test is 4.0 percent. If profit after tax (PAT) exceeds the after-tax financing costs of $9.7 million, the deal will be accretive to (i.e., add to) earnings. Since the purchase price of the acquisition, including assumed debt, is $243.8 million, the hurdle rate is 4.0 percent, as follows:

$$\frac{\text{After-Tax Financing Expense}}{\text{Transaction Value}} = \frac{\$9.7 \text{ million}}{\$243.7 \text{ million}} = 4.0\%$$

Is 4.0 percent an appropriate return for shareholders on this transaction? Hardly. Investors could typically earn a higher rate by investing in essentially risk-free Treasury notes. In all investment decisions, the hurdle rate should be based on the specific risk associated with the investment. In acquisitions, the hurdle rate should be based on the target's risk profile adjusted for any perceived addition/reduction in risk due to the acquisition.

In spite of the reduced usefulness of the accretive/dilutive metric under the new rules eliminating goodwill amortization, bankers, managers, and analysts continue to use it as a primary measure of the financial performance of an acquisition. If you listen to any conference call announcing an acquisition, EPS accretion/dilution will likely be prominently featured. It is certainly important to understand and communicate the EPS effect of a deal. However, it is not a comprehensive economic test.

Comparable or Relative Pricing Methods: Multiples of Revenues, Earnings, and Cash Flow   Nearly all acquisition decisions include an analysis of the pricing of similar companies in recent acquisitions. It is an important tool to determine whether pricing of a proposed transaction compares with the pricing of other recent deals. This process is no different than evaluating the pricing of residential real estate. Prior to negotiating on the purchase price of a home, real estate brokers provide a "comp listing," which summarizes transaction prices on recent home sales in the area. In a similar way, investment bankers and corporate development managers will identify recent transactions in the industry and compute key valuation metrics such as enterprise value/EBITDA and EV/revenue. These valuation metrics are then used to set or evaluate the pricing of the deal under review.

Generally, companies must pay a "full" or "strong" value in order to convince the target's management and board that they should sell the company. Sometimes acquirers offer preemptive bids to discourage the target from considering other potential acquirers. Further, many companies are sold through auctions, where they are essentially marketed to a large number of potential buyers. The winner of this process is typically the highest bidder. All of these factors put upward pressure on the transaction prices. Therefore, managers who wish to build economic value through an acquisition program must recognize that the comparable transaction valuation methodology has a strong upward bias on transaction pricing.

Control Premium Analysis   A control or acquisition premium is the difference between the acquisition price and the market value of a public company prior to the acquisition announcement. Control premiums are often measured from the date preceding the announcement of a transaction. If the market is anticipating an acquisition, it is likely that a substantial part of an expected premium is already reflected in the stock price. Therefore, it is important to examine the stock trading history for the target over the prior 12 to 18 months. It is possible that investors are expecting an acquisition and have partially or fully reflected an acquisition premium in the price of the stock.

Table 12.3 shows the control premiums for the ACI–Simple Co. transaction.

ACI's proposed purchase price of $13.75 per share represents a 30

TABLE 12.3   Control Premiums

Simple Co. Shares Outstanding: 17 million			
		%	$ M
Acquisition Price (per Share)	$13.75		$233.7
Price (1 Day Prior to Announcement)	10.59		180.0
Acquisition Premium	$ 3.16	30%	$ 53.7
12-Month Trading Range: High	$10.59	30%	
Low	$ 9.22	49%	

percent premium over Simple Co.'s stock price on the day preceding the announcement of the deal. It represents a 30 percent premium over the 12-month high and a 49 percent premium over the 12-month low.

Economic-Based Measures

Despite their shortcomings, both the accretive/dilutive test and comparable methods are useful tools in the decision process. The danger in placing too much reliance on these methods results from two factors. First, neither method reflects the full economics of the deal, since they do not utilize an appropriate measure of return on the capital invested. Second, the measures do not require explicit assumptions about the total performance of the combined businesses. Therefore, it is difficult to understand the performance expectations that are built into a comparables pricing analysis. How can operating managers understand what performance they are signing up for under these measures?

The use of the EPS accretive/dilutive test and multiples pricing methods should be complemented by economic tools, including discounted cash flow (DCF). The DCF analysis should include a base case valuation and sensitivity analysis to understand the impact of critical assumptions on valuation. Similarly, acquirers should estimate the expected economic return using return on invested capital (ROIC) or similar measures.

Discounted Cash Flow   Discounted cash flow should be an integral element of any acquisition analysis. In addition to being an economic measure, the primary advantage in using DCF is that it requires managers to make explicit assumptions about future performance. We would start with the discounted cash flow projection presented in Table 3.1. This DCF for Simple Co. would be for a stand-alone or independent valuation, since we have not considered any changes that may result from an acquisition by another company. A simplified version of the stand-alone DCF for Simple Co. is presented in Table 12.4.

We must now determine the potential value of Simple Co. if acquired by ACI. There are two ways to estimate the economic value of proposed synergies. One method is simply to change the financial projections in the DCF for higher sales growth or reduced costs arising from the acquisition in the DCF analysis and record the revised value (Table 12.5).

The second method is to compute the economic value of the synergies directly. The projected cash flow for each synergy is discounted to estimate the economic value today in Table 12.6. Note that the two methods result in the same value.

TABLE 12.4 Stand-Alone DCF ($000s)

Simple Co.		2006	2007	2008	2009	2010	2011	2012	2013	2014
Sales	55%	$100,000.0	$108,000.0	$116,640.0	$125,971.2	$136,048.9	$146,932.8	$158,687.4	$171,382.4	$185,093.0
Gross Margin			59,400.0	64,152.0	69,284.2	74,826.9	80,813.0	87,278.1	94,260.3	101,801.2
%			55%	55%	55%	55%	55%	55%	55%	55%
Cost Synergies										
SG&A			$ 43,200.0	$ 46,656.0	$ 50,388.5	$ 54,419.6	$ 58,773.1	$ 63,475.0	$ 68,553.0	$ 74,037.2
Total Operating Expenses			$ 43,200.0	$ 46,656.0	$ 50,388.5	$ 54,419.6	$ 58,773.1	$ 63,475.0	$ 68,553.0	$ 74,037.2
%			40%	40%	40%	40%	40%	40%	40%	40%
Operating Income			$ 16,200.0	$ 17,496.0	$ 18,895.7	$ 20,407.3	$ 22,039.9	$ 23,803.1	$ 25,707.4	$ 27,764.0
%			0.2	0.2	0.2	0.2	0.2	0.2	0.2	0.2
Tax	34%		5,508.0	5,948.6	6,424.5	6,938.5	7,493.6	8,093.1	8,740.5	9,439.7
EBIAT			$ 10,692.0	$ 11,547.4	$ 12,471.1	$ 13,468.8	$ 14,546.3	$ 15,710.1	$ 16,966.9	$ 18,324.2
Depreciation			$ 5,000.0	$ 5,400.0	$ 5,832.0	$ 6,298.6	$ 6,802.4	$ 7,346.6	$ 7,934.4	$ 8,569.1
Capital Expenditures	-30%		-5,400.0	-5,832.0	-6,298.6	-6,802.4	-7,346.6	-7,934.4	-8,569.1	-9,254.7
WC Increase			-2,400.0	-2,592.0	-2,799.4	-3,023.3	-3,265.2	-3,526.4	-3,808.5	-4,113.2
Free Cash Flow (FCF)			$ 7,892.0	$ 8,523.4	$ 9,205.2	$ 9,941.6	$ 10,737.0	$ 11,595.9	$ 12,523.6	$ 13,525.5
Acquisition Costs			0.0	0.0	0.0	0.0	0.0	0.0	0.0	0.0
Terminal Value										$293,187.3
Cash Flow (CF)			$ 7,892.0	$ 8,523.4	$ 9,205.2	$ 9,941.6	$ 10,737.0	$ 11,595.9	$ 12,523.6	$306,712.8
Present Value CF (Discount Rate):	12%		$ 7,892	$ 7,610	$ 7,338	$ 7,076	$ 6,824	$ 6,580	$ 6,345	$138,741
Sum PVFCF		$188,406						TV P/E 16×	16.00	
Excess Cash		7,944								
Estimated Value of Enterprise		196,350								
Value of Debt		10,000								
Estimated Value of Equity		$186,350								

243

TABLE 12.5 DCF Synergy + Stand-Alone ($000s)

Simple Co.		2006	2007	2008	2009	2010	2011	2012	2013	2014
Sales		$100,000.0	$108,000.0	$136,640.0	$145,971.0	$156,049.0	$166,933.0	$178,687.0	$191,382.0	$205,093.0
Gross Margin	55%		59,400.0	75,152.0	80,284.0	85,827.0	91,813.0	98,278.0	105,260.0	112,801.0
%			55%	55%	55%	55%	55%	55%	55%	55%
Cost Synergies			$ 2,200.0	$ -6,000.0	$ -6,000.0	-6,000.0	-6,000.0	-6,000.0	-6,000.0	-6,000.0
SG&A			$ 43,200.0	$ 52,656.0	$ 56,388.5	$ 60,419.6	$ 64,773.1	$ 69,475.0	$ 74,553.0	$ 80,037.2
Operating Expenses			$ 45,200.0	$ 46,656.0	$ 50,388.5	$ 54,419.6	$ 58,773.1	$ 63,475.0	$ 68,553.0	$ 74,037.2
%			42%	34%	35%	35%	35%	36%	36%	36%
Operating Income			$ 14,200.0	$ 28,496.0	$ 29,895.7	$ 31,407.3	$ 33,039.9	$ 34,803.1	$ 36,707.4	$ 38,764.0
%			13.1%	20.9%	29.5%	20.1%	19.8%	19.5%	19.2%	18.9%
Tax	34%		4,828.0	9,688.6	10,164.5	10,678.5	11,233.6	11,833.1	12,480.5	13,179.7
EBIAT			$ 9,372.0	$ 18,807.4	$ 19,731.1	$ 20,728.8	$ 21,806.3	$ 22,970.1	$ 24,226.9	$ 25,584.2
Depreciation			$ 5,000.0	$ 5,400.0	$ 5,832.0	$ 6,298.6	$ 6,802.4	$ 7,346.6	$ 7,934.4	$ 8,569.1
Capital Expenditures			-5,400.0	-5,832.0	-6,298.6	-6,802.4	-7,346.6	-7,934.4	-8,569.1	-9,254.7
WC Increase	-30%		-2,400.0	-8,592.0	-2,799.4	-3,023.3	-3,265.2	-3,526.4	-3,808.5	-4,113.2
Free Cash Flow (FCF)			$ 6,572.0	$ 9,783.4	$ 16,465.2	$ 17,201.6	$ 17,997.0	$ 18,855.9	$ 19,783.6	$ 20,785.5
Acquisition Costs			—	—	—	—	—	—	—	—
Terminal Value										$353,687.3
Cash Flow (CF)			$ 6,572.0	$ 9,783.4	$ 16,465.2	$ 16,465.2	$ 17,201.6	$ 17,997.0	$ 18,855.9	$ 19,783.6	$374,472.8
Present Value CF (Discount Rate):	12%		$ 6,572	$ 8,734	$ 13,126	$ 12,244	$ 11,437	$ 10,699	$ 10,023	$169,392
Sum PVFCF		$242,229								
Excess Cash		7,944								
		250,173								
Estimated Value of Enterprise		250,173								
Value of Debt		10,000								
Estimated Value of Equity		$240,173								

Terminal Value Estimate

TV Simple Co.: P/E Ratio	16	293,187.3
TV PHG Synergies: 0% Growth (Table 12.6)	18.32	60,500.00
		353,687.3

Test		
DCF Value Stand-Alone	$186,350.3	
DCF Value Synergies	53,822.9	
	$240,173.2	

The value of equity from Table 12.5 is $240.2 million. This is consistent with the sum of:

Simple Co. stand-alone (Table 12.4)	$186.4 million
Value of synergies (Table 12.6)	53.8 million
Total	$240.2 million

The advantage in using the detail synergy method in Table 12.6 is that managers understand the specific contribution to value of each projected synergy as well as the stand-alone value of Simple Co. This is useful in evaluating the probability and risks associated with each synergy. Not all synergies are created equal. For example, there may be substantially more risk associated with sales growth expected in three to four years. However, the probability of achieving expected administrative savings should be relatively high.

In addition to estimating the value of each synergy, this analysis indicates that the total value of estimated synergies approximates the control premium in this deal. Presuming that the market is valuing Simple Co. at close to its economic value (indicated by the DCF analysis), the full value of potential synergies is being transferred to the shareholders of the selling firm. Comparing the value of potential synergies to the control premium is a useful test. The dynamics of this macro test are shown in Figure 12.2.

Combining the estimated stand-alone valuation with the estimates of each projected synergy results in the DCF valuation summary shown in Figure 12.3.

Economic Profit Test   Another sobering test in M&A analysis is to estimate the economic profit required to earn an acceptable return on the capital invested to acquire the business. Management must earn a return at least equal to the firm's cost of capital to create value for shareholders. Table 12.7 illustrates the economic profit/ROIC test for the Simple Co. acquisition. The total economic purchase price of $243.7 million will include the market value of the target (stand-alone), the control premium, and assumed debt. Based on the estimated cost of capital of 12 percent, the required economic profit can be computed and compared to the projections of the target and estimated synergies. In this case, the projected EBIAT over the forecast horizon doesn't reach the level required to achieve economic breakeven until sometime beyond 2014. Consistent with this result, the analysis also indicates that the ROIC will not achieve the cost of capital of 12 percent until some point beyond the forecast period.

TABLE 12.6 Synergy Valuation and Control Premium Test: Simple Co. ($ Millions)

		EBIT	EBIAT/CF	PV
Cost of Capital	12%			
Tax Rate	34%			
Synergy Valuation				
Revenue	$20.0	$ 5.0	$ 3.3	$27.5
Cost Savings				
G&A		$ 2.0	$ 1.3	$11.0
R&D		1.0	0.7	5.5
Material Cost Savings		1.0	0.7	5.5
Plant Closings		2.0	1.3	11.0
Total		$11.0	$ 7.3	$60.5
PV Annuity in Perpetuity, Beginning in 2008			$60.5	
Less: Working Capital on Revenue Growth	30%		$−5.4[a]	
Implementation Costs (Synergies)	$ 2.0		−1.3[b]	
PV of Estimated Synergies			$53.8	
Control Premium			$53.7	

Excess (Gap)
$ 0.1

[a]$6 million in year 2008, discounted for 1 period.
[b]$2 million pretax in 2007.

246

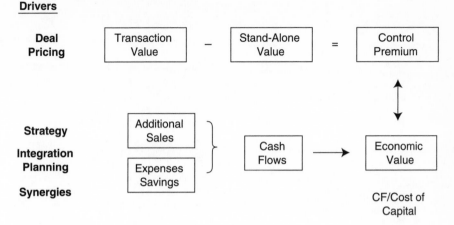

FIGURE 12.2 Control Premium–Synergies Macro Test

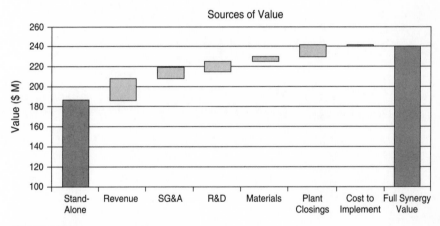

FIGURE 12.3 Equity Value Recap

The management team of the acquiring organization has several options in this situation:

1. Consider reducing the acquisition price.
2. Walk away.
3. Increase the projected performance to justify the price.
4. Proceed with the transaction (and overpay).

TABLE 12.7 Economic Profit and ROIC Test: Simple Co. ($ Millions)

Market Value of Company (Prior to Announcement)	$180.0
Control Premium	53.7
Assumed Debt	10.0
Total Transaction Value (Invested Capital)	$243.7
Cost of Capital	12%
Required Annual EBIAT for Economic Breakeven	$29.3

	2007	2008	2009	2010	2011	2012	2013	2014
Projected EBIAT (Table 12.5)	$ 9.4	$ 18.8	$19.7	$20.7	$21.8	$23.0	$24.2	$25.6
Required	29.3	29.3	29.3	29.3	29.3	29.3	29.3	29.3
Excess (Deficit) EBIAT	$–19.9	$–10.4	$–9.5	$–8.5	$–7.4	$–6.3	$–5.0	$–3.7
ROIC (on Total Transaction Value)	3.8%	7.7%	8.1%	8.5%	8.9%	9.4%	9.9%	10.5%

Unfortunately, too often managers select either option 3 or 4. Many proceed with the deal terms and argue that the economic analysis is not relevant or indicative of the value in the transaction. Often they argue that the deal is strategic and that the financial analysis does not properly capture the strategic value. If the financials do not fully reflect the strategic case and expected synergies, then they should be revised. However, in other cases, the financial projections are increased merely to support the deal price. Presuming that the base projections were realistic estimates of future performance, this option may increase the risk of failing to achieve the financial results.

Internal Rate of Return and Net Present Value Analysis   An acquisition of a company is a complex form of a capital investment. Therefore, it should be subject to the same tests as a new product proposal, plant expansion, and other capital expenditures described in Chapter 9.

Present value of cash flows—stand-alone	$186.4
Present value of cash flows—synergies	53.8
Total present value of cash flows to equity	$240.2
Purchase price of equity	(233.7)
NPV	$ 6.5
IRR	12.5%

The NPV is a small positive result and the IRR just exceeds the cost of capital of 12 percent. This test indicates that the economics of the transaction satisfy the economic tests, although marginally. These results in NPV and IRR are consistent with the economic profit/ROIC test that indicated that breakeven returns would not be attained until sometime after 2014. While technically satisfying the economic tests, management of ACI should consider whether the value created and returns earned are commensurate with the effort and risk in proceeding with the transaction.

Comparative Summary of Valuation Methods

We have reviewed a number of different valuation methodologies and metrics. It is helpful to summarize the indicated values from these differing methods, as illustrated in Figure 12.4. It is quite common for the methods to result in a wide range of potential transaction values. A useful exercise is to compare and contrast the estimated value ranges and understand the underlying factors resulting in wide valuation ranges and sometimes even inconsistent results.

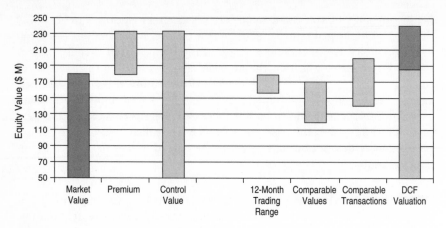

FIGURE 12.4 Comparative Value Summary

FASB Rule Change Reconciles Economics to Accounting

As discussed earlier, the Financial Accounting Standards Board (FASB) introduced a new standard for accounting for business combinations in 2001. The "pooling of interest method of accounting for business combinations" was officially put to death (the SEC had been nailing the coffin shut over time by requiring strict adherence to the conditions requisite to using this method) because it was not consistent with the underlying economics of M&A transactions. Goodwill is now carried on the books of the acquiring company and is not amortized. Intangibles and other assets are typically still amortized under the new method.

The goodwill resulting from an acquisition (illustrated in Table 9.2) will be tested for recoverability at least annually under the new rules. This test will require an annual review to determine if the acquisition is performing at levels sufficient to justify carrying the assets on the balance sheet. The test utilized is essentially a market-based valuation, often utilizing discounted cash flow. This annual test has resulted and will continue to result in a day of reckoning for many acquisitions. In fact, since the new standard was adopted, billions of dollars of goodwill have been written off, indicating that the acquisitions did not perform at a level that would earn an acceptable return on the original purchase price.

COMMON MISTAKES IN M&A

A number of common mistakes contribute to the difficulty in earning a return for shareholders of the acquiring firm. Many managers feel compelled to pursue acquisitions because the organic growth rate has slowed or is about to slow. Sales growth is a key value driver, and the public capital markets place a huge premium on growth. Managers and boards want to serve growing organizations. As the business matures and organic growth begins to slow, they may embark on an acquisition program. This is fine if the program is well thought out and if the team acquires/develops competencies necessary to execute an effective acquisition program. Many do not.

Poor Strategic Rationale and Fit

Some acquisitions are based on soft strategic cases. On the surface, the acquirer believes and articulates a strategy for the combined companies and points to synergistic benefits. Observers who are knowledgeable of the markets and the companies involved may recognize that the strategic case is weak and that some or all of the expected synergies may be difficult to attain. In these cases, a year or two after the deal is closed the company will announce that the acquisition is not meeting expectations and will have difficulty in achieving the strategic and economic goals.

Poor Planning, Communication, Integration, and Execution

Well-planned and well-executed integration activities and strong communication plans are essential to achieve the objectives of an acquisition. Most successful acquirers also advocate speed in integrating acquisitions. Time is money, and getting the benefits of the acquisition earlier is better. More importantly, there is likely to be significant uncertainty and concern in the management and employee ranks about the potential impact of an acquisition. The sooner changes are made, the sooner employees will settle down to the tasks at hand. In the absence of well-planned, well-communicated, and timely changes, employees will lose significant productivity to speculation and fear. In addition, many will explore opportunities outside the firm.

Overpaying

A number of factors cause managers to overpay for an acquisition. Paying too much for an acquisition may make it next to impossible to earn an acceptable rate of return on the investment, even if all other aspects are executed flawlessly. Many advisers and academics believe that it is difficult to purchase a public company at a price that will allow the acquiring shareholders to earn a return. Managers and boards have a fiduciary responsibility to maximize shareholder value. They have an obligation when selling a company to obtain the highest potential price for shareholders.

Managers often become emotionally charged when engaged in the acquisition process. After spending a great deal of time and emotional energy, it feels like losing to walk away from a deal. Winning is defined as "doing the deal," contrasted with doing the deal at a sensible valuation. Projections are often modified upwards to support a higher offer. It is very easy to change expected savings or growth rates on a spreadsheet to yield a higher potential transaction value. Of course, achieving those lofty projections is another matter. The objective should be to buy a good company at a sensible price, not to buy a good company at any price. Ground the pricing discussions with DCF and other economic tests so that all parties understand the assumptions about future performance required to earn an economic return.

Managers should establish walk-away boundaries on price and other terms early in the process. The walk-away price should be supported by key assumptions. By putting a stake in the ground (or at least on paper), it will be easier for managers to recognize the inevitable upward pressure in transaction pricing. Only when significant changes in assumptions can be validated should managers consider migrating to another pricing level.

Unrealistic or Unspecified Synergies

Watch unrealistic or unspecified synergies. Red flags include unsupported statements similar to these:

- Sales growth rates will increase from 3 percent to 10 percent as a result of the acquisition.
- SG&A levels will decrease 5 percent after the acquisition.

Test the preceding statements with questions such as these:

- What new products will contribute to this growth?
- What territories and customers will contribute to the growth?
- Has the sales organization signed up to these projections?
- How many jobs will be eliminated to achieve the lower SG&A levels?
- Have these positions been identified?
- When will they be eliminated?
- Do we have commitment from the line managers for the financial projections?

Failure to Anticipate and Address Soft Issues

People make acquisitions work. Too often, key managers are excluded from early stages of the M&A process. Unless everyone is in the boat and rowing hard, it will be difficult to make forward progress and achieve the challenging objectives of most acquisitions. Clear, timely, and well-communicated decisions about organizational structure are essential.

Inadequate Due Diligence

Due diligence must go far beyond traditional areas such as accounting, legal, and environmental. Strong acquisition programs will test the key areas contributing to future value, including people, intellectual property, and customer relationships.

BEST PRACTICES AND CRITICAL SUCCESS FACTORS

Companies that have a track record of success with acquisitions avoid the aforementioned common mistakes and potential pitfalls with a strong acquisition process.

Sound Strategic Justification

Acquirers always present a strategic case for a transaction. The key for managers, directors, and investors is to understand and test the strength of the strategic case. Most deals make sense, at least at a high level. Some questions to consider:

- Is this a move that is consistent with stated strategy and prior actions? Or did it come out of the blue?
- Does the acquisition address a competitive disadvantage?
- Does it strengthen a key advantage?
- Does it accelerate progress on a key strategic initiative?

Discipline in Valuation

The objective of an M&A program is to acquire a strategic asset at a price that will create value for shareholders. It should not be to complete a transaction at any price. It is very useful to establish a walk-away price at the beginning of an acquisition review. Managers and boards must not view walking away from a potential deal that is overpriced as a failure. After passing up or being outbid on a potential deal, managers do a lot of hand-wringing and questioning. What is wrong with our valuation methodology? Are we too conservative?

Different buyers will determine value very differently. Some buyers will perceive and be capable of realizing higher synergies from a potential deal than others. It is always possible that another buyer may not have priced the deal on a rational basis. Remember that most acquisitions are not successful and many are overpriced. After one particularly emotional postmortem session with a management team over a deal that got away, some members of the team predicted that the buyer would have substantial difficulty in earning an acceptable return at the final price. Within a short time, the acquirer announced that the deal would not meet expectations, wrote off the goodwill, and announced that the company was exploring "strategic options" for the unit. That company was available again, for substantially less than the value that would have been required to win the deal over an irrational buyer the first time around.

Identify Specific Synergies

Synergies must be specific. They must be supported by detailed estimates and implementation plans. There must be buy-in by key managers, and accountability must be established. Incentive and compensation plans must incorporate key value drivers in the deal, including achieving projections.

Strong Acquisition Process

Companies with solid track records in M&A have a strong acquisition process. Candidates are identified in the context of the firm's strategic assessment and plan. These companies devote considerable attention and resources to identifying, evaluating, and valuing potential targets. Thorough due diligence is conducted well beyond the legal and financial basics to confirm key value drivers, including customer relationships and intellectual property. Synergies are confirmed and detailed execution plans are developed. Substantial effort is made to communicate the deal to key constituencies, including employees, customers, and investors. Integration is achieved as quickly as possible and monitored against the detailed implementation plans. Postacquisition reviews are conducted to ensure follow-through and to identify lessons learned to improve the process for future transactions.

Identify and Address Key Issues Before Finalizing Deal

Successful acquirers identify and address key issues before announcing and proceeding with a deal. These issues often relate to posttransaction organization and people issues. How will the combined organizations be structured? Who will be the CEO and CFO of the combined organizations? What will happen to redundant organizations and positions? Will compensation and benefit plans be changed?

Communicate with, Retain, and Motivate Key Human Resources

It is extremely important to reduce uncertainty in the workforce as soon as possible. Details of integration plans and combined organizations should be communicated soon after the deal is announced. Key employees must be signed up and on board on day one to ensure a smooth transition and integration. Employees whose positions will be eliminated should be informed and provided details of termination dates and benefits.

BEST PRACTICES SUMMARY

- Sound strategic justification.
- Discipline in valuation: success defined as acquiring a strategic asset at the right price.
- Identify specific synergies: action plan and timely execution.
- Solid acquisition programs:
  - Objectives.
  - Acquisition criteria.
  - Process: predeal planning, due diligence teams and rigor, integration speed.
  - Establish line manager ownership early in process.
- Address key issues before finalizing deal.
- Retain and incentivize critical human resources.

UNDERSTANDING SELLER BEST PRACTICES

I learned as much about acquisitions by participating in the sale of several companies as I had learned by participating in the acquisition of businesses. In addition to watching buyer behavior and practices, it was enlightening to understand the advice of investment bankers and consultants retained to assist in selling these businesses. Here is what I took away as seller best practices.

"Dress the Performance"

Most sellers of businesses attempt to improve the performance of the business to increase the potential sale price. Obviously it makes sense to paint the house and clean the carpets before listing the house. It also makes sense to address any areas that may detract from the value of a business that will be sold. However, no home buyer would be happy if a major flaw was hidden by some surface paint. Similarly, potential buyers of companies need to be thorough in their evaluation of businesses. For example, a business may be sold because of an emerging competitive or market risk. Other sellers may reduce investment in R&D to increase profitability in the short term; this may have a negative impact on the competitiveness of the company and future sales and earnings.

Meet the Current Plan

Sellers are advised to meet or exceed their current operating plan. Falling short of the current plan provides a potential buyer with an opportunity to question future projections and the ability of the organization to execute to those plans. Buyers should beware of modest plans or Herculean, unsustainable actions to meet the current plan.

Sell through an Auction Process or Sell to Best Potential Parent

Sellers and their advisers recognize that they are likely to realize a higher selling price if they create a competitive bidding activity. Many establish processes that encourage as many as 20 to 30 companies to consider preliminary bids for a business. Obviously, the relative bargaining position tilts to the seller in these situations. In addition, sellers should identify the best potential parents or strategic partners. These potential buyers are likely to identify the highest level of potential synergies and therefore likely to offer a higher price.

Sell into a Strong Market

This is a variation of the investment advice to "buy low and sell high." Managers tend to offer businesses for sale at the top of valuation/market cycles. If the company is cyclical, the valuation will be substantially higher at the top of the business cycle than at the bottom.

KEY PERFORMANCE INDICATORS FOR M&A

Managers can use a number of performance measures to evaluate the effectiveness of the M&A process and to track progress in achieving the objectives for a specific acquisition.

Effectiveness of M&A Process

Companies that are serial acquirers should look at the performance of each of their acquisitions to evaluate the overall effectiveness of the entire process. Are we achieving the sales, profits, and returns anticipated in the acquisition proposal? What is the level of intangible assets arising from acquisitions? Have these acquisitions resulted in subsequent write-down of goodwill? This evaluation may identify potential improvement opportunities in the acquisition process.

Actual versus Planned Sales   Compare the actual sales to the level planned for in the acquisition proposal for the current year. Are the acquisitions achieving the sales estimates in the plan? If not, then the team should identify the reasons for the shortfall and consider these in future acquisition proposals.

Actual versus Planned Return on Invested Capital   Are the acquisitions achieving the return on invested capital (ROIC) projected in the acquisition proposal? Again, what changes should we contemplate for future acquisitions?

Goodwill and Intangible Turnover   This measure provides a view into the relative significance of acquisitions to the firm. For highly acquisitive firms, this ratio will likely be low and will have a significant impact on return measures such as ROE and ROIC.

Asset Write-Offs and Impairment Charges   Goodwill impairment charges result from acquisitions failing to perform to expectations that supported the original purchase price. Significant charges to write off or write down assets may indicate an ineffective decision or implementation process for capital investment. Companies that have frequent asset write-offs and impairment charges (and other nonrecurring charges) likely have an opportunity to improve capital investment, acquisition, and strategic processes.

Specific Acquisitions

These measures are intended to provide real-time feedback on the performance of a specific acquisition. The objective is to select measures that provide a leading indication of progress toward achieving the financial and strategic objectives of the transaction.

Progress on Key Acquisition Activities   During the acquisition process, a number of actions are identified that are vital to achieving the objectives of the acquisition. These may include retention of critical human resources, benefits integration, and consolidation of the sales force and manufacturing plants. Progress on these action plans is a leading indicator of being able to achieve the financial goals of the acquisition.

Acquired Sales and Synergies   Most acquisition plans anticipate growing the acquired sales base from the time of the acquisition and realizing revenue synergies from the combined companies. Both of these components should be closely monitored on a frequent basis.

Annualized Cost Synergies Achieved   Cost savings from combining organizations are an important contributor to the economic success of the merger or acquisition. Progress toward achieving the annual synergies included in the acquisition proposal should be tracked frequently (e.g., monthly or quarterly).

Key Human Resource Retention   The success of most acquisitions is predicated on retaining and motivating key human resources. Key human resources may include some or all of the executive team, functional managers, and technical, manufacturing, and customer relationship personnel. These individuals are identified during the acquisition planning process, and a program is put in place to encourage continuation of employment. Success in retaining the key people should be closely monitored.

Dashboards for M&A

Based on the specific facts and circumstances, several of these performance measures may be combined to measure the overall effectiveness of the M&A activity and the progress in achieving the objectives for a specific acquisition. These dashboards are illustrated in Figures 12.5 and 12.6, respectively.

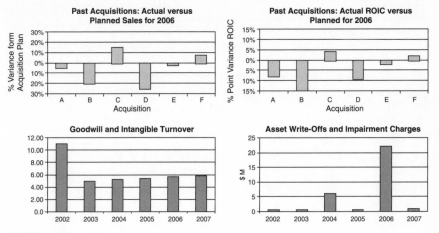

FIGURE 12.5   M&A Dashboard

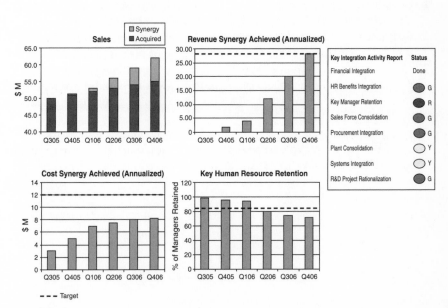

FIGURE 12.6   Dashboard for a Specific Acquisition

SUMMARY

Do acquisitions create value for shareholders? Value is nearly always created for the selling shareholders, but not as consistently for the shareholders of acquiring firms. Firms that have strong acquisition programs have developed competencies to execute well on all steps in the acquisition process. A key element of a successful acquisition program is to be disciplined in setting pricing and other terms. Ensure that the acquisition pricing is supported by economic analysis based on realistic projections of future performance. *Synergies* is not a bad word if they are specifically identified and supported by a detailed implementation plan with clear accountability. The objective should be to do a good strategic deal at a reasonable price.

QUESTIONS FOR CONSIDERATION

1. Consider a recent acquisition or a potential transaction. Identify and quantify potential synergies. Estimate the value of the potential synergies.
2. Estimate the full potential value of the combined entities, reflecting the stand-alone value of the target and the value of potential synergies.
3. Compare the full potential value to the current trading price of the target and estimated acquisition premium. Is/was it possible to acquire the company at a price that will allow the acquiring company to earn an economic return?
4. Identify critical success factors and key performance indicators that would be necessary to ensure that the deal would achieve strategic objectives and create value for the acquiring shareholders.

CHAPTER 13

Benchmark Takeaways and Summary

In this chapter, we discuss the results and conclusions from the Value Performance Framework (VPF) benchmark study, including a summary of the findings, identification of standout performers, and a discussion of key pressure points that tend to have a significant impact on building and sustaining value. We also review key themes presented throughout the book.

THE VALUE PERFORMANCE FRAMEWORK BENCHMARK STUDY: SUMMARY FINDINGS

What factors lead to the creation of long-term, sustainable shareholder value? Throughout this book, we have examined value drivers and the impact that each can have in creating and sustaining shareholder value. In Chapter 3 we reviewed discounted cash flow and other valuation tools that allow us to test the sensitivity of these drivers on shareholder value. We introduced an approach in Chapter 5 to evaluate performance on each driver and to identify and quantify potential improvement opportunities. In Chapters 6 through 10, we reviewed each driver in detail, discussing methods to measure and improve related business activities and processes. We now turn to a review of performance and valuation measures that provide additional context.

The objective of the VPF benchmark study is to capture operating, financial, and value measures from a broad array of companies in order to understand the dynamics of performance and value creation. The study includes over 125 companies across a broad set of industries. The companies were selected to provide a diverse mix of performance characteristics, and include high-growth, best-practice, mature, and underperforming firms. The study evaluated the performance of these companies on various operating and financial measures. For a number of these companies, this analysis has been combined with an understanding or assessment of key business processes and internal performance measures. The range of performance within the database is very wide on nearly all variables. While there tend to be some patterns within industry groups, there is also a wide range of performance on key variables within each industry.

Table 13.1 presents a summary of the VPF benchmark findings, highlighting performance in key areas, including growth, profitability, asset management, capital structure, and returns. While interesting, the information on individual measures is of little use to managers without an understanding of the industries, practices, and other factors leading to the performance levels. In addition, the objective for managers should not be to optimize performance on a single variable. The objective is to maximize long-term shareholder value. Accordingly, managers should set goals for each variable within the context of an overall business model that will maximize shareholder value.

There are many different business models and combinations of value drivers that will lead to building long-term shareholder value. For example, some companies operate with very low operating margins, but earn

TABLE 13.1   Summary of Benchmark Study: Key Performance Measures

		Percentile				
Driver	Measure	5%	25%	Median	75%	95%
Revenue Growth	3-Year CAGR	82%	16%	8%	0%	−20%
Operating and Capital Effectiveness						
Profitability	Operating Profit % Sales	33%	15%	9%	4%	−24%
DSO	Accounts Receivable × 365/Sales	3	37	55	71	99
DSI	Inventory × 365/COGS	11	40	60	111	215
Asset Turnover	Sales/Assets	2.9	1.6	1.0	0.6	0.4
Financing						
Financial Leverage	Assets/Equity	7.6	2.8	2.0	1.4	1.1
Capital Structure	Debt/Total Capital	83%	45%	30%	2%	0%
Returns						
ROIC	OPAT/Invested Capital	41%	16%	9%	4%	−25%
ROE	Net Income/Equity	50%	21%	12%	6%	−23%

Source: Reprinted by permission of Value Advisory Group, LLC.

respectable levels of return on invested capital (ROIC) based on effective utilization of assets. Others earn high margins but are very capital intensive. Companies that have built and sustained shareholder value over an extended period of time have blended a mix of the three critical ingredients for value creation: revenue growth, return on invested capital, and cost of capital.

Revenue Growth

Revenue growth is one of the primary drivers of shareholder value. Recall that a critical aspect for valuation is the expectation of *future* revenue levels. Not only is sales growth one of the most important drivers of value, it is also typically the most difficult to evaluate and estimate for a number of reasons. First, revenue growth rates are very sensitive to the selection of the measurement period. For example, the measurement period can begin with a low point for an organization just commencing operations or experiencing a rebound in a cyclical market. In addition, small, high-growth companies have very high growth rates due to the small revenue base. Growing sales 100 percent from $10 million to $20 million may be challenging, but it is a different challenge altogether to grow sales from $1 billion to $2 billion. As a result, growth rates tend to decline as the sales base grows larger. Another issue to consider when evaluating growth rates is to remember that historical revenue growth may not be indicative of future growth potential. Many managers and investors have a tendency to extrapolate historical rates into the future. Future expectations of revenue should consider historical performance but also consider many other factors, such as market forces, competitive issues, and product cycles.

The benchmark top-quartile performers posted revenue growth ranging from 16 percent to more than 700 percent. The top performers fall into four groups:

1. Start-up companies such as Google, Netflix, JetBlue and XM Satellite Radio.
2. Companies with extended high-growth track records, including Genzyme and Dell.
3. Companies that have completed large acquisitions. Growth by acquisition typically has different economic characteristics from organic growth and may not be repeatable in the future. Growth by acquisition can create value for shareholders if transactions are priced appropriately and the acquisition strategy is successfully executed. For these reasons, it is important to identify and separately evaluate acquired growth from organic growth.

4. Companies participating in recoveries in cyclical industries. Companies in cyclical industries experience high growth rates during market recoveries and slow or even negative growth rates during periods of contraction. In order to evaluate long-term growth rates for cyclical companies, it is necessary to take a longer-term view covering a full market cycle or cycles over an extended period.

Return on Invested Capital

In Chapter 2 we identified that return on invested capital (ROIC) is a function of profitability and asset utilization expressed as follows:

$$\text{ROIC} = \frac{\text{Operating Profit After Tax (OPAT)}}{\text{Invested Capital}}$$

ROIC expanded formula:

$$\text{ROIC} = \text{Profitability} \times \text{Capital Turnover}$$
$$= \frac{\text{OPAT}}{\text{Sales}} \times \frac{\text{Sales}}{\text{Invested Capital}}$$

Several factors may contribute to high levels of return on invested capital.

Operating and Capital Effectiveness   Overall measures of operating and capital effectiveness include profitability and asset turnover. Both of these drivers contribute directly to the ROIC expanded formula. In Chapters 7, 8, and 9 we reviewed the critical business processes, measures, and best practices related to operating and capital effectiveness. Operating and capital effectiveness measures, including gross margins, expense ratios, profitability, days sales in inventory (DSI), days sales outstanding (DSO), and asset turnover are also extremely sensitive to the specific industry and business model. Dell stands out as a great example of a firm that has achieved a very effective operating model, leading to very low DSO and DSI and very respectable levels of profitability and ROIC.

Strong Competitive Position   In addition to highly effective operating practices, high margins can result from a strong competitive position leading to pricing strength. Examples include Microsoft and Procter & Gamble (P&G).

Introduction of Radical Changes to Business Model and Industry Practices
A number of very successful companies have achieved very high returns
(and growth rates) by reinventing the business model for a particular industry. Examples include Southwest Airlines, Dell, and Wal-Mart. The development of a comprehensive business model was explored in detail in
Chapter 4.

Other Factors   Several other factors account for high rates of ROIC. One
is the life cycle stage of the firm. Older, mature companies with moderate
growth levels tend to have higher ROIC. This is due to reduced levels of investment for growth and also due to one of the quirks in basic financial
statements discussed in Chapter 2. Assets are stated at historical cost and
depreciated over time. Older firms may have a substantial number of assets
acquired over an extended period of time at lower historical values and
these assets may be substantially depreciated. High-growth companies typically have lower ROIC rates since both the profit and loss (P&L) and balance sheet will reflect investments toward future growth. This is acceptable
so long as the firm is on track to achieve long-term rates of return exceeding the cost of capital over time.

The benchmark results for ROIC are surprising. While a number of
firms posted high levels of ROIC, the overall results are lower than expected. The top-quartile performers posted ROIC levels from 16 percent to
166 percent, but the median of all companies is just 9 percent. Top performers include Weight Watchers, Gillette, Dell, Google, Procter & Gamble, and Wal-Mart. The low overall performance on this metric may be
attributed to two factors. First, a number of high-growth companies, including many technology firms, have low ROICs. Second, the public capital markets and managers have become very focused on sales and earnings
growth in recent years, often at the expense of economic returns.

Cost of Capital

In order to fully assess the adequacy of returns, ROIC and return on equity
(ROE) results must be evaluated in the context of the firm's cost of capital.
The return spread—the difference between ROIC and weighted average
cost of capital (WACC) or ROE and the cost of equity—is the important
measure. Many of the companies in the study utilized debt as part of their
permanent capital structure. Using a reasonable level of debt in the capital
structure reduces the WACC and provides financial leverage to equity earnings and returns. Many of the companies also achieve lower cost of capital
by recording lower betas, based on building credibility with investors and a
track record of consistently achieving performance objectives.

Standout Performers

A number of companies stand out from the pack in terms of the value created and sustained over extended periods. These companies have recorded sales growth and above-average returns, leading to significant growth in market capitalization. We review a few of these to highlight the combinations of growth and ROIC that led to this performance. For each company, a 10-year history is provided covering revenue, profitability, capital effectiveness, ROIC, and market capitalization measures. In addition to posting strong sales growth, ROIC, and growth in market cap, these companies were chosen because most of us are aware of them and likely have some exposure to their business practices and operating models. While the companies have posted strong results over time, each of the performance trends reflects a few kinks, underscoring the reality of business and valuation. In addition, it is important to remember that in spite of very strong historical track records, value for these companies will continue to be a function of future expectations of performance.

Wal-Mart   The company that Sam Walton founded has grown to become one of the largest corporations measured in terms of market capitalization and sales levels. (See Figure 13.1.) Sales exceeded $250 billion in 2005. While growth rates have slowed in recent years, they remain at or above 10 percent per year. This is no small accomplishment. Growing $25 billion in a year is the equivalent of creating a Fortune 100 company each year. The company has posted consistent profitability, asset turnover, and ROIC over the period. Market capitalization has grown significantly, although the rate is down from peak levels of 2000–2001 due to the market bubble and the general reduction in growth rates.

Dell, Inc.   Dell has one of the highest levels of ROIC in the study. (See Figure 13.2.) It should come as no surprise that Dell has used a variation of ROIC as its primary performance measure and decision criterion. Dell's revolutionary business strategy results in a powerful combination: 8 percent operating margins (5 to 6 percent after tax) and asset turnover of nearly 2.5 times. Dell has reduced inventory levels to four to six days of inventory on the strength of a highly effective supply chain process. Dell's growth rate has slowed as the sales base increased, but the trend was reversed in 2003 as Dell expanded product offerings. The company's market cap has grown at a compound annual growth rate of approximately 20 percent over this period, although down from peak levels in 1999 due to extraordinary sales growth and the market bubble, and again in 2005 due to lower expected sales growth.

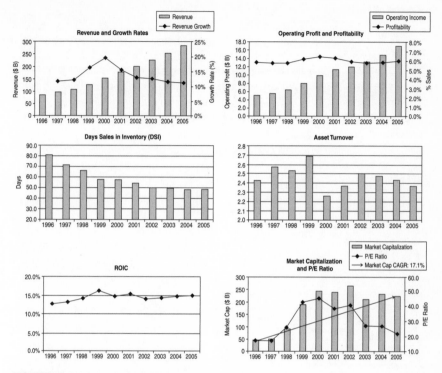

FIGURE 13.1 Wal-Mart Performance Trends
Source: Annual and other company reports, Value Advisory Group analysis. Reprinted by permission of Value Advisory Group, LLC.

Procter & Gamble This 167-year-old company is an icon for strong brands and brand management with sales exceeding $50 billion. (See Figure 13.3.) Over the years, P&G has consistently been profitable with high ROIC. Under the leadership of a new CEO in 2001, the company embarked on a number of initiatives to improve performance, including portfolio changes to accelerate growth rates. A substantial increase in market cap followed. Management uses a variation of total return to shareholders as a key performance measure and has a strong focus on DSO and inventory turns. Note the change in P/E multiple over the 10-year horizon and the relationship to market cap, profitability, and growth. Recall that the P/E multiple is a function of market cap and a single (in this case, trailing) earnings period, while the market cap will be set on the basis of future expectations.

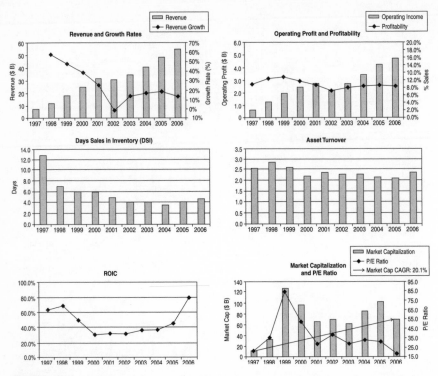

FIGURE 13.2 Dell Performance Trends
Source: Annual and other company reports, Value Advisory Group analysis. Reprinted by permission of Value Advisory Group, LLC.

VALUE PRESSURE POINTS

Certain business processes, practices, and other factors have a significant impact on performance across one or more value drivers. These pressure points represent areas that deserve significant management attention.

Innovation and Growth

Many companies grow revenue and command pricing premiums as a result of innovations in product performance or functionality. Innovation is not limited to product attributes. Many companies have been very successful at introducing innovative business practices, including distribution and customer fulfillment, supply chain management, operating practices, and entire business models. Chapter 6 covers innovation and growth in

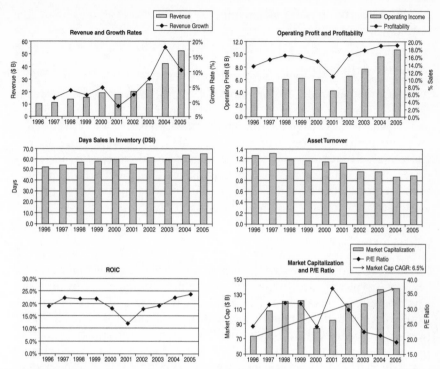

FIGURE 13.3 Procter & Gamble Performance Trends
Source: Annual and other company reports, Value Advisory Group analysis.
Reprinted by permission of Value Advisory Group, LLC.

revenue; innovative business practices are also discussed in Chapters 7 through 10. Chapter 4 provides a framework for evaluating and improving business models.

Attractiveness of Markets (or Identifying Attractive Opportunities in Ugly Markets)

The importance of choosing to participate in markets with potential for growth and higher returns cannot be underestimated. Unattractive markets present some real challenges for market participants, including low or negative sales growth rates, excess capacity, and poor returns. However, consider that Southwest Airlines and JetBlue identified and captured opportunities to thrive in a very difficult market by introducing radically different business and operating practices. Unattractive markets may also present opportunities for companies to restructure or consolidate the industry.

Customer Satisfaction

An important factor in maintaining current sales levels and in growing sales is customer satisfaction. Dissatisfied customers find other suppliers and alternatives. Satisfying customers builds loyalty, leading to future orders and perhaps an opportunity to provide other products or services. Customer satisfaction is based on customers' total experience, including price, quality, delivery, and service. Companies should objectively measure performance on these factors frequently and from a customer perspective. Customer satisfaction was explored in Chapter 6.

Revenue Linearity

Monitoring and improving the pattern of revenue within quarters and years will typically lead to performance improvements across several drivers, including operating and capital effectiveness and cost of capital. While revenue patterns may be dictated to some extent by industry practices or seasonality, there is typically a long list of self-imposed practices that lead to revenue "hockey sticks." These hockey sticks cause higher costs, operating inefficiencies, increased working capital levels, and operating risks. Revenue linearity was explored in Chapters 6 through 8.

Process Effectiveness and Quality Management

A focus on improving the efficiency and quality of critical business processes from manufacturing to forecasting can reap benefits across *all* key value drivers. Quality problems and failures can jeopardize existing revenue streams and future growth and result in high costs and working capital levels. Process effectiveness and quality were discussed in Chapter 7.

Predictability and Consistency of Performance

Forecasting future business levels is almost always a significant challenge. In addition to providing a projection of future performance for planning, budgeting, and investor communication, the revenue forecast typically drives procurement and manufacturing schedules and activities. Improving a company's ability to forecast *and achieve* projected performance levels and eliminate wide variations in performance will impact key value drivers, especially operating and capital effectiveness and the cost of capital. Lower cost of capital will result from increased confidence and credibility with investors, leading to reduced levels of perceived execution risk.

Performance Visibility, Execution, and Accountability

Companies are complex organizations, and business is becoming more challenging and time sensitive. Managers need timely, accurate, and relevant information to run the business. All too often, critical information is not available to managers on a timely basis. Ensuring that managers have visibility into key business activities, processes, and leading performance indicators is essential. Companies that establish a culture of meeting commitments, from development schedules to sales projections, outperform other companies. People in high-performing companies focus on top business objectives and know what they should be working on *today* in order to ensure that these objectives are achieved.

Focus on the Right Measures: Growth and Economic Returns

By carefully selecting measures that support long-term growth and economic returns, managers establish a framework to build long-term sustainable shareholder value. These measures should be the key decision criteria for critical business decisions and the basis for manager and employee performance evaluation and compensation. Companies that use incomplete measures such as sales growth or earnings as the primary performance measure and decision criterion often do not focus on other value drivers and may miss opportunities to maximize shareholder value over the long term.

SUMMARY

Long-term sustainable value is built by strong performance on key value drivers (Figure 13.4). These value drivers aggregate to a firm's ability to grow and earn rates of return in excess of the cost of capital. Each value driver can be further disaggregated and linked to specific business activities, processes, and performance measures that can be easily understood by managers and employees. Successful performance measurement systems will create a context for measures based on the firm's strategy and value drivers and will link operating, financial, and value measures.

Managers can utilize valuation methods, especially discounted cash flow, to identify critical value drivers and estimate the sensitivity of changes in key performance factors on value. By evaluating performance

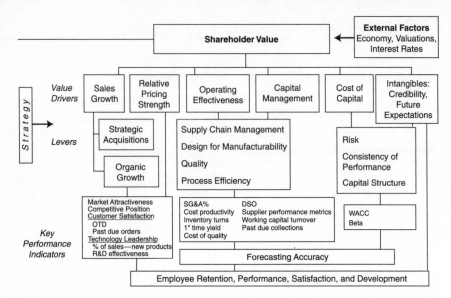

FIGURE 13.4 Building Shareholder Value Requires Performance across All Value Drivers
Source: Reprinted by permission of Value Advisory Group, LLC.

utilizing benchmark comparisons of key measures of performance and valuation, managers can identify potential improvement opportunities and quantify the potential effect each would have on shareholder value.

Acquisitions can contribute to building long-term shareholder value, in spite of significant challenges and a long history of transactions that fail to do so. Discipline in valuation and pricing and a focus on executing to achieve the strategic objectives and synergies are essential to successful M&A projects.

To run a business effectively, managers need information on the performance of their company on a timely basis. Building a system of performance dashboards to present critical business information in a timely and visual manner is a significant improvement over traditional financial and operating reports. Key performance measures must be carefully selected to ensure that they represent the company's strategic objectives and goals for value creation.

In spite of the advantages of performance measures and dashboards, managers should never rely exclusively on these tools. Successful managers will combine this perspective with their intuition, judgment, and direct feedback from customers, suppliers, employees, and other stakeholders.

Utilizing a performance management framework established to support the company's long-term goals for value creation provides a terrific context. Viewing the business through the six value drivers—sales growth, pricing strength, operating and capital effectiveness, cost of capital, and the intangibles—provides managers with a structure to evaluate and drive performance and value.

QUESTIONS FOR CONSIDERATION

1. Compare the results for your company to the benchmark findings in Table 13.1.
2. What performance "gaps" on individual measures does the comparison highlight?
3. Is your current business strategy likely to result in revenue growth and ROIC consistent with your objectives for value creation?

accrual accounting   A basic principle of accounting that requires revenues to be recorded when earned and expenses recorded when incurred, regardless of the timing of cash payments.

amortization   A periodic charge to earnings to reduce the book value of intangible assets including goodwill.

asset   Any tangible or intangible item or claim owned by a firm.

asset turnover   A measure of how efficiently assets are being used to generate revenue, computed by dividing sales by total assets.

backlog   The level of open (i.e., not shipped) customer orders at a point in time.

balance sheet   One of the three primary financial statements, providing a schedule of assets, liabilities, and owner equity.

benchmarking   A process of comparing processes, performance, and valuation of one company to a group of other companies.

beta   The risk associated with a specific investment or security estimated by the correlation of price movements in an individual stock to the market as a whole.

book value   The value of an asset on the balance sheet, reflecting original cost less any accumulated depreciation.

breakeven   The level of a particular assumption (e.g., sales) that results in a measure, such as net present value (NPV) or income, equaling zero.

business model   A financial representation of a firm's strategy and operating practices, usually expressed as a percentage of each income statement line item (e.g., SG&A) to sales.

capital asset   A tangible asset of a firm, such as real estate and machinery.

capital effectiveness   A key driver of value, representing the firm's ability to manage and control capital levels in the business, computed as sales/net fixed assets.

capital intensity   A measure of the level of capital requirements for a business, which varies significantly across industries.

capital structure   The mix of capital sources for a company, including debt and equity.

cash flow statement   One of the three primary financial statements, providing a reconciliation of accounting income to cash flow.

common stock equivalent   An instrument, such as stock options and convertible bonds, that can be converted into common stock under certain conditions.

comparables   A method used to value a company that involves selecting similar public companies to compare valuation measures such as the price-earnings (P/E) ratio.

compound annual growth rate (CAGR)   A multiyear measure of growth that reflects compounding.

control premium   The premium over market value required to purchase a company.

cost of capital   The weighted average return expected by all investors in a firm, based on the opportunity cost and risk incurred in making an investment in that firm.

cost of equity   The return expected by shareholders in a firm, based on the opportunity cost and risk incurred in making an investment in that stock.

cost of goods sold (COGS)   The total cost of products sold, including material, labor, overhead, and other manufacturing costs and variances.

dashboard   A one-page summary or screen presenting graphs and charts of key performance measures.

days sales in inventory (DSI)   A measure of the level of inventories on hand relative to sales.

days sales outstanding (DSO)   A measure of the average time to collect accounts receivable from customers.

debt   A formal borrowing obligation of the firm including bonds, notes, loans, and short-term financing.

depreciation   A periodic charge to earnings to reduce the book value of long-term assets such as equipment.

depreciation and amortization (D&A)   Periodic charges to earnings to reduce the value of long-term and intangible assets. D&A is a noncash charge and is often an adjustment to income to estimate cash flows for valuation purposes.

discounted cash flow (DCF)   A valuation and decision tool that considers the cash flows of an asset or project and the time value of money.

distribution channel   Refers to the method of selling and distributing the firm's products including internal sales force, third party distributors, and value-added resellers.

earnings before interest after taxes (EBIAT)   Also called net operating profit after taxes (NOPAT), this measure estimates the after-tax operating earnings. It excludes financing costs but does reflect income tax expense. It is useful in comparing the operational performance of firms, excluding the impact of financing costs.

earnings before interest and taxes (EBIT)   This measure reflects the income generated by operating activities before subtracting financing costs (interest) and income tax expense. Also called operating income.

earnings before interest, taxes, depreciation, and amortization (EBITDA)   EBITDA adjusts EBIT (operating income) by adding back noncash charges, depreciation and amortization. This measure is used in valuation and financing decisions, since it approximates cash generated by the operation. It does not reflect capital requirements such as working capital and expenditures for property and equipment.

earnings per share (EPS)   The accounting net income per each share of common stock and equivalents outstanding.

earnings per share (EPS) accretive/dilutive test   A decision test to determine if a project, acquisition, or financing alternative will increase or decrease earnings per share.

economic profit A financial measure of performance that subtracts a capital charge from earnings to arrive at an economic profit, consistent with other economic techniques including NPV and DCF.

engineering change notice/order (ECN/O) A document or order used to initiate changes in a product's bill of materials or manufacturing process.

enterprise value The sum of a firm's market value of equity and debt.

equity The book value of shareholders' equity or investment in the firm, including common stock and earnings retained in the business.

Financial Accounting Standards Board (FASB) The accounting standards setter in the United States.

financial leverage The use of debt and other liabilities to leverage the investment of equity investors. Computed as assets divided by equity.

fixed assets A term used to describe property, plant, and equipment.

fixed cost A cost that cannot be eliminated in the short term (e.g., six months) and does not vary with changes in sales levels.

free cash flow to equity (FCFE) The cash flow available to equity investors after providing for working capital requirements; investments in property, plant, and equipment; and payments to service debt (interest and principal).

free cash flow/free cash flow to the firm (FCF/FCFF) The cash flow available to all investors after providing for working capital requirements and investments in property, plant, and equipment.

generally accepted accounting principles (GAAP) The cumulative body of accounting rules issued by the FASB, SEC, and other rule-making organizations.

gross margin The residual of sales minus cost of goods sold (COGS).

income statement One of the three primary financial statements, providing a summary of the firm's sales, costs, and expenses for a period.

intangible assets Assets of a firm that are not physical assets, such as reputation, brands, trademarks, patents, and goodwill.

internal rate of return (IRR) The economic return of a project based on its cash inflows and outflows.

invested capital The total capital invested in a business, including equity and interest-bearing debt.

key performance indicator/measure (KPI/M) A measure of a business process, activity, or result that is significant to the overall performance of the firm.

lagging performance measure A measure that is computed after an event, transaction, or the close of an accounting period, such as DSO or ROE.

liability An amount or service due another party.

market capitalization (value) The market value of common stock outstanding, computed as the price per share times the number of common shares outstanding.

multiples A ratio of value to one of several financial measures, including price-earnings and price-to-sales ratios. These ratios are used to compare values of similar companies.

net income Represents the bottom line of the income statement, the excess of sales over all costs and expenses for a period.

net operating profit after taxes (NOPAT) Same as EBIAT.

net present value (NPV) The present value of cash inflows less the present value of cash outflows.

operating capital The level of net working capital required to support the business, reflecting the excess of current operating assets over current operating liabilities. The measure excludes financing components of working capital such as cash and debt.

operating effectiveness An important value driver that reflects the effectiveness and efficiency of the firm's business processes and activities.

operating income/profit A pretax measure of operating performance, reflecting all operating income and expenses for a period.

operating leverage A measure of the proportion of fixed costs to total costs that causes wider variations in profits resulting from changes in sales levels.

operating profit after taxes (OPAT) This measure estimates the after-tax operating earnings. It excludes financing costs but does reflect income tax expense. It is useful in comparing the operational performance of firms, excluding the impact of financing costs.

payback The period of time it takes to recover the original investment in a project.

performance management framework (PMF) A comprehensive system of management practices to measure, report, and improve business performance.

perpetuity A measure of time, typically used in valuing an asset or cash flow, meaning forever.

predictive (leading) performance measure A measure that covers a key business process and activity on a current basis and provides an early indication of future business and financial results.

present value The value today of a future payment or cash flow, reflecting a discount for the time value of money.

price-earnings multiple (P/E) A key valuation measure representing the ratio of the firm's share price to earnings per share.

pricing strength The ability of a firm to command a premium price for its products and services based on a competitive advantage that will result in acceptable or above-average economic performance for the firm.

proxy statement A filing with the SEC required for publicly traded companies that presents matters to be voted on by shareholders. The proxy statement also contains disclosures on the company's stock performance or total return to shareholders (TRS) and management compensation levels and policies.

return on assets A measure of overall effectiveness, computed as net income divided by total assets.

return on equity (ROE) A measure of overall effectiveness, computed as net income divided by total shareholders' equity.

return on invested capital (ROIC) A measure of overall effectiveness, computed as after-tax operating profit divided by the total of shareholders' equity and interest-bearing debt. Since it considers all capital invested in a firm, this measure is independent of the mix of capital.

revenue linearity The pattern of revenue within a period (e.g., quarter). A linear pattern would result from a constant level of shipments over the entire period.

revenue process The entire process that supports delivering a product or service to a customer, commencing with presales activities and concluding with the collection of cash from the customer.

scenario analysis A projection or forecast version based on a specific set of conditions (e.g., a recession).

Securities and Exchange Commission (SEC) The U.S. federal agency tasked with monitoring securities markets and financial reporting of publicly traded companies.

selling, general, and administrative expenses (SG&A) An income statement line item that captures all costs and expenses associated with sales, marketing, and administrative activities of the firm.

sensitivity analysis A summary of the changes in a decision outcome (e.g., net present value) based on changes in one or more input variables.

supply chain management A key business process incorporating all aspects of planning, procuring, manufacturing, and distributing a firm's product.

synergies The incremental savings or income that results from an acquisition or merger beyond the sum of the two independent companies.

terminal value The estimated value of a company at the end of the forecast period in discounted cash flow valuations.

times interest earned (TIE) A measure of the ability to service debt, computed by dividing profit before tax by interest expense.

total return to shareholders (TRS) An overall measure of returns earned by shareholders that reflects both capital appreciation and dividends paid over a period of time.

valuation The process of estimating the value of an asset or company using one or more commonly accepted techniques such as comparable pricing, and discounted cash flow analysis.

value driver A factor that has a significant impact on the value of the firm for example sales growth.

Value Performance Framework (VPF) A comprehensive performance management framework that emphasizes building and sustaining long-term shareholder value.

variable cost A cost that varies with changes in sales levels.

vertical integration The extent to which a firm directly owns its supply chain and distribution channels.

weighted average cost of capital (WACC) The blend of returns expected by all suppliers of capital to the firm (weighted by market value).

working capital The excess of current assets (cash, accounts receivable, inventories, and prepaid expenses) over current liabilities (accounts payable, debt, and accrued expenses).

yield to maturity The current rate an investor will earn on a bond, adjusting the bond's stated (coupon) rate for current market conditions.

About the CD-ROM

INTRODUCTION

This appendix provides you with information on the contents of the CD that accompanies this book. For the latest and greatest information, please refer to the ReadMe file located at the root of the CD.

SYSTEM REQUIREMENTS

- A computer with a processor running at 120 Mhz or faster.
- At least 32 MB of total RAM installed on your computer; for best performance, we recommend at least 64 MB.
- A CD-ROM drive.

Note: Many popular spreadsheet programs are capable of reading Microsoft Excel files. However, users should be aware that a slight amount of formatting might be lost when using a program other than Microsoft Excel.

USING THE CD WITH WINDOWS

To install the items from the CD to your hard drive, follow these steps:

1. Insert the CD into your computer's CD-ROM drive.
2. The CD-ROM interface will appear. The interface provides a simple point-and-click way to explore the contents of the CD.

If the opening screen of the CD-ROM does not appear automatically, follow these steps to access the CD:

1. Click the Start button on the left end of the taskbar and then choose Run from the menu that pops up.
2. In the dialog box that appears, type *d:\setup.exe*. (If your CD-ROM drive is not drive d, fill in the appropriate letter in place of *d*.) This brings up the CD Interface described in the preceding set of steps.

WHAT'S ON THE CD

The following sections provide a summary of the software and other materials you'll find on the CD.

281

Content

A number of illustrative performance dashboards and Excel models used in the book are included in the accompanying CD-ROM. These items are identified in the book with a CD-ROM logo ⊙ . The dashboards and spreadsheets are intended as working examples and starting points for the reader's use. An important theme of this book is to underscore the importance of selecting the appropriate measures and dashboards. It is very important to carefully select the measures and analytical tools that are most appropriate for each circumstance. Accordingly, most of the dashboards and models will have to be tailored to fit the specific needs of each situation. Please note that in order to facilitate changes to the analyses, none of the formulas in the worksheets are "protected." A copy of the original files should be retained in the event that formulas are inadvertently changed or deleted.

The spreadsheets contain the data used in the examples provided in the book. In order to fully understand the worksheets, including the objective, context, and logic of the analysis, the user should refer to the appropriate example in the text. For each worksheet, the data input fields are high-lighted in blue. All other fields contain formulas. The reader should save these files under a different name and use them to begin developing dash-boards and analysis for the reader's specific needs. Using the models on the CD-ROM requires Microsoft Excel software and an intermediate skill level in the use of that software. Most of the worksheets are stand-alone analy-ses that are not linked to the other spreadsheets. However, the files for Chapters 2 and 3 contain models that require data input on the first work-sheet to drive the models on subsequent worksheets in that file. In these two cases, additional instructions are provided on the first worksheet in that file.

The CD-ROM also includes a Quick Reference Guide (Table 2.8) that can be printed, laminated, and retained as a reference for financial terms and ratios and key aspects of valuation and performance measurement.

All contents are Excel spreadsheets unless otherwise noted.

Chapter 2

Table   2.5   Simple Co. Historical and Estimated 2006 Financials
Table   2.7   Simple Co. Performance Assessment
Figure 2.3   Key Performance Trends
Table   2.8   Key Terms and Measures: Quick Reference Guide (Adobe PDF)

Chapter 3

Table   3.1   Discounted Cash Flow (DCF) Valuation Model
Table   3.2   Valuation Summary Table
Figure 3.2   Valuation Summary Graph

Chapter 4

Table   4.6   Cost and Breakeven Analysis
Table   4.7   Operating Leverage Illustration

Chapter 5

Table   5.1   Discounted Cash Flow (DCF) Sensitivity Analysis
Figure 5.4   Sample Quarterly Corporate Dashboard
Figure 5.7   Estimating Full Potential Value

Chapter 6

Table   6.1   Revenue Planning Worksheet: Product Detail
Figure 6.2   Revenue Change Analysis
Table   6.2   Forecast Evaluation Worksheet
Table   6.3   Market Size and Share Analysis
Figure 6.3   Forecast Trend Analysis
Table   6.4   Revenue Forecast Accuracy
Table   6.6   Revenue in Product Development Pipeline
Figure 6.5   Revenue Growth and Innovation Dashboard
Table   6.7   Gross Margin Analysis
Figure 6.7   Gross Margin and Pricing Strength Dashboard

Chapter 7

Table   7.1 Value Added per Employee
Table   7.2 Head Count Analysis
Table   7.3 Critical New Product Development Status
Table   7.4 Natural Expense Code Analysis
Figure 7.4 Natural Expense Code Analysis—Pie Chart
Figure 7.5 Operational Effectiveness Dashboard
Figure 7.6 New Product Development Dashboard

Chapter 8

Table   8.2 Operating Capital Budget
Table   8.3 Working Capital Improvement Illustration
Table   8.4 DSO Countback Illustration
Table   8.5 Best Possible DSO Estimate
Figure 8.4 Revenue Process Accounts Receivable Dashboard
Figure 8.5 AR DSO Driver Chart
Table   8.6 Accounts Receivable Aging Report
Figure 8.9 Supply Chain and Inventory Dashboard

Chapter 9

Table   9.1 Capital Investment Evaluation
Table   9.3 Estimating the Economic Cost (Penalty) of Retaining Excess Cash
Figure 9.3 Long-Term Capital Dashboard

Modifying the Charts and Graphs

The user may need to modify some of the charts and graphs on the CD-ROM in order to substitute specific performance measures for those contained in the sample dashboard. In order to modify chart titles, alter axis labels, and make other changes to charts, click on the chart, then select Chart in the menu commands and then select Options. A menu of available chart options will be presented, including titles, labels, and scale selections.

The user may also want to change the scale of the charts to better present the data for each situation. This can be accomplished by double clicking on the "Value Axis" label on the graph and selecting Scale to change axis minimum and maximum values.

CUSTOMER CARE

If you have trouble with the CD-ROM, please call the Wiley Product Technical Support phone number at (800) 762-2974. Outside the United States, call (317) 572-3994. You can also contact Wiley Product Technical Support at http://www.wiley.com/techsupport. John Wiley & Sons will provide technical support only for installation and other general quality control items. For technical support on the applications themselves, consult the program's vendor or author.

To place additional orders or to request information about other Wiley products, please call (877) 762-2974.

Index of Performance Measures

Subject Index

**For more information about the CD-ROM, see the
About the CD-ROM section on page 281.**

John Wiley & Sons, Inc.